THE SECRETS OF
AI VALUE CREATION

THE SECRETS OF

AI VALUE CREATION

PRACTICAL GUIDE TO BUSINESS VALUE CREATION WITH ARTIFICIAL INTELLIGENCE FROM STRATEGY TO EXECUTION

MICHAEL PROKSCH
NISHA PALIWAL
WILHELM BIELERT

WILEY

This edition first published 2024

©2024 Michael Proksch, Nisha Paliwal, and Wilhelm Bielert

All rights reserved. No part of this publication may be reproduced, stored in a retrieval system, or transmitted, in any form or by any means, electronic, mechanical, photocopying, recording or otherwise, except as permitted by law. Advice on how to obtain permission to reuse material from this title is available at http://www.wiley.com/go/permissions.

The right of Michael Proksch, Nisha Paliwal, and Willhelm Bielert to be identified as the authors of this work has been asserted in accordance with law.

Registered Office(s)
John Wiley & Sons, Inc., 111 River Street, Hoboken, NJ 07030, USA
John Wiley & Sons Ltd, The Atrium, Southern Gate, Chichester, West Sussex, PO19 8SQ, UK

For details of our global editorial offices, customer services, and more information about Wiley products visit us at www.wiley.com.

Wiley also publishes its books in a variety of electronic formats and by print-on-demand. Some content that appears in standard print versions of this book may not be available in other formats.

Trademarks: Wiley and the Wiley logo are trademarks or registered trademarks of John Wiley & Sons, Inc. and/or its affiliates in the United States and other countries and may not be used without written permission. All other trademarks are the property of their respective owners. John Wiley & Sons, Inc. is not associated with any product or vendor mentioned in this book.

Limit of Liability/Disclaimer of Warranty
While the publisher and authors have used their best efforts in preparing this work, they make no representations or warranties with respect to the accuracy or completeness of the contents of this work and specifically disclaim all warranties, including without limitation any implied warranties of merchantability or fitness for a particular purpose. No warranty may be created or extended by sales representatives, written sales materials or promotional statements for this work. This work is sold with the understanding that the publisher is not engaged in rendering professional services. The advice and strategies contained herein may not be suitable for your situation. You should consult with a specialist where appropriate. The fact that an organization, website, or product is referred to in this work as a citation and/or potential source of further information does not mean that the publisher and authors endorse the information or services the organization, website, or product may provide or recommendations it may make. Further, readers should be aware that websites listed in this work may have changed or disappeared between when this work was written and when it is read. Neither the publisher nor authors shall be liable for any loss of profit or any other commercial damages, including but not limited to special, incidental, consequential, or other damages.

Library of Congress Cataloging-in-Publication Data

ISBN 9781394233625 (Cloth)
ISBN 9781394233632 (ePub)
ISBN 9781394233649 (ePDF)

Cover Design and Image: Wiley

SKY10068126_022324

This book is dedicated to our spouses and children – the value creators in our lives.

With love and appreciation,
Michael, Nisha, and Wilhelm

We would like to express our gratitude to all contributing experts, reviewers, and especially our editor, Sheshagiri Hegde. Their contributions and guidance have been invaluable, and we are tremendously grateful for their dedication to this book.

Contents

Introduction

There is no passion to be found playing small – in settling
for a life that is less than the one you are capable of living.
—Nelson Mandela (politician, former
president of South Africa)

Welcome to the world of AI, where the pace of change is relentless, and the opportunities and stakes seem higher than ever – especially with the latest buzz surrounding AI's tremendous potential for value creation. Through the newest developments in generative AI with solutions such as ChatGPT and Midjourney, the age-old question of AI hype versus reality takes center stage once more. Although there's undoubtedly substantial potential for this technology to create value (McKinsey 2023), Sequoia, a prominent venture capital firm known for its early investments in companies such as Apple, Google, Oracle, YouTube, WhatsApp, and Airbnb, has pointed out that even though it has outperformed the SaaS market and generated more than $1 billion in revenue within a mere few months, 'generative AI's biggest problem [right now] is not finding use cases or demand or distribution, it is proving value' (Huang and Grady 2023). But this challenge is by no means new to the field of AI and forms the central theme of this book.

Whether you're just someone interested in exploring the subject or a seasoned business leader, an AI expert, an enterprise data and AI manager, a data scientist, an engineer, or an AI start-up, you might be seeking guidance on how to create value with AI. Regardless of your background, you may find yourself wrestling with the puzzle of AI's value creation. You may have even turned to some of the greatest minds across algorithmic, data, and information technology – legends like Alan Turing, Geoffery Hinton, Marvin Minsky, Trevor Hastie, Yoshua Bengio – in your quest for insights and inspiration. In your search for answers, you might have even sought advice from others within your network of AI experts. Engineers stress the importance of deploying AI algorithms quickly with the right software and hardware, whereas data scientists insist that a more accurate algorithm is the key to value creation. Data management experts emphasise the critical role of data quality and accessibility, and business experts highlight the need to connect AI outcomes to key performance indicators (KPIs). Each answer provides a valuable piece of the puzzle, but none offers a comprehensive solution. The fact is that the creation of value through AI necessitates a more holistic perspective. If this story sounds familiar to you, you are not alone. Even AI experts lack the view of the entire value creation process and its multifaceted components.

Although AI's value creation indeed entails unique nuances, this book demonstrates that AI-mature organisations leverage proven methodologies to sustainably generate value with this technology. This insight stands in contrast to the belief that AI is an entirely unprecedented and exclusively distinctive domain, rendering past experiences irrelevant. This contrast underscores the fact that despite the influx of new algorithms, cloud computing capabilities, and access to big volumes of data during the latest AI wave, only a limited number of organisations have successfully created business value with AI (Rayome 2019). Consequently, the questions that remain are as follows:

- How can you create value with AI?
- What are the challenges of AI value creation, and how can they be overcome?
- What kind of methodologies and capabilities are needed for your AI initiative to succeed?

Overcoming the Challenges of a Multimillion-Dollar AI Project

Let's explore some of the AI value creation challenges through a fictitious example. Your organisation, a company that produces and sells a wide range of family care, health care, and beauty products is experiencing a decline in its market share and sales volume. An increase in competition and changing consumer preferences have influenced your industry and created pressure on your leadership team to adapt. The leadership team puts you in charge to leverage data and AI to gain a competitive edge with the goal to improve sales.

Creating a Business Opportunity

As you are trying to improve sales, you treat the sales team as your stakeholders. When you ask the sales team how AI could help augment their operations, their initial response is to focus on forecasting sales volume. However, even with accurate sales volume forecasts generated by AI, a significant challenge remains: how does that insight create a business opportunity for the sales team? The salespeople will not know how, where, and which actions to take to affect the predicted sales volume.

You know that the real business opportunity in your AI project comes from providing insights to drive actions with AI's capabilities on an individual store level. For example, AI could be applied to predict sales opportunities for each store instead of just predicting sales volume that creates a valuable business opportunity and helps to prioritise stores based on their business potential. However, AI's output not only equips the sales team with the necessary insights to identify which stores to prioritise but also empowers them to take high-impact actions that can drive sales growth. For instance, if an AI algorithm predicts that a store has the potential to increase sales volume by 10% in a given month, the sales team can take targeted and high-impact actions, such as keeping more stock to avoid stock-outs, making promotional offers, adjusting pricing strategies, increasing product visibility, and improving customer engagement.

Building a Feasible AI Solution

By harnessing the power of data and connecting it with the help of AI to business outcomes, organisations can optimise their sales operations. However, managing the decision-making process of AI in augmenting or automating business decisions with accurate information poses its challenges. Selecting the right algorithmic approach to explain the reasons behind business opportunities requires a keen understanding of the limitations and capabilities of AI.

The feasibility challenge of your AI project is related to choosing the right approach to not only accurately predict sales opportunities but also identify the actions to drive sales. Selecting the wrong approach and data can easily lead to taking the wrong actions and a negative business outcome. For example, the variables you choose have to accurately represent potential actions, the data has to accurately reflect them, and the solution's output has to align with the business operations of the sales team. However, AI is not infallible and market and environmental conditions might change, and, therefore, proper monitoring of AI's decision-making has to be implemented, and limitations defined.

The Importance of AI Adoption

Last, but not least, the adoption of the AI solution is crucial for driving business outcomes. Without adoption, even the most sophisticated AI algorithms will fail to deliver the desired business value. Therefore, you prioritise understanding the motivations, risks, and concerns of all stakeholders involved in your AI project and build trust with each of them.

For example, the sales team has a central role in the success of your AI solution aimed at growing sales volume through impactful actions. Therefore, it is essential to understand how the AI solution will affect the commission and incentives of the sales team, align with the goals and bonuses of team leadership, and fit within the budget of the sales department. It is also important to address any potential risks or concerns, such as fears of job loss due to increased efficiency or the perception of the AI solution as a tool for monitoring and tracking sales representatives' performance and actions. Concerns are often subjective, but you take them seriously and proactively address them to gain buy-in ideally from all stakeholders.

This example about your imaginary organisation illustrates that creating business value with AI requires an understanding of various value creation factors and their connected challenges. No worries, you did a great job and were successful in creating a significant business impact in that project. Your project was rolled out in various countries and created a tremendous multibillion dollar value for your organisation. However, you might not be that lucky in the next project and are looking for a repeatable framework to reduce the risk of failure.

The goal of developing value-creating AI solutions is an ambitious one due to the origin of those challenges in business, data and algorithmics, psychology, and technology. This book aims to help you have an impact on your organisation by providing a holistic framework for delivering value with AI.

Three Authors, Three Perspectives, One Framework

We – Michael, Nisha, and Wilhelm ('Wil') – wrote this book in order to share our experience. We integrate multiple perspectives to provide a holistic understanding of AI and its impact in the world of business. Collectively we have a wealth of knowledge and experience, with a combined 65+ years of expertise in AI, psychology, business, data, and technology. Having led data and AI organisations, dozens of AI projects for various global organisations, and engaged in many conversations with hundreds of experts in AI, we offer you a comprehensive and multifaceted view of the complex and rapidly evolving field of AI value creation to help you make your AI opportunity reality. We will help you figure out how to unlock the value of AI in your context. Each of us provides answers evolving from different experiences in AI value creation.

Michael is an AI strategy and execution expert with an academic background in business and economics. His work focusses on the importance of creating a competitive advantage, building customised analytics solutions, and driving AI adoption through the creation of value and trust. He emphasises the execution and successful integration of AI solutions into enterprise business processes.

Nisha is a senior technology executive with an academic background in microbiology. She is known for her expertise in various technology services, focussing on the importance of bringing AI technology, computing resources, data, and talent together in a synchronous and organic way. She highlights the capabilities required to drive value for all stakeholders across a multinational organisation.

Wil is a seasoned senior executive with an academic background in management and extensive experience in digital transformation, program and project management, and corporate restructuring. He specialises in the strategic implementation of AI technology in organisational infrastructure. He stresses the significance of implementing AI solutions that fit into business processes and are able to support and guide business decisions.

Though we have each travelled different roads, we realised that we are missing a cohesive framework that can bring together the essential elements of AI and analytics, business and culture management, technology and data. Drawing on our diverse backgrounds and perspectives, all three of us held a piece of the overall value creation framework in our hands. As we compared our individual pieces, a more significant big picture emerged, with many connections and interdependencies. With this larger, holistic perspective, we set out to propose a comprehensive framework for creating business value with AI – one that would be practical, actionable, and effective for organisations seeking to integrate this powerful technology.

Who This Book Is For

This book's goal is to provide you with a framework to unlock the potential of AI for business value creation. Our aim is to guide you through potential pitfalls by sharing our learnings on our journey to AI value creation. It offers approaches for your own evolution to become an AI value creator, helping you to make the most of this powerful technology. With actionable advice and insights from our industry experts, this book is essential reading for you to explore the subject, especially if you are one of the following:

- **Business leader:** AI and other digital technologies are a key part of your overall digital transformation journey. You know many business areas where you see optimisation potential but do not know how AI can help. What best practices can you learn from those like you who have been creating value with AI? What are the required capabilities and what is the necessary budget to build your own AI initiative?

- **Analytics/AI/data science leader:** You've accepted the challenge of guiding your organisation's journey to success. You have excellent technical skills to manage AI projects, but some pieces for value creation seem to still be missing. How can you overcome the various challenges of value creation and build AI capabilities as a solid foundation to create tangible business value?

- **Enterprise data and AI manager:** You are tasked with leading multiple data and analytics projects within your organisation, working with business stakeholders and heading a team of data scientists, analysts, or engineers. But how can you be sure that these projects will be successful and create value? What factors can help ensure that business value is created from these initiatives? How can you plan your capabilities and resources efficiently?

- **Data scientist/analyst/AI and data engineer:** If you are part of the data science department of your organisation, you are responsible for building solutions and providing insights that support business outcomes. Although you are aware of the scope of your individual contribution, you might feel that you are missing the bigger picture. How can you make sure that your contribution fits into the overall value-creating solution? How can you increase the individual impact of your work to increase your value within your organisation?

- **Technology/engineering leader:** You are well positioned to collaborate with digital leaders and drive enterprise IT operations. However, with new AI technology innovations you might need to adjust your technology stack and want to know what are the required capabilities that AI requires within your technology environment. Moreover, some of your engineers may need to acquire new skills, but what are the skills that are required for the integration of AI into your organisation's technology stack?

- **AI software vendor/start-up:** Your company has so much to offer to its clients, but you recognise the hesitancy they may have when it comes to the adoption of your AI solution. So, how do you find the right clients, showcase the right elements of your AI solution, and effectively focus your business development? How can you construct a strategy that will not only enable you to secure the right clients but also ensure the successful adoption of your product?

No matter your role, from executives to employees, leaders to collaborators, this book will help you understand how to maximise the value of AI. With practical advice and real-world examples, you will be able to make an impact that is felt far beyond your job title.

What You Will Learn

This book provides a comprehensive overview of the processes for and capabilities needed to create business value with AI, from understanding what AI value creation means and how it can be achieved, to overcoming the challenges on the journey, to integrating AI in the enterprise to scale it, to understanding the capabilities needed for successful AI value creation. However, there is no guarantee for success and every framework has to be adjusted to be successful in your context. Illustrated in Figure I.1 is our framework for AI value creation, connecting the various topics within this book.

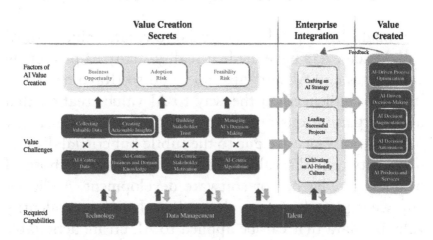

Figure I.1 Framework for AI Value Creation

Part I: Value Creation Potential

In Part I of this book, we explore how AI can be applied to create business value. We will provide an inside look at how AI achievers such as John Deere, Coca-Cola, Google, Microsoft, and IBM have used it to successfully create sustainable value for their operations. We will investigate the journey AI achievers went through and show best practices of how to create value with AI. We will introduce the major factors of AI value creation explained in various use cases across industries and functional areas, from sales and marketing to customer management and underwriting. We'll also introduce a classification of different types of AI value creation with detailed examples to help you identify potential AI use cases in your own business environment. By the end of the first part of this book, you'll have a good overview of how to approach the topic of AI value creation.

Part II: Overcoming Value Challenges

Although there is a clear potential to create value with AI and AI achievers have made it reality, many AI projects in enterprises and AI start-ups fail to do so (Rayome 2019). It is the challenges on the way to AI value creation that many organisations are not aware of. The hurdles many organisations face are due to the subtle but crucial distinctions between AI's value creation elements and those of business intelligence or software development. Additionally, we explore how to evaluate the value of data, identify valuable data that can be applied to AI, create actionable insights, and ultimately turn those findings into a business opportunity. Although AI is typically seen as a way to generate business value for organisations, its successful adoption depends on the trust from all of its stakeholders and so we explore how to build it. The last hurdle to AI value creation is understanding how AI supports and makes decisions. Although we may assume that mastering the math behind an algorithm is enough to comprehend how it works, this is not the case. Managing AI's decision-making is therefore critical to develop solutions that deliver sustainable value.

Part III: Enterprise Integration

You've done it: you've successfully implemented an AI project, and it's already creating value. But now the real challenge begins: how do you scale AI value creation across your organisation? How do you drive enterprise-wide adoption and maximise the potential of your AI capabilities? And, most important, what do you need to do to ensure that your AI adoption efforts don't backfire? The answers to these questions will determine the success or failure of your AI initiative. Therefore we address the enterprise-wide integration of AI, demonstrating how to craft an executable AI strategy that aligns with your business's overall strategy. Doing so will enable you to drive AI adoption at the leadership level, focus on the AI value areas within your organisation; plan for the necessary capabilities, budgets, and measures of success; and showcase the initiative's value contribution. Although it might seem obvious that AI projects should be managed, the appropriate steering of AI projects with the appropriate methodologies is often missing. To overcome their value creation challenges we discuss various development approaches related to AI projects, crucial project planning elements, and how to lead change to drive AI adoption within AI projects. Organisations that have achieved success with AI implementation understand the importance of cultivating an AI-friendly culture. To foster an AI-friendly environment, AI achievers have understood the depth of corporate culture and implemented tools to facilitate the right corporate values of experimentation, collaboration, and innovation. This has enabled them to unlock the potential of AI, scaled the technologies' decision-making capabilities across the enterprise, and maximised its benefits.

Part IV: Required Capabilities

Tackling AI value creation is a complex challenge, one that can only be overcome with the right capabilities in place. To enable AI value creation, organisations must have the necessary technology, data management, and, most important, the right talent. We therefore dive into the fundamental capabilities and elements of AI value creation. Understanding the technical capabilities required to build an AI pipeline that brings value to an organisation is essential. We explore the hardware and software requirements that are necessary to develop AI algorithms and to ensure the successful deployment of AI in the production environment. There is no AI at scale without data at scale. To realise value creation with AI, your data must be managed properly, and the right data storage and processes must be employed to develop and deploy AI algorithms. From an AI talent perspective, data scientists and data engineers may be crucial roles for successful AI initiatives, but the experience of AI achievers shows that a broader set of competencies and skills is necessary for value creation. We describe the tasks at hand, the required competencies and skills to fulfil, and the specifics of the roles that need to be defined for an AI initiative to be successful. Additionally, we address various organisational structures of the AI initiative to tackle the various challenges presented throughout the book.

Reading this book, you'll learn that there are many misconceptions about how to generate value with AI. We'll discuss the misconception that a large investment in AI is necessary to create value, that AI value creation is a purely technological issue, that an AI project should start with a business problem, and that complex algorithms are necessary to produce the best business results. We focus on the value creation we have experienced and seen and will not focus on the hype about AI's potential future risks or value creation potential. With a wealth of examples and use cases, this book will show you how to unlock immense value with AI. This book is also about giving you the skills to become an AI value creator regardless of the industry you are in, whether you work for someone or have your own company. (See Figure I.2.)

You don't have to do it alone; join the conversation with our authors on our website (www.aivaluesecrets.com), give us feedback, and access more content. Unlock your potential and become an AI value creator today.

Figure I.2 Scan to Discover Exclusive Insights at www.aivaluesecrets.com

Part I

Value Creation Potential

As the excitement surrounding AI continues to grow, the question remains: what is the real potential of AI to create value? Although the overall answer may not always be clear, one thing is certain: few organisations, which we will refer to as *AI achievers*, have leveraged AI to create significant business value. Although there are some industry-specific use cases that contribute to value creation with AI for all organisations, there are company-specific best practices that drive AI business value creation.

By studying their AI journeys and mindsets, we can gain invaluable insight into the potential of AI, the best practices for leveraging it, and how to create sustained business value with it. In Part I of this book, we will uncover the primary factors to AI value creation, examine when it might be wise to buy AI solutions rather than building your own, and outline detailed examples of how to create business opportunities and reduce the risks in AI. We will also provide a classification of AI value creation types, which make it possible to identify the right AI use cases for any organisation.

1

The Journey of AI Achievers

In the coming years we will be limited not by technology but by imagination.
        —John Leonard (CEO of Intellia Therapeutics)

As we look at the history of various organisations, we see that all evolved and adapted to new technologies over the years. But what sets apart the AI achievers is not their sole focus on AI, but rather their ability to incorporate AI into their tool set and drive sustainable value for their organisation. We will take a closer look at some of the AI achievers, including Amazon, John Deere, Chipotle, Commonwealth Bank of Australia, Coca-Cola, IBM, Intel, Microsoft, and Google, among others. These organisations are examples of how innovative applications of AI can create value within and beyond the enterprise.

However, success did not happen overnight. Their AI journey, often spanning two decades or more, has been a marathon, which required not just time but dedication. But, it's not the total time invested that yields results at the end of their AI journey, it's the milestones they set along the way that have created value. The secret of their persistence seems to be their mindset. Similar to marathon runners, who visualise the finish line to fight the pain and discomfort on the way, AI achievers have a specific mindset to stay focussed on the long and winding journey ahead of them.

Although many manufacturing organisations have recently made significant investments in their AI capabilities, one particular industrial manufacturer stands out as an AI achiever: John Deere. With nearly two centuries of history, John Deere is recognised as one of the world's foremost industrial manufacturers. Today, they extensively integrate AI into their agricultural equipment and operations to the extent of providing AI-driven services to farmers (Meffert and Swaminathan 2017).

It was 2013 when John Deere introduced a visionary approach to the future of agriculture, placing significant emphasis on cutting-edge technologies such as AI. Their 'Farm Forward' vision showcased the concept of an autonomous farm, where machinery could be centrally controlled and managed. During a compelling demonstration, a farmer was portrayed monitoring data and supervising machinery from a home console, while AI made real-time operational decisions (21 Century Equipment 2013). This demonstration effectively communicated the company's forward-thinking vision. John Stone, senior vice president of the Intelligent Solutions Group (ISG) at John Deere, captures the future role of AI in farming, stating, 'Farmers have long served as the primary "sensors" on their farms, relying heavily on visual observations. The appearance of the soil, the health of the plants indicated by their visual cues, the presence of pests—these visual elements play a crucial role in farming. The ongoing revolution in deep learning has opened up exciting possibilities to solve long-standing problems that farmers have dreamt of solving for years. Computer vision systems and deep neural networks present a highly promising future for these technologies within the agricultural sector' (Marr 2020).

The Finish Line

Running a marathon requires its participants to deal with challenging terrain, varying environmental conditions, and a constantly changing landscape. But how do marathon runners stay in the zone for more than four hours and make it to the end? Those successful in finishing the marathon keep track of their progress and stay focussed on the finish line (Samson et al. 2015). In the same way, the journey of our AI achievers shows that their success requires the focus on the state of the possible with AI. It is that unique perspective that will shape the business opportunities of AI and define what organisations are able to do with the technology.

However, what is the unique perspective AI achievers have in common, that enables them to truly tap into the technology's potential? Some of the AI achievers think about AI in the following way:

- Ginni Rometty, CEO and president of IBM, has articulated IBM's mindset towards AI: 'Some people call this artificial intelligence, but the reality is this technology will enhance us. So instead of artificial intelligence, I think we'll augment our intelligence' (Marr 2017b).
- Microsoft CEO Satya Nadella talks about the company's efforts to develop an AI 'with human preferences and societal norms and you're not going to do that in a lab. You have to do that out in the world' (O'Brien 2023).
- Elon Musk, CEO of SpaceX and Tesla, issued a stern warning about AI: 'Robots will be able to do everything better than us. I have exposure to the most cutting edge AI, and I'm telling you, the future is worrying' (Clifford 2017).

Drawing on the mindset of AI achievers and the experiences of organisations that have embraced AI, Sebastian Thrun, German innovator, entrepreneur, and computer scientist, summarises the shared vision of AI in the following way: 'Nobody phrases it this way, but I think that artificial intelligence is almost a humanities discipline. It really is an attempt to understand human intelligence and human cognition' (Marr 2017b).

In other words, AI achievers are those who embrace the idea that AI can augment humans to overcome their limitations. This collective belief in AI is propelling AI achievers closer to a new horison of business opportunities and keeping them on their AI marathon journey. This very belief forms the foundation that we share, and the core theme of this book is based on the augmentation of human potential through AI.

The Milestones

AI achievers had to overcome their fair share of obstacles on their long and rocky journey, but each milestone they achieved helped to spur them on to reach their ultimate goal. Furthermore, each milestone brought them significant value, new insights, and propelled them ever closer to their finish line.

Data-Driven Decision-Making

The first step of the journey, however, did not begin with AI for many AI achievers, but with an ambition to revolutionise their organisations with a data-driven mindset. A data-driven mindset is rooted in the application of data to improve the quality of human decision-making. It involves collecting and analysing data to gain insights that can help guide decisions in a complex environment where intuition does not lead to good decisions.

John Deere has emerged as a shining example of an AI achiever, successfully integrating AI into its product portfolio. As a prominent and longstanding enterprise, the company's journey serves as a north star for others on the path to AI maturity. Established in 1837, John Deere holds a substantial revenue of approximately $52.57 billion in 2022 and employs a global workforce of about 75,000 individuals (Global Data 2022).

The path to AI maturity was not instantaneous for John Deere. They embarked on a progressive journey characterised by the first stage of data-driven decision-making. In the early 2000s, John Deere started its journey by investing in sensor technology and harnessing its data. As part of their precision agriculture initiatives, the company deployed sensors in farm fields and equipment, with the aim of collecting data to enhance farmers' yields. Additionally, John Deere made strategic investments in GPS technology, starting in the mid-1990s and culminating in the acquisition of NavCom, a GPS technology firm, in the late 1990s (Mergr 1999). This GPS system facilitated the tracking of harvesting equipment and tractor movement, resulting in reduced labor costs and increased convenience for farmers. By combining GPS location data with their sensor-equipped harvesting equipment, John Deere gained valuable insights about grain quality, crop and seed types, and soil conditions (Horwitz 2020). These insights contributed to internal product development efforts and advisory services provided to farmers. For example, John Deere offered services to optimise crop health and nutrition, leading to enhanced agricultural productivity (Horwitz 2020; Marr 2020). Over the following decade, John Deere continued its journey of experimentation and data-driven decision-making, gradually realising the transformative power of data-based insights.

Similarly Coca-Cola has been taking measured strides on the same journey. Since its inception in 1886, Coca-Cola has become the undisputed leader in the beverage industry, with more than 200 brands and various beverages, serving millions of customers in over 200 countries. Each day, Coca-Cola's customers drink more than 2.2 billion servings of their products, creating a treasure trove of data that can be used to optimise production and distribution, as well as analyse sales and customer feedback (The Coca-Cola Company 2023a).

Though it took some time, Coca-Cola's journey from launch to creating value eventually paid off. At the 2013 Transforming Data with Intelligence (TDWI) Business Intelligence (BI) Executive Summit, Justin Honaman, former vice president of customer intelligence at bottling operation Coca-Cola Refreshments, recounted a decade-long battle the company had begun waging in 2003 to tackle the obstacles associated with collecting data across the different databases and software systems used by the company's bottlers (Burns 2013). But it was less a technical challenge than an organisational one, as Honaman pointed out, one that was worth taking on, especially since it enabled data-driven decision-making through the quick generation of sales reports, information about production output management, and helped to proactively resupply retailers to avoid out-of-stock situations, a problem that can have a 10% revenue impact on fast-moving consumer goods companies (Andersen Consulting 1996).

In 2014, Coca-Cola conducted an analysis of sensor data collected from 60 vending machines to examine the transaction patterns associated with these machines. The results of this project were highly impactful, resulting in a significant reduction in instances of stock-outs and a notable increase in sales within the areas where the pilot was conducted. Specifically, transactions saw a remarkable increase of 15%, and the need for restocking visits was reduced by an impressive 18%. The success of this pilot project served as the foundation for the establishment of the vending analytics platform HIVERY. This platform has since been deployed across the company's vending machines in multiple countries, including Australia, New Zealand, and the United States (Prime 2021).

As more and more businesses are entering their AI journey, Coca-Cola's and John Deere's stories serve as inspiring tales of success and resilience as well as where to start – with a data-driven mindset. According to *Harvard Business Review*'s 2012 survey, that first milestone of the AI journey has been shown to create value for many organisations. Data-driven enterprises have outperformed their competitors by up to 6% in profitability and 5% in productivity (McAfee and Brynjolfsson 2012).

Supporting Human Decision-Making

As organisations are gaining the means to live up to the challenge of becoming data-driven, they are also overcoming a major obstacle to the next step of their journey: the application of AI.

By 2013, John Deere had embarked on several ambitious big data projects, showcasing their commitment to effectively harnessing data. They have state-of-the-art data and technology platforms that enable them to process data and deploy AI at scale. For instance, a vast amount of data is telematically streamed from thousands of connected machines from about 100 locations in 30 countries where the company operates. All this raw data from agricultural machines and sensors flows into their cloud-based enterprise data lake, and from there, it is transferred to their data factory. Here, the data is stored, curated, and made accessible to analytics and AI algorithms to generate valuable insights (Marr 2020).

Through the integration of data and AI, John Deere has reached a stage where their AI-driven products actively support human decision-making. Their online platform, www.myjohndeere.com, provides highly personalised AI-driven recommendations to farmers based on weather data, soil conditions gathered from field sensors, and information about the seeds being used (Meffert and Swaminathan 2017). By analysing these data points, John Deere assists farmers in maximising their crop yields. However, John Deere's AI-driven approach extends beyond yield optimisation. Through continuous equipment monitoring using sensors installed in vehicles, John Deere helps farmers reduce repair costs and extend the life span of their machinery through timely maintenance. The collected data is sent to a central data center, where AI algorithms convert it into valuable insights about their equipment maintenance requirements that farmers can access conveniently through the platform or the Farm Manager app on their smartphones or tablets (Horwitz 2020). Through its adoption of data and AI-based services, John Deere, despite being a traditional manufacturing company, has evolved to a stage where it actively supports human decision-making. This transformation aligns with the viewpoint expressed by Jeff Immelt, the former CEO of GE, who stated that every industrial company today is a software and analytics company (Rose 2015).

Coca-Cola's next step in their journey was to leverage AI to support human decision-making through insights from their vast amounts of data, especially social data. In 2017, Greg Chambers, global director of digital innovation at Coca-Cola, declared, 'AI is the foundation for everything we do. We create intelligent experiences. AI is the kernel that powers that experience' (Brandon 2017). For example, the company used AI to gain customer targeting insights. With more than 105 million Facebook followers and 3.3 million followers on X (formerly Twitter), Coca-Cola has a substantial fan base (Twitter 2023). By using image recognition to track when customers post images with the Coca-Cola logo across these social media channels, the company can gain an understanding of the surrounding context. AI can recognise people along with Coke in posted images, and also enable Coca-Cola to track the brands of its competitors. This insight helps Coca-Cola better understand its target group and support human decision-making in reaching those individual customers (Marr 2017a).

As most AI achievers today are in their journey stage in leveraging AI for supporting human decision-making, recent research shows that AI's impact can be up to 30% of an organisation's revenue (Vohra et al. 2019), or 20% of earnings before interest and taxes (Chui et al. 2021), and 42% of organisations report that the ROI of their AI initiatives exceeded their expectations (Vohra et al. 2019).

Exceeding Human Decision-Making Capabilities

The last milestone and finish line of the journey of our two AI achievers is an outcome of acknowledging human limitations and embracing AI's potential to exceed human capabilities.

Thanks to their early investments in data, coupled with a decade of experience in adopting relevant technologies such as GPS, John Deere has been able to take bold steps towards leveraging AI to surpass human capabilities, particularly in the realm of intelligent agricultural machinery and robotics.

In 2017, the company acquired Blue River Technology, a robotics start-up based in California, followed by the acquisition of Bear Flag Robotics in 2021, both of which contribute to John Deere's AI strategy (Colodony 2017; Vincent 2017). These acquisitions have integrated unique AI capabilities into John Deere's AI initiatives, particularly in the development of autonomous-driving technology. Merely a year later, John Deere proudly showcased their state-of-the-art AI technology at the esteemed 2022 CES (Consumer Electronics Summit) in the US. The spotlight was on their flagship AI product, the autonomous and self-driving tractor. This advanced machine is equipped with six pairs of cameras that possess the capability to detect obstacles in all directions and calculate distances. Images captured by these cameras are swiftly processed through AI algorithms, enabling pixel classification in a mere 100 milliseconds, thereby facilitating the tractor's movement (John Deere 2022a). The autonomous tractor continuously verifies its position relative to a geofence, ensuring precise operation within an inch of accuracy. Remarkably, farmers can control the tractor conveniently using their mobile phones.

Their unwavering dedication to embracing innovation, coupled with the utilisation of data and AI, has resulted in substantial value creation for their customers. This accomplishment has been recognised and appreciated not only by their customers but also by investors, resulting in a remarkable stock price premium in comparison to their competitors. From 2020 to 2023, John Deere's stock witnessed an impressive appreciation of about 200% (Google Finance 2023).

In a similar fashion as John Deere, Coca-Cola made their next step by leveraging AI to overcome human limitations. In order to improve sales, the Coca-Cola Company is taking their vending machines to the next level by incorporating AI's automated decision-making, creating intelligent vending machines that can adjust their 'mood' to fit in any setting. For example, a vending machine placed in a gym would focus more on selling water and energy drinks than sugary beverages. These intelligent machines use customer data to further customise the products they advertise in a given area, while offering exclusive discounts and deals for the targeted audience (Chaturvedi 2021). But not just vending machines will become smarter with AI's capabilities. Even coolers will become smarter and take over some of the sales representative's tasks. Coolers will provide real-time visibility and control to continuously manage stock levels to avoid out-of-stock situations. Furthermore, they can alert on price changes, provide information on competitor products and maintenance, as well as offer insight into customer traffic and purchase behaviour. This can help to identify intraday consumption patterns, giving businesses such as Coca-Cola a competitive edge (Trax 2016).

Moreover, as one of the first organisations to appoint a head of generative AI, the company just recently appointed their head of generative AI and professionally applied this new technology to their advertising. They created an

AI-generated campaign that was able to show how AI, combined with human creativity and skills, can create something very new that is able to 'bring the wow factor' (Marr 2023). In their first AI-generated advertisement in 2023, Coca-Cola brings some of the world's most popular artifacts of art to life. On their journey of creative enablement, the company integrated generative AI capabilities into their free music-making platform Coke Studio, where visitors are able to generate their own songs, music videos, and album covers (Marr 2023).

The potential of AI to exceed human decision-making capabilities is a game-changer for many organisations. It presents an enormous opportunity to create new business models, gain a competitive edge against rivals, and even forge new industries. One prominent example is Tesla, whose self-driving car technology created a new market demand for this feature and inspired several other car manufacturers to pursue similar technology developments. For Tesla, this innovation resulted in $300 million in additional revenue as per Marketwatch in 2022 (Poletti 2023). Another example is Amazon, whose AI-powered product recommendation system is estimated to generate 35% of its online sales revenue. Similarly, AI plays a critical role in Netflix's content recommendation system, influencing 75% of its viewers (McKinzie et al. 2013). However, particularly with the innovation of generative AI, AI has now ascended in an area that people have not been dreaming of and accomplishes tasks that were traditionally considered exclusive to human skills. From text and image generation to audio and video creation, AI has attained a new area of human capabilities, which opens up a new field of AI applications, such as creating media campaigns as in the example of Coca-Cola (Marr 2023).

Radha Subramanyam, Chief Research and Analytics Officer at CBS Corporation

As the chief research and analytics officer at CBS Corporation and in my roles at Yahoo, Nielsen, and iHeartMedia, I've had the privilege of being part of the AI journey in the media industry. Media might not be the first thing that comes to mind when discussing AI, and I may not fit the conventional image of a data and AI leader either. Working in the highly creative field of TV, often stereotyped as more 'art' than science, has been a unique experience. However, I've found that data and AI hold immense value and is embraced by top-tier creators and artists. I'm sharing my story and AI journey within the media industry.

The journey of media organisations began as early as the 1950s and took on greater urgency in the 1990s with the digitisation and collection of data. This marked the shift from analog to digital content creation, storage, and distribution, leading to the accumulation of vast amounts of digital data, including consumer data, but especially text, image, audio, and video data related to content. This foundational step was pivotal for the subsequent phase in the 2000s: content management and analytics. During this period, companies focussed on developing digital assets, and analytics became increasingly valuable, providing data-driven insights for audience segmentation, content recommendations, and targeted advertising. Over the past decade, AI has been seamlessly integrated into the digital platforms of many content providers, enabling personalised content delivery through recommendation systems. Notably, in the last 12 months, the creative field has come into sharp focus with the advent of generative AI.

The various stages of the AI journey can be seen as points along a continuum, where the original approaches represent one end and generative AI, the most recent development, the other end. Our latest tools do not break with the past; rather, they exponentially scale and accelerate previous approaches. In the TV industry, performance data and market research data have been used for years to optimise our products – from creating characters to the overall storytelling. When I moved into AI,

(*continued*)

I used the technology's insights to complement our existing practices. We conducted extensive R&D and experimentation to determine if these newer approaches yielded meaningful results, adding value at each step of our journey. Equally important, we did not impose these new approaches on our stakeholders. We always kept our eyes on the finish line, which centered on people. Our journey was mostly smooth and characterised by trust and a focus on actionable insights, emphasising outcomes to make better television, not methodology or technology discussions.

2

Three Factors of AI Business Value Creation

And because the upsides are so obvious, it's particularly important to step back and ask ourselves, what are the possible downsides? . . . How do we get the benefits of this while mitigating the risk?

—Emily Bender (professor of computational linguistics at the University of Washington)

The interest in AI remains substantial due to its anticipated influence on value creation in the coming decade. According to PWC, the potential contribution of AI to the global economy could reach $15.7 trillion by 2030, fostering a 26.1% GDP enhancement for China and a 14.5% growth for North America (PwC 2017). This potential impact constitutes approximately 70% of the worldwide value creation of AI. Similarly, McKinsey has estimated an annual global impact of AI of $13 trillion by 2030 (McKinsey 2018b).

Particularly with the advent of cutting-edge AI technology such as generative AI and its potential to influence workforce productivity, these forecasts might require adjustments. According to a study by McKinsey, generative AI could potentially add $2.6 to $4.4 trillion in value to the global economy alone (McKinsey 2023). However, these assessments often overlook the associated implementation costs and are contingent on the extent of AI adoption within corporations and government bodies, as well as their proficiency in deploying this new technology (McKinsey 2018b).

At an organisational level, AI's influence is evident in the accomplishments of various AI achievers who have effectively integrated AI into their operations. Research indicates that AI-mature organisations attribute up to 30% of their revenue to AI (Vohra et al. 2019), or 20% of

EBIT (Chui et al. 2021). Therefore, it is hardly surprising that numerous businesses are enthusiastic about drawing lessons from these AI achievers to emulate their successes.

In this chapter, we'll explore how AI can generate value for businesses of all sizes. We'll present compelling case studies that demonstrate how AI can be used to drive revenue, reduce costs, and create a significant business opportunity. However, we'll also explore the potential risks associated with AI and how to avoid falling into the trap of pursuing a use case that ultimately ends up draining resources and yielding little or no return on investment.

The AI Industry Use Case Approach

One of the most popular approaches AI practitioners have taken to answer the question of how to create business value with AI is to leverage potential industry use cases and emulate their business value generation (Davenport and Mittal 2023, 123–61).

Industry use cases usually describe various opportunities for the application of AI to activities that organisations within one industry have in common. For example, activities that could be supported by AI for manufacturing can relate to maintenance, industrial robots, and quality control to drive efficiency and effectiveness. Health care organisations can apply AI to support activities such as risk analytics, in-patient care, and hospital management, and telecommunication providers could apply AI to customer and network analytics in order to remain competitive (Markets and Markets 2018).

Those use cases can serve as a good starting point and foster a conversation about the business application of AI: 'When our competitors are doing it, why are we not doing it?' Although industry use cases can create a sense of urgency and can spark interest in AI, the key challenge of the industry use case approach is the difficulty of replicating AI value creation achieved in one organisation across others.

The challenge becomes evident when we experience the AI readiness and distinctive AI capabilities of individual organisations. Although organisations within an industry might share the need for a specific AI use case, their capabilities to execute them might be very different. However, industry use cases published by various research institutes and consulting companies usually do not address which capabilities are needed to create value with them. To make that more visual, let us compare use cases to an iceberg. Although the visual outcome of a use case describes the tip of an iceberg above water, the capabilities that are required to execute it is everything below the surface. Let us consider an example of a company in the brewing industry that has recently employed AI. This decision was influenced by the notable investment made by a competitive organisation in the same area and a use case was selected from a use case catalog. However, it is worth noting that the rival company has accumulated over a decade of experience in working with AI, whereas our subject organisation is venturing into uncharted territory. The selected use case is connected to an industry-wide activity within the sales domain and includes the optimisation of the actions of their sales team. However, the use case presents a tremendous challenge, involving the adoption of an AI solution by 2,500 sales representatives who possess no prior experience with AI. Additionally, our organisation lacks the necessary internal capabilities to construct a viable AI solution, as well as the essential reservoir of internal and external data and its management (data governance capabilities). Hence, it becomes evident that this particular use case may be better suited for organisations well-versed in AI with the right capabilities, as opposed to those new to this domain.

Another challenge of AI value creation with industry use cases is related to their ability to create a competitive advantage. Years of experience drawn from AI achievers such as John Deere, Tesla, and Amazon make it clear: creating the highest business value with AI requires the development of AI use cases that create an advantage over industry competitors. It was management expert Michael Porter who pointed out that the competitive advantage for organisations come from discrete activities that are unique to an organisation and different from its competitors (Porter 1985). When AI provides the potential to improve the efficiency or effectiveness of *discrete core operations that differentiate an organisation from others,* it is able to create viable opportunities for a competitive advantage. Jeff Bezos, former CEO of Amazon, pointed out some examples for Amazon's targeted application of the technology to achieve that 'machine learning drives our algorithms for demand forecasting, product search ranking, product and deals recommendations, merchandising placements, fraud detection, translations, and much more. Though less visible, much of the impact of machine learning will be of this type – quietly but meaningfully improving core operations' (Soper 2017) Those operations enable Amazon to create a competitive advantage by being faster in delivery operations and create a higher customer satisfaction compared to other online retailers (Amazon 2023; Malik 2023).

However, industry use cases hold significance and offer value. Organisations not pursuing them might face a disadvantage against competitors. Furthermore, these use cases provide valuable direction, helping organisations pinpoint areas where building their own AI solutions might not be worthwhile, because the acquisition of an AI solution can be faster and simpler.

The AI Value Factor Approach

Identifying AI use cases with the potential to unlock a competitive advantage starts with an evaluation of their business value by focussing on value impact factors. The foundational principle for success is simple: the evaluation of AI use cases comes down to weighing potential future business opportunities against the risks that could diminish their potential. The conceptual formula shown in Figure 2.1 provides a simple way to assess the business value a use case might be able to provide.

The *business opportunity* offered by AI is one that can significantly affect a company's bottom line, from boosting revenue to reducing costs. However, a business opportunity is only an opportunity if it exceeds the costs to create it. Those AI-related costs include the resources related to

$$\text{AI Business Value} = \text{AI Business Opportunity} - \text{AI Risks}$$

Figure 2.1   Value Creation Formula

the technology, data management, and talent required to successfully build and maintain an AI solution.

Evaluating the *risks of AI* value creation requires an extensive view that incorporates multiple disciplines, from computer science and algorithmics, data science, law, and social sciences to organisational management, health and motivational psychology, and behavioural economics (Buckingham and Coffman 2005; Vreede et al. 2021). Those areas can be further deconstructed into various topics. For example, computer science risks involve topics such as AI security and algorithmic performance, whereas legal risks include the possibility of AI bias and discrimination, impact on human safety, as well as compliance with applicable regulations (Mikko et al. 2018).

Broadly, we can categorise all AI risks into two groups: *feasibility and adoption*. The evaluation of feasibility is required to ensure a successful AI implementation and the fulfillment of stakeholder expectations. Therefore various capabilities related to technology, data, and algorithmics must be taken into consideration. The second category of *adoption* is based on the costs incurred when stakeholders are not leveraging the benefits of an AI solution or not collaborating with the initiative in its creation. This can manifest in customers and employees rejecting or not utilising the technology to its fullest potential. Furthermore, it also includes the potential negative effects on an organisation's workforce that can arise from the introduction of AI into an organisation. Legal risks can be included in both categories. Although legal limitations can have a substantial impact on the feasibility of an AI solution, the potential to violate them adds to the adoption risk of AI. These legal constraints often pertain to specific industries and vary among countries.

In order to unlock the business value of AI, it is essential to consider the opportunities and risks associated with it. A comprehensive evaluation of a particular use case must therefore incorporate the three key factors: AI business opportunity, AI adoption risk, and AI feasibility risk (see Figure 2.2).

Creating sustainable value with AI, achievers have built a balanced portfolio of use cases that simultaneously reap the benefits of 'low-hanging fruits' (low opportunity, low risk) but create passion for AI and trigger the imagination of stakeholders with visionary use cases (high opportunity, high risk). For instance, Alphabet Inc., the holding company of Google, has a subsidiary called Verily Life Sciences that focuses on using AI and advanced technologies to improve health care outcomes (Ram 2019). Verily has undertaken a high-risk use case to develop a smart contact lens capable of measuring glucose levels in tears, which has the potential to revolutionise diabetes management. However, this visionary project entails cutting-edge technology,

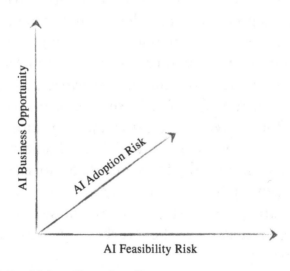

Figure 2.2 Value Creation Factors

substantial investment, and regulatory challenges. To drive value in the short term, Verily has also pursued low-hanging fruit use cases that offer lower opportunities but also lower risks. For example, Verily has formed partnerships with health care providers to apply AI algorithms for analysing large datasets to detect diseases such as diabetic retinopathy and cardiovascular conditions at an early stage. These projects leverage Verily's AI capabilities to provide value-added services to health care providers, generate revenue, and build valuable partnerships. By adopting a strategic portfolio approach that includes both visionary high-risk use cases and low-hanging fruit use cases, Alphabet's Verily Life Sciences demonstrates a strategic approach to driving innovation and value in the health care industry through AI technologies (Al-Heeti 2019).

Evaluating AI's Business Opportunity

In today's world, AI has started to transform various industries, including health care, telecommunication, manufacturing, and finance. Companies are utilising AI to increase revenue, improve operational efficiency, and create value through better decision-making. However, assessing the business opportunity of an AI use case seems to provide a challenge for many AI practitioners. Even more concerning, our experience has shown that AI initiatives often prioritise technological advancements or novelty over projects that genuinely affect the organisation's bottom line. In other words, the pursuit of AI for the sake of AI is still a common practice (Forbes Technology Council 2022; Gartner 2019a).

AI business opportunities arise out of the enhancement of critical performance indicators that have a direct or indirect effect on the bottom line, such as customer satisfaction, customer loyalty, or Net Promoter Score. Although focussing on secondary performance indicators may seem appealing, it is crucial to quantify their financial impact. Doing so not only aids in obtaining funding and organisational support for the AI project but also helps uncover shortcomings in the business opportunity of an AI use case.

Example: Customer Retention Opportunity for an Insurance Company

Let's explore how to evaluate the business opportunity of a fictitious customer retention use case. Various studies in the field of customer retention show that new customer acquisition is between 5 to 25 times more expensive than retaining an existing one (Gallo 2014). Therefore, if an enterprise can keep their existing customers, there can be a significant financial gain for the enterprise. For example, according to Bain & Company, increasing the customer retention rate by as little as 5% can have a dramatic effect on an enterprise's profits, boosting them by anywhere from 25% to 95% (Gillis 2021; Reichheld 2001).

Using AI to enhance customer retention in the insurance industry has been a popular use case for more than a decade (IBM 2010). Car insurance providers, in particular, have faced persistent challenges related to maintaining satisfactory customer retention rates. In 2019 and 2020, the sector's retention rate in the US stood at a mere 80%–83%, causing significant financial strain for insurance providers (OECD Statistics 2023; Super 2019). For instance, an exemplary insurance company with an 80% retention rate may lose up to $200 million in revenue annually from a pool of $1 billion in insurance premiums. To address this challenge, insurance companies have turned to AI-driven customer retention initiatives to predict which customers are at risk of leaving and implement strategies to retain them. However, it is important to recognise that the magnitude of the problem does not necessarily equate to the business opportunity that can be unlocked through AI. AI algorithms in the car insurance industry exhibit impressive predictive capabilities. A study by the University of Groningen shows that AI algorithms can predict customers who will not renew their contracts with an accuracy of 80% or higher several weeks in advance (Spiteri and Azzopardi 2018). In other words, out of 10,000 customers predicted to leave (not renew), approximately 8,000 (80% accuracy) will indeed leave the following month. Considering that the average cost of car insurance in the US for full coverage is about $1,620 per year, this translates to a monthly revenue potential of $12.96 million, or approximately $156 million annually (Pope 2022).

However, while discussing the potential of AI to mitigate revenue loss, it is crucial to understand that the true business opportunity lies in taking action based on these predictions. What happens after the customers at risk of leaving have been identified? To fully capitalise on the business opportunity, it is necessary, after taking into account the customer costs, to explore the potential actions that insurance companies can take. In this scenario, the most likely response from the car insurance company would be to initiate outbound contact center phone calls to address potential customer churn. When a customer answers the call, they may engage in a conversation with an agent or terminate the call. It is important to note that most customers who answer the phone are unlikely to openly express their dissatisfaction, feeling rushed, or unwilling to discuss renewing their insurance contract. However, assuming that some customers are willing to discuss their contract, the contact center agent's next task is to resolve the customer's concerns. According to market research, the primary reasons for voluntary insurance churn are related to customer issues with the product or the price (Accenture 2014). Although adjusting pricing to address the issue is challenging due to regulations in the US, changing the customer's negative experience with the company's product can also prove difficult, especially considering that car insurance companies typically offer only one insurance product. Taking all these factors into account, the success rate of retaining a customer through call center calls could be as low as 2% (Kolmar 2023).

Translating this to our example, the situation becomes clear: if the AI project were to proceed, only 144 individuals out of the initial 10,000 would remain, resulting in a potential monthly avoided revenue loss of as low as $233,280 or $2.8 million annually, compared to the projected $200 million of the business problem. But this figure does not reflect the real business opportunity, because the associated costs need to be taken into account. For example, the expenses for damages settled by the insurance provider account for about 70% of the premium (Gerbis 2022). The contact center's outreach efforts to contact up to 8,000 people per month could accumulate to approximately $80,000 per month (assuming an average expense of $10 per call), thereby reducing the business opportunity to approximately –$120,000 annually (for the calculation, we refer to Table 2.1).

Table 2.1 AI Business Opportunity Calculation
for Insurance Retention

(A) Customers leaving every month	$ 10,000
(B) Customers accurately predicted to leave (80% of A)	$ 8,000
(C) Average revenue earned per customer – premium p.a.	$ 1,620
(D) Number of people who respond to the call – 30% (30% of B)	$ 2,400
(E) Number of people who are willing to talk – 30% (30% of D)	$ 720
(F) Customers who finally agree to renew – 20% (20% of E)	$ 144
(G) Monthly revenue loss avoided by AI (F * C)	$233,280
(H) Monthly expenses for damages settled (70% * G)	−$163,296
(I) Monthly call center costs – $10 on average per call (B * $10)	−$ 80,000
AI Business Opportunity per year*	−$120,192
Total annual loss	

*Does not include costs related to AI project.

However, this calculation does not include the costs associated with the AI project related to data, technology, talent, and the risks related to AI adoption and feasibility. Furthermore, we have not considered the possibility of being slightly incorrect in our assumptions.

Although car insurance retention might not be a business opportunity in the US, it can still provide a business opportunity in other countries. In other countries, where pricing for insurance products is less regulated, leveraging a contact center to offer discounts to customers to win them back could still deliver a business opportunity.

In conclusion, although the business problem is significant, AI will not be able to solve it and create a business opportunity if the insights it provides cannot lead to actions that drive a positive business outcome.

Evaluating AI's Feasibility Risk

Assessing the feasibility of an AI business opportunity is crucial for creating value. From a technical and algorithmic standpoint, the risk of feasibility is related to the management of AI's decision-making capabilities, the availability of the required technology, the talent to use that technology effectively, and the data and its management needed to build that solution. From a project management perspective, we must also assess whether the project can realistically be accomplished within the given budget and time line (Bloch et al. 2012). Feasibility depends largely on the expectations established when defining the business opportunity. For example, augmenting human decision-making with AI is typically more feasible than automating it (Cremer and Kasparov 2021).

Let us get back to the previously mentioned car insurance example. The business opportunity evaluation assumed that the AI algorithm could predict customer churn with 80% accuracy, 30% of customers would answer the phone, 30% would be willing to talk to a contact center agent, and 20% could be convinced to not cancel their policy. This was based on the assumption that AI could predict potential customer retention four to six weeks in advance, giving the contact center enough time to act on AI's recommendation. Yet, what happens if the algorithm can only reach an accuracy of 80% in predicting customer churn *with a two-week forecast horison?* The contact center would have a much smaller time window to act before the customer officially cancels their policy, likely too late with only 20% of customers contacted being open to talk and almost no customers willing to renew. This renders the predictions less useful and increases the feasibility risk of the AI project, thereby not meeting the project's initial business opportunity expectations. Or what would happen if the call center outreach would cost $20 instead of $10? The objective is therefore to develop an end-to-end view of and processes for AI projects evaluating all possible risks for it.

Example: Evaluating AI's Feasibility Risk for Apple's Voice Assistant Siri

Let's explore another example to understand how AI feasibility affects AI value creation: the example of Apple's virtual assistant Siri. In October 2011, Apple executive Phil Schiller excitedly introduced Siri as the 'intelligent assistant' that would help its users 'get things done just by asking', anticipating the dawn of a new era in human-machine interaction. Calling it 'a dream technologists have teased us with for decades', Schiller hailed the advancement of AI-driven voice recognition and natural language user interface capabilities. And, indeed, Siri promised users could rely on it to schedule events and reminders, search the internet, pay bills, order rides, and much more. It had seemingly limitless opportunities revolutionising the way we interact with technology, transforming the way we work and live. Brian Chen, reporter for the technology magazine *Wired*, described Siri as 'like having the unpaid intern of my dreams at my beck and call, organising my life for me' (Chen 2011).

A decade after Siri's introduction, the verdict is largely in: what was promised as the world's first intelligent personal assistant was still far from that. When The Verge called Siri 'largely half-baked' in 2017, it was clear that the dream of an assistant that could understand its users as if it were a real person had fallen short. Despite the progress made in being able to retrieve sports news and helping users know whether to bring an umbrella, the smart assistant was still frequently misunderstood in noisy environments and lacked the reliability to accurately interpret its owners' questions (Gartenberg 2017; Vincent and Krales 2021). In the end, Schiller's bold promise that Siri would understand its users on a human level was a little bit too lofty a goal for the technology of the day. The expected potential for Apple's Siri was tremendously hyped when it was first introduced in the iPhone 4s, with its sales more than doubling those of its predecessor (Chen 2011). However, customer expectations couldn't be met because the virtual assistant's functionality was not up to the high bar that had been set. Despite some small improvements to Siri over the years, the assistant quickly lost attention in press conferences and reviews and was rarely even mentioned on the newest iPhone product websites.

However, the hype around the potential of virtual assistants led to the launch of several competitors including Samsung's S Voice, Google's Now (which later became Google Assistant in 2016), Microsoft's Cortana on Windows Phone in 2014, and eventually Amazon's Alexa. These competitors were able to catch up with and exceed Siri's capabilities and integrate voice recognition for tasks that could be realistically managed by AI. Amazon's Alexa, for instance, could be used to find the right song to play or set a reminder to take a cake out of the oven. This fruitful alignment of AI capabilities and customer expectations has proven to be a success because more than 25% of US households owned an Amazon Alexa speaker by 2020 (Vincent 2021). Although Amazon's devices are among the top-selling items on its online platform, recent developments indicate that Alexa has encountered challenges in generating a consistent revenue stream. Although the devices are sold at cost, the plan to generate revenue through their use has supposedly not materialised. Apparently, the virtual AI assistant has not been widely adopted by spending money on Alexa's skills related services or purchasing products on Amazon's online platform without first seeing a picture of the product or reading reviews about it (Naughton 2022).

In conclusion, it is imperative to grasp the intricacies of the business model and consistently validate assumptions. In our experience, we have frequently observed an emphasis on the technical solution and heard phrases like 'let's bring it to fruition; the world eagerly anticipates this feature'. Even though creating an AI solution presents a significant challenge, the real uphill battle often lies in its adoption. This is particularly true when users are required to alter their behaviour (such as transitioning from online browser shopping to voice-activated shopping).

Evaluating AI's Adoption Risk

When assessing the possible value of an AI business opportunity, the adoption risk, which refers to the extent of stakeholder motivation in embracing an AI solution, is frequently disregarded. This oversight is particularly evident in the context of employees. A comprehensive survey conducted by McKinsey in 2019 revealed that 48% of leaders regarded employee resistance as the foremost risk associated with automation in any capacity (Gomez et al. 2019). Renowned Harvard professor Rosabeth Kanter describes 'resistance to change manifests itself in many ways, from foot-dragging and inertia to petty sabotage to outright rebellions' (Kanter 2012). But what is the motivation that can reduce resistance and positively affect the future adoption of an AI solution? For example, an employee who is supposed to use an AI solution might be motivated through AI's impact on a reduced workload, a performance boost, a learning experience through the involvement in the AI project, a development towards a new skill set and even the promise of a future career advancement. However, an employee can be demotivated by the anticipation of job loss, an increase in micro management, the potential impact on their variable salary, or a decrease of perceived competence (Candelon 2022; Power 2018).

Previous research and the experience of many AI achievers indicate that the understanding of the motivation and the creation of value for all stakeholders might be the missing piece to AI value creation for many organisations (Chatterjee and Bhattacharjee 2020; Kar and Kushwaha 2021). To ensure successful adoption, AI achievers have taken a multi-stakeholder approach and acknowledge the critical role of people in AI's design, operation, and use. Successful AI stories, such as those of John Deere, Google, and IBM, demonstrate that the key to successful AI adoption lies in ensuring that the objectives of all stakeholders – from enterprises (represented by their shareholders, board, and leadership) to employees and customers – are properly aligned, conflicts of interest avoided, and that its expected value creation is motivating for all parties involved. Although we will primarily focus on those three stakeholder groups, there are additional stakeholders, such as regulators, partners, third-party providers, and more. (See Figure 2.3.)

Research shows that stakeholder value is determined by the expected stakeholder benefits and risks of an AI solution. Expected benefits are related to the anticipated outcome created in alignment with an employee's motivation, such as saving time, personal development, and increasing efficiency and salary (Kelley et al. 2023). A customer's benefits could be a better product or service experience, time savings, and reduced costs. An enterprise's benefit is usually related to the business opportunity and the impact on the organisation's bottom line. However, when stakeholders are required to expend effort designing and using the solution, the estimated stakeholder value will decrease, for example, the amount of information a customer has to provide to leverage the solution, the time an employee has to spend building or using the solution, or the money an organisation has to invest building it can reduce the value perception for its stakeholders (Kuhberger et al. 1999).

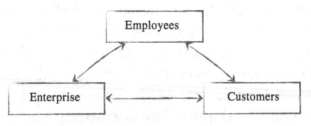

Figure 2.3 Core AI Stakeholders

However, when calculating stakeholder value, it is not just the direct costs that should be taken into consideration but also the associated risks. Although stakeholder costs are relatively straightforward to define and measure, assessing risks presents a different challenge. Research in behavioural economics has demonstrated that risks are often magnified, and their impact on decision-making can outweigh the actual costs involved. For example, the risks associated with leveraging consumer data, for example, can lead to a negative perception of value among an organisation's customers, whereas the risk of being monitored and evaluated based on performance can affect an employee's assessment of value. An illustrative example is the announcement made by WhatsApp in January 2021, when they updated their privacy policy to allow the use of customer conversations for analytical and promotional purposes. This sparked a widespread backlash, prompting millions of users to seek alternative messaging apps such as Telegram and Signal. A survey conducted among 1,525 WhatsApp users in Mexico, Spain, South Africa, and the United Kingdom revealed that 25% expressed a desire to reduce their use of the application, with approximately a quarter of them following through on that intention (Griggio et al. 2022, 1–23).

Example: Employee Adoption Risk for a Pharmaceutical Company

Let us take a closer look at another example. An AI solution developed by a pharmaceutical company's AI initiative was intended to assist the media planning team in allocating budget in real time. It was projected that this could lead to a business opportunity with an increase in ROI of up to 200%.

This could mean investing the same budget to reach 200% more media-related sales, or reducing the media budget by 50% while maintaining the same outcome. The potential stakeholders involved in designing, operating, and taking advantage of the AI solution include the enterprise, the media planners and their management, and the customers of the enterprise. Although this AI solution would benefit the enterprise as a whole, each stakeholder might not see the same value. The media planner team is typically incentivised to increase media reach. However, targeting ROI improvement might reduce this performance indicator. Furthermore, the time and money saved through the AI solution could potentially decrease the media team's head count. Hence, the potential benefit of showing a higher return on investment in their campaigns might likely be overshadowed by the fear of their media budget being reduced or their team size being cut. The risk of such a costly outcome might be comparatively small, but the fear of it has the potential to significantly reduce the team's motivation to adopt and work with the AI solution.

Bibhuti Anand, CEO of Vitt.ai

As CEO of a start-up company specialising in AI solutions, I have observed many organisations facing the dilemma: whether to develop their own AI solution or purchase one from a vendor. Building an in-house solution often requires substantial investments and specific expertise, leading many organisations to opt for vendor solutions in hopes of reducing risks and expediting implementation. However, even when organisations choose to buy a solution, they frequently overlook critical factors, resulting in significant financial losses down the line. When selecting a vendor for AI implementation, organisations have to carefully consider three key success factors presented in this chapter: business opportunity, feasibility risk, and adoption risk.

The business opportunity has usually been shown before, is at least partially transferable from company to company, and can be validated by projects from previous customers using a vendor solution. Nevertheless, the feasibility and adoption risks still persist.

Although choosing an external AI solution usually reduces feasibility risks significantly, there are still many elements to consider. For instance, the integration framework provided by the vendor plays a crucial role, as a poorly designed architecture can lead to challenges in integration of an AI solution or lead to extensive operational costs. Evaluating the data flow from the AI solution, to the company environment, and to third-party applications is necessary to ensure smooth integration with existing systems and to comply with legal constraints. For example the chosen deployment environment, such as a private or public cloud, significantly affects AI security and compliance. Additionally, evaluating the reliability and diversity of data is essential to create an accurate, unbiased, and reliable outcome.

However, in addition to feasibility, the adoption risk can still be the determining factor for success. Successful adoption often hinges on the involvement of key business stakeholders rather than solely relying on IT in choosing a vendor for a specific business problem. That approach can significantly improve the understanding of the full business problem, requirements, and barriers for value creation and the ownership of the outcome of the implementation of the solution. Eventually, it is the business owner who is creating value by using an AI solution.

3

Four Types of AI Value Creation

What all of us have to do is to make sure we are using AI in a way that is for the benefit of humanity, not to the detriment of humanity.

—Tim Cook (CEO of Apple)

Although the three-factor approach presented in Chapter 2 can help to create clarity about the value creation potential of use cases, it lacks insight on where to find areas of AI application with high potential business value. Various perspectives have been used to classify areas of AI application in the past. From a technical perspective, AI can be seen in the form of chatbots and natural language processing, computer vision and image recognition, pattern recognition, and robotics. However, neural networks, random forests, and gradient boosting machines are some of the algorithms that have been used to create value analytically. From a business perspective, AI's use cases can range from network optimisation in the telecommunications sector to drug discovery and diagnostics in health care, to budget optimisation for media departments to lead generation for sales teams.

We have identified four distinct ways in which AI can create value: process optimisation, decision-making augmentation, decision-making automation, and AI products and services. By mastering these AI value creation types, businesses can develop a road map for sustainable value creation. Each type of AI value creation presents unique opportunities and also carries its own feasibility and adoption risks. It is critical to understand the nuances of each approach to ensure successful AI value creation for your specific use cases.

Process Optimisation

The fundamental building blocks of organisations are capabilities (e.g. skills, competencies, resources, and expertise) that eventually give rise to what are known as value chains (Porter 1985). A value chain is a sequence of activities involving the application of capabilities transforming inputs into valuable outputs. Although value chains provide a high-level perspective on how value is delivered across an organisation, processes detail the specific steps and activities required to make that value a reality (Porter 1985). Process optimisation entails the discipline of adjusting a process to optimise its parameters, with the goals of minimising process costs or maximising process throughput, thereby increasing efficiency.

For example, the shipping process of an online retailer may include various steps with the activities of taking products off the warehouse shelf, packing them in cardboard boxes, and placing them on a truck for delivery. The goal is to maximise efficiency and throughput by completing this process as quickly as possible for each item. To increase efficiency, it is possible to plan the order in which products are retrieved from the shelf; this can be done by finding the fastest route from product to product and taking into account an individual's capacity for carrying multiple products of a certain weight. Additionally, when packing, a customer's products should be ideally placed in one box rather than multiple boxes. The last step in the process is the optimal truck loading, identifying the best combination of parcels to maximise the use of the truck's capacity.

Example: Optimising a Direct Mailing Process

Many companies are beginning to explore how AI can create value through process optimisation, including in the area of direct mailing. Although the direct mailing industry has seen a decline in mail volume over the last 15 years (from 215 billion pieces in 2006 to 128.9 billion in 2021), it remains an important customer touchpoint, with response rates significantly higher than digital mail (0.5% to 2% compared to 0.1%; Placek 2022). The telecommunications industry is still one of the most prominent users of direct mailing, spending millions of dollars each year on campaigns targeting potential customers to purchase communication and entertainment services and products (American Litho 2022). By leveraging AI, telecommunications companies can optimise their direct mailing process to maximise returns. AI-driven algorithms can analyse customer data such as demographic and real estate information, location, and other factors to identify the most likely prospects for their products and services. This can help telecommunications companies target their campaigns more effectively and efficiently, ultimately leading to increased customer acquisition rates.

At the start, the telecommunications company as sender must select its target group based on key criteria. Once the target group is identified, an offer letter is sent out. Finally, the customer is prompted to respond to the offer either via an online or offline application for a product or service.

Let's look at the business opportunity that could be created on a yearly basis by optimising outreach campaigns using AI. To determine this, it's important to consider that the average response rate for a direct mailing campaign is about 1%. Customers are typically charged about $150 per household per month for a family of two to three people for their cell phone plans, which can vary based on provider, and the average profit margin of a telecommunications company is about 12.5% as of 2022 (Maverick 2022; Sheehy et al. 2020). The average cost for a direct mail contact is between $0.5 and $1.50, but we'll use $1 per letter for simplicity (Schulz and Shepard 2023). In this example the company is reaching out to about 1 million randomly selected potential customers with a cost of $1 per letter. An average yearly profit per household of $225 (12.5% of $150 over 12 months) is creating a total profit per campaign of $2,250,000. After subtracting the mailing costs of $1 million the net profit is $1,250,000 per campaign. If the company is running four campaigns a year, the annual net profit would be about $5 million.

From an optimisation standpoint, the direct mailing process involves two key parameters: the number of customers to whom letters are sent and who they get sent to. By leveraging the customer information gleaned from previous campaigns, AI can be used to calculate the likely response rate of customers based on demographic factors such as age, gender, and location. In sorting customers by their predicted probability of campaign response, businesses can strategically target those most likely to respond and thus generate the highest campaign profit. For example, if the telecommunications company reaches out to 1 million potential households and has an average profit of $225 per year, sending an offer to just 300,000 of those customers with the highest predicted response probability (of 3% instead of 1%) could generate $2,025,000 for the campaign. Even though the total profit earned would be

$225,000 less, it would save $700,000 in direct mailing costs, resulting in a business opportunity/additional net profit of $475,000 per campaign or $1,900,000 if the company is running four of them per year. This strategy of minimising direct costs through AI-driven decision-making would increase the ROI from 125% to 575% for the outreach campaign. Table 3.1 shows the comparison of the traditional versus the AI-driven campaign.

Table 3.1 AI-Process Optimized Versus Traditional Campaign Comparison

	Condition	Traditional Campaign	AI-Driven Campaign
		> Targeting whole population	> Targeting sample with the highest response likelihood
A	Number of people contacted	1 million (full population)	300,000 (sample of full population with highest response likelihood)
B	Number of people converted with response rate	10,000 (1% response rate)	9,000 (3% response rate)
C	Average profit earned per customer per year	$225	$225
D	Total profit earned	$2,250,000	$2,025,000
E	Total cost of letters sent ($1 per letter * A)	$1,000,000	$300,000
F	Net profit from the campaign (D – E)	$1,250,000	$1,725,000
G	ROI from the campaign – F/E * 100	125%	575%

AI's business opportunity is a direct outcome of the overall process costs and revenue impact and can be measured in terms of the change in contribution margin received through cost savings or revenue increase achieved through improved process efficiency – in this example, the mailing costs saved from the outreach campaign. The business opportunity stems from the ability to act on the result and to affect its outcome. The telecommunications company in the example of the direct mail effort was able to reduce the number of customers targeted and to find those best suited for their product offer. We can further break down the segmentation, targeting, and positioning process to add more parameters and enhance our ability to shape the result. For instance, we can optimise the message of the letters or decide on the best day or month to send them. A red letter might draw more attention than a blue one and a letter sent at the end of the month when people are anticipating their paycheck might be more effective than one sent at the beginning of the month when they just got paid.

AI adoption and *feasibility risks* are usually lower in use cases that are related to process optimisation. When there is a limited number of stakeholders or their responsibilities remain unaffected, the risk of rejecting a solution is low and optimising an existing process entails only increasing the overall efficiency of its activities, not the creation of a new one. Consequently, the benefits of AI applied to process optimisation can be accrued rather quickly. For example, when the telecommunication company needed to send a list of customers to its mailing agency, AI could be used to identify the ideal target population and optimise the response rate without affecting the tasks of the stakeholders involved. With AI, the response rate increased and the business value created was $1,900,000 – the size of the AI business opportunity

Table 3.2 Value-Driving Factors for Process Optimisation

AI Value Creation Type	Value-Driving Factors		
	Business Opportunity	Feasibility Risk	Adoption Risk
Process optimisation	Business opportunity is usually connected to a process's total costs and revenue impact. Business opportunity is an outcome of the ability to take action on process outcome or ability to impact input. Business opportunity increases with disaggregation of the process and adding parameters to affect outcome.	Feasibility risk is usually low if processes already exist and expectations are related to any improvement compared to the original process outcomes.	Low risk for enterprise Low risk for employees in case of low process involvement Low risk for customers only if it reduces customer value through optimisation

minus the adoption and feasibility risk. Table 3.2 summarises the value-driving factors for process optimization.

Decision-Making Augmentation

The second type of AI value creation focuses on the potential of AI to augment stakeholder decision-making. AI aims to support stakeholder decision-making through providing actionable insights. However, it does not autonomously make decisions. Examples of AI decision-making augmentation include AI solutions that provide insights on valuable sales leads, estimations of customer lifetime value, and customer segmentation.

The AI business opportunity in decision-making is born out of the technology's potential to surpass the limitations of human decision-making capabilities. Psychology tells us that human decision-making is a cognitive process that produces a course of action from among a set of possible options. However, research in the field of behavioural economics has demonstrated consistently that these decisions are often not rational, leading to missed opportunities and lost profits. As a Nobel Prize winner and one of the forefathers of the field of research in economics, Daniel Kahneman has long explored why people often make irrational economic decisions. He explains that the combination of cognitive biases, limits of attention, and the tendency to overestimate our expertise in areas where we lack knowledge can lead to poor judgement. In regard to the business world, Kahneman offered a critical assessment, saying, 'You look at large enterprises that are supposed to be optimal, rational. And the amount of folly in the way these places are run . . . is actually fairly troubling' (Boyd 2017). According to a recent study of 500 managers and executives 98% fail to apply best practices in their decision-making (Larson 2018). It's time to face the facts: we may think we're using logic and expertise, but the reality is that we're often lying to ourselves. With the help of AI augmentation, we can unlock the potential for improved decision-making and increased decision quality. By better understanding the ratio of good decisions to bad decisions, we can better gauge the quality of our decisions and determine whether we made the right call in hindsight.

Although AI decision-making augmentation presents a tremendous opportunity, Gartner research vice president, Svetlana Sicular, warns that the confusion between AI and automation often overshadows the true power of AI augmentation: 'AI augmentation is the greatest benefit, a combination of human and artificial intelligence where both complement each other – something that is too often overlooked in the face of calamitous warnings of job losses' (Gartner 2017).

Example: Augmenting Credit Underwriting

AI-augmented decision-making is transforming the way credit card underwriting is done (Lee 2023). When a potential customer applies for a credit card, the credit card company usually requests a personal credit score from a credit agency. This score, calculated by the credit agency, is the result of a person's payment history and behaviour over many years. In the past, the underwriters from the credit card company focussed heavily on that credit score when making a decision about a potential customer's credit card application. However, this may not always be the best approach. For instance, a highly skilled technology manager with an income of $350,000 who just moved to the US can be denied a credit card or given a low credit limit due to the lack of credit history and therefore a low credit score. AI-based tools, however, can go beyond this limited view of credit worthiness and analyse a wider range of information, leading to better decisions to accept a wider range of customers and therefore providing greater returns. AI's credit recommendation can augment the underwriter's information basis by providing further insights in addition to the usual credit score.

The *business opportunity* of decision-making augmentation with AI is directly related to AI's ability to improve human decision-making quality by providing actionable insights, which could be a risk score in case of underwriting. By taking advantage of a vast amount of custom data beyond credit score and income, AI solutions can realise a 20%–30% increase in approval rates, while also reducing risk (Zest AI 2022). Indeed, the use of AI in decision-making has been found to reduce charge-offs and defaults by 30%–40% compared to human-only decision-making (Zest AI 2022). The *AI feasibility risk* for AI decision augmentation is often data and business domain knowledge-related. In the case of the underwriting example, AI feasibility risk is tightly linked to the availability of historical data. For instance, when forecasting credit default, there may be insufficient data to replace the current practice of using the credit score. In general, the information provided for through AI augmentation has to support the ability to take action in order to create a business opportunity. However, a big challenge of AI decision augmentation use cases is *stakeholder adoption*. Employees have to be willing to accept the AI solution's advice in order to realise business value, but this can only be done if the AI is trusted and stakeholder value is created. Without trust, the AI solution will not be adopted, and the potential value it could have created will remain unrealised.

The business opportunity for decision augmentation use cases is not always obvious, and the value creation is not as closely aligned with the opportunity as with process optimisation. Table 3.3 summarises the value-driving factors for decision-making augmentation.

Table 3.3 Value-Driving Factors for Decision-Making Augmentation

AI Value Creation Type	Value-Driving Factors		
	Business Opportunity	Feasibility Risk	Adoption Risk
Decision-making augmentation	Improved decision-making quality by providing prioritisation and insights on what actions to take	Identifying and providing relevant data that are business opportunity predictors Identifying actionability Availability of historical data	Low risk for the enterprise Medium risk for employees Relatively low customer risk; only if it reduces customer value

Additionally, the implementation of AI-driven decision augmentation projects can come with higher feasibility and adoption risks. The business impact of such projects may be delayed, because it might take time for its stakeholders to develop familiarity with the AI's recommendations and to adopt new behaviours and actions accordingly.

Decision-Making Automation

The automation of decision-making with AI is extending the decision augmentation process by offering not only actionable insights but also taking action itself. Although AI automation is often seen as a way to save costs by substituting human decision-making, its true potential lies in optimising it.

Although decision augmentation can improve the quality of human decision-making, decision-making automation with AI has the potential to increase decision yield and speed. Decision yield, or the success of a given decision when it is acted on, can be greatly improved through the use of AI. By providing clear instructions on what to optimise, AI can be capitalised on to increase efficiency, for example, providing the optimal discount to retain a telecommunication customer (Davenport et al. 2023). This can also lead to a business benefit because speed can be improved markedly; selling or purchasing stock or granting a customer's credit application faster, for example, can increase financial gains or reduce costs such as by swiftly shutting down low-performing media campaigns. Ultimately, the rise in speed and drop in cost per decision enables businesses to leverage it to previously unviable arenas. Take, for instance, the ability to alert customers ahead of time and block any potential fraudulent credit card charges – an activity that would be impossible to achieve with human intervention.

Example: Automating Credit Underwriting

AI has revolutionised the underwriting process by not just augmenting human decision-making but also by its potential of automating the process. A growing trend of software-as-a-service solutions from companies such as Zest.ai, Upstart, Scienaptic AI, and Pagaya is creating significant business opportunities for organisations looking to take advantage of this technology from an automation perspective. The increased decision yield and speed enabled by the automation of underwriting with AI provides credit card companies with a unique opportunity. An increased customer satisfaction and a more competitive underwriting offer provides a unique business opportunity. Not only are credit card applications now approved within seconds, but AI also enables companies to provide a risk adjusted credit line or personalised product recommendations. Furthermore, this automation eliminates the bottleneck of having to hire additional underwriters to handle more credit card applications, making it easier than ever for companies to grow their business. The potential of automated decision-making in the credit and lending industry is immense, and it goes beyond just replacing the manual process of underwriting. Cred.ai, Kabbage, Lending Club, On Deck, and others are leveraging the power of AI to unlock a new market segment, offering credit cards and loans to small businesses and consumers who would be rejected by established banks (Costa 2020; Erman 2015). The algorithms used by these companies draw conclusions from a broad range of data to evaluate risk and are very cost-effective, enabling them not just to accept different clientele but also pass savings onto their customers.

Although decision augmentation can be considered a pre-step to decision automation, they have a markedly different risk and opportunity profile. Not only do these use cases present the possibility to improve decision yield and speed on top of decision quality but also they could provide a lucrative *business opportunity* through the cost savings from replacing human decision-making. The learnings from use cases in decision automation are that AI's business opportunity and value creation are usually not closely aligned because the business opportunity of AI automation seems to be creating a higher feasibility risk as well as higher adoption risk. Table 3.4 summarises the value-driving factors for decision-making automation.

Table 3.4 Value-Driving Factors for Decision-Making Automation

AI Value Creation Type	Value-Driving Factors		
	Business Opportunity	**Feasibility Risk**	**Adoption Risk**
Decision-making automation	Business opportunity is an outcome of not just making higher quality decisions but also taking actions. Businesses can increase decision yield and speed compared to human decisions. Decision automation allows for disaggregation of decision-making.	Identifying and providing actionable decision options that have a direct impact on the outcome of a decision Increase of the risk of non-responsible and generalisable decision-making of AI	High risk for enterprise related to AI's decision management High risk for employees because use case could affect their value negatively High customer risk related to responsible AI decision-making and reduction of customer experience

The AI *feasibility risk* is highly related to identifying actionable decision options that have a clear business impact. In other words, the actions taken from AI must be able to improve the outcome of a decision. Although the risk of making a mistake with AI-automated decisions is omnipresent and a general concern, it can be managed by monitoring AI's decision outcomes. For example, car driving support capabilities such as lane assist or adaptive cruise control have been embraced by consumers while self-driving cars are still struggling with edge cases and unique situations in daily traffic in 2023 (Helmore 2022). Additionally, the risk of automation may be high for the employees leading to a lack of motivation to get involved with the AI initiative and *adopt* the final AI solution, because AI might take over their decision-making. However, AI can liberate employees from repetitive tasks.

AI Products and Services

AI is creating tremendous business opportunities as a product, service, or feature. In economics, a product is defined as a combination of benefits derived from its attributes, and a service refers to activities that benefit a company without tangible products (Parry et al. 2011). By using AI to enhance the perceived benefits of a product or service, companies have the potential to increase its value, enabling them to charge a higher price. The automotive industry is witnessing the growing adoption of AI as a product attribute, exemplified by Tesla's autonomous driving feature. Studies have demonstrated that consumers are willing to pay an additional 24% for a vehicle equipped with this capability. Starting in 2022, Tesla's full self-driving feature will be available for an extra $15,000 on cars priced between $50,000 and $150,000. This highlights the significant value AI can add to products, particularly in the automotive sector (Roth and Castro 2022). Essentially, AI has the capacity to enhance the perceived value of a product.

Expedia, a leading travel service giant with 168 million loyal customers, provides another example of an AI-powered service. It offers online flight and hotel bookings, travel packages, and more to consumers worldwide and connects them to 50,000 B2B partners, 3 million hotels, and 500 airlines globally (Murthy 2023). In an interview, CTO/president of Expedia Product and Technology, Rathi Murthy, highlighted that Expedia's various AI products make approximately 600 billion decisions to deliver their services. For instance, one of their AI products assists customers in finding the optimal price to pay for a flight to a chosen destination and advises them on the best time to travel within their desired price range (Murthy 2023).

Example: Building an AI Product for Detecting Diabetic Retinopathy

Google Health's AI application for detecting diabetic retinopathy had the potential to revolutionise the health care industry. With an estimated 415 million patients at risk worldwide, diabetic retinopathy is the fastest-growing cause of blindness, yet can be treated when diagnosed early (Peng 2016). To put the power of AI to the test, Google chose to launch its product in Thailand. The Thai Ministry of Health had set a goal of screening 60% of patients with diabetes, a seemingly impossible task given that only 200 retinal specialists served the country's 4.5 million patients. To bridge this gap, Google outfitted 11 clinics across the country with AI-trained systems to detect the disease, replacing a system in which nurses take photos of patients' eyes and send them off to specialists, a process that can take up to 10 weeks. But with 90% accuracy in a lab environment in less than 10 minutes, Google's AI solution had the potential to revolutionise the way the world diagnoses and treats diabetic retinopathy (Peng 2016).

But, when it was put into practice, the laboratory environment could not be replicated, leading to mixed results over time. In areas where the system was able to work well, it could be a great asset, but the varying quality of images and the presence or lack thereof of an internet connection posed real problems. Patients were being asked to travel to different clinics or, when that wasn't possible, to wait hours for their images to be processed. Nurses were even having to edit images by hand to make them acceptable for the AI solution. Despite the potential business opportunity, the AI solution proved to be rather disappointing. Hamid Tizhoosh, a medical researcher at the University of Waterloo in Canada, calls this 'a crucial study for anybody interested in getting their hands dirty and actually implementing AI solutions in real-world settings' (Douglas 2020).

Despite AI's tremendous capabilities to create valuable product features and services, its feasibility and adoption risks are high. Michael Abramoff, an eye doctor and computer scientist at the University of Iowa Hospitals and Clinics, highlights and urges caution against hastily implemented solutions and the potential for negative reactions from those who have had a bad experience with AI in the health care field (Heaven 2020). Table 3.5 summarises the value-driving factors for building AI products and services.

The value creation potential of AI products and services is a significant advantage over other types of AI value creation because it represents an opportunity for long-term, monetary gains. Other types of value creation are mostly limited in their business opportunity, whereas AI-driven customer value creation through a

Table 3.5 Value-Driving Factors for AI Products and Services

| AI Value Creation Type | Value-Driving Factors | | |
	Business Opportunity	Feasibility Risk	Adoption Risk
AI products and services	Business opportunities are an outcome of the increase in customer value compared to competitive products and the customer's willingness to pay a price premium for it	High risk of feasibility because real-world application might not align with lab environment and unforeseen problems can significantly affect customer expectations	High risk related to AI's ability to create customer value in real-world environment Low risk for employees because AI mostly does not affect their operations High customer risk related to value creation and trust in AI's responsible decision-making and its decision-making quality

customer-oriented product or service can provide a competitive differentiation, leading to increased market share or a price premium.

However, what use cases for AI products and services have proven is that their business opportunity and value creation are not easy to connect as an outcome of high feasibility and adoption risks.

Dr. Adam Bujak, CEO at KYP.ai

As the CEO of an AI company specialising in process mining and a former global head of intelligent automation at Capgemini, I have had the privilege of collaborating with numerous organisations in creating business opportunities through process optimisation. Allow me to share an exemplary story that I have encountered on multiple occasions.

Within a global business services organisation, a 47-year-old leader has successfully consolidated and optimised operations across various departments including finance, supply chain, human resources, marketing, information security, IT, and legal services in more than 55 different countries. With a strategic plan in place to not rehire retiring roles and effectively manage attrition cases, combined with ongoing improvement initiatives, the leader is confident in achieving the targeted 6% productivity improvement within the upcoming 12 months. However, the organisation faces complications due to the current economic turmoil. In response, the chief financial officer decides to raise the productivity improvement target from 6% to 14%. Recognising that their initial plans won't suffice to meet this new objective, the leader realises the need for a different approach.

Inspired by the concept of process optimisation, our leader sets a goal to analyse and optimise a subset of the 1,500 identified business processes that have been accumulated by the organisation over the past decade. However, on consultation with the team, it becomes apparent that manually analysing and identifying opportunities within these business processes would require an estimated 15 years to complete.

In response, the company's chief digital officer proposes a data-driven approach, advocating for the adoption of a platform capable of capturing patterns for AI-driven decision-making. The head of process improvement within the organisation builds on this idea, suggesting and implementing a digital value stream mapping strategy on a large scale. This data-driven approach not only reduces the effort required to identify potential process optimisation opportunities but

(continued)

also illuminates how to optimise them, thereby creating value optimisation opportunities that go beyond the targeted 14% productivity improvement.

This story exemplifies the daily challenges faced by shared services and global business services organisations. In the face of economic turmoil and ambitious targets, the key lies in making data-driven decisions on a large scale. Informed decision-making based on actual data and business cases becomes imperative in order to effectively navigate the economic pressures at hand.

Part II

Overcoming Value Challenges

Within the complexities of creating a business opportunity and mitigating the risks associated with AI adoption and feasibility, we start on a journey to explore the primary challenges of AI value creation. It is only by exploring the details, addressing, and comprehending the core of these value creation challenges that we can overcome them.

Among all of the potential challenges, we focus on some of the most prominent ones – challenges that have demonstrated their ability to significantly reduce the value of AI. We therefore discuss the unique elements of AI's value generation, the complexities of sourcing valuable data, approaches of generating actionable insights, the management of AI's decision-making, and the delicate task of building trust among stakeholders.

We provide you with real-world examples and practical use cases to demonstrate how these challenges can be overcome. Conquering these challenges is not merely about overcoming each individual obstacle; it's also about understanding the complex connection among them.

4

AI-Centric Elements

By far, the greatest danger of artificial intelligence is that people conclude too early that they understand it.
—Eliezer Yudkowsky (decision theorist and computer scientist, Machine Intelligence Research Institute)

Regardless of the type of value creation discussed in Chapter 3 (process optimisation, augmented or automated decision-making, or product and service creation), four essential elements must be taken into account when utilising AI to create value: business domain knowledge, algorithmic, data, and stakeholder motivation.

Business Domain Knowledge

In order to unlock the business opportunities unique to the application of AI, it's critical to come to a shared understanding of what constitutes business domain knowledge. As an economist, professor at Harvard Business School, and cofounder of the reputable consulting firm Monitor Group, Michael Porter has been credited with redefining the way in which companies and corporations think and act when it comes to their business strategies and operations. His work on strategic business development has demonstrated the existence of common strategies across industries and highlighted their potential to achieve a competitive advantage.

According to Porter, the goal of every business is to establish a competitive advantage by leveraging our knowledge of the distinctive components of designing, producing, marketing, delivering, and supporting a product or a service (Porter 1985). By fine-tuning each of these areas, organisations can build a sustainable competitive edge and

69

differentiate themselves from their competitors. Ultimately, this can result in better cost positioning and improved customer value (Porter 1998). That objective aligns with the categorisation of types of AI value creation described in the first part of this book. Whereas process optimisation, the augmentation or automation of decision-making, can offer business opportunities mostly related to increased efficiency, AI-driven product and service creation can enable business opportunities related to differentiation that is customer value focussed.

Constructing a Value Chain

As described by Porter, by breaking down an organisation into its strategic activities, a value chain can help companies better recognise existing or potential sources of differentiation in order to gain a competitive advantage (Porter 1985). The value chain is a collection of all activities with the intention to design, produce, market, deliver, and support a product, which are a reflection of an organisation's strategy, the underlying economics, and the activities themselves. The construction of a value chain is based on an organisation's activities in a particular industry.

However, an industry-wide value chain might not provide a competitive advantage according to Porter. This is why an industry-based use case approach for AI business opportunities has been found to be of limited value creation potential, as discussed in Part I of this book. Despite many organisations within an industry having similar value chains, each organisation's value chain is slightly different. For example, although the US retail giants Walmart and Target are competitors, the nuances of their respective value chains – from business strategy to product assortment to customer focus – illustrate the distinct paths each organisation has chosen to thrive. Walmart has taken a cost leadership approach, offering low-cost products across a variety of categories to households of lower incomes. Target, however, has opted for a higher-end shopping and service experience, offering a higher quality product assortment to its middle class target demographic. Although both organisations operate in the same industry, the areas in which AI can offer value are different.

A value chain is indicative of the total value an organisation creates, based on their primary and support activities. Primary activities, such as inbound and outbound logistics, operations, marketing and sales, and services, involve the physical creation and transfer of a product to the buyer. Meanwhile, support activities encompass the infrastructure, HR management, technology, and procurement functions of the organisation. By examining and understanding both types of activities, organisations can optimise their value chain and maximise the value of their product. After understanding the various activities that embody the value chain of an organisation, the next step is to assess if an organisation can effectively execute on it. To execute a value chain, an organisation must possess the necessary capabilities. A capability denotes an organisation's capacity to perform specific tasks, functions, or processes. They form vital components of business architecture because they articulate how an organisation's resources, processes, and technology synergise to deliver value. If an organisation lacks the capabilities necessary for a value chain, establishing those capabilities becomes imperative. The effort required varies from case to case; for instance, outsourcing a capability for a service provider might take just weeks, while building the 'data governance' capability for a century-old established company poses a challenge.

Identifying Business Opportunities

Identifying and leveraging discrete value activities as building blocks of a company's value chain and to establish the needed capabilities is the key to successful AI value creation. Porter's approach of starting with a generic perspective and then subdividing activities into increasingly specific ones is particularly effective here. For example, if a factory is to be assessed, it would make sense to break down all activities until each machine is examined individually, because each could potentially bring its own value to the equation (Porter 1998). Every activity is the result of the cumulative value created from its deconstructed subactivities. For example, inbound logistics can be broken down into distinct activities: receiving, storing and disseminating inputs to the product, and activities such as material handling, warehousing, inventory control, and vehicle scheduling, as well as returns to suppliers (Porter 1998). Those sub-activities can each be broken down further. Though it might seem simple in theory, practical situations frequently introduce further complexities. For instance, a value chain and the underlying processes often lack documentation because they have evolved over generations in legacy organisations. In such cases, gaining insight into the execution of these processes becomes a priority. Or if company growth has been driven by acquisitions, the execution of an enterprise value chain relies on diverse and unrelated technology stacks, leading to varying underlying value chains.

Each instance of breaking down value chain activities presents an opportunity to harness AI for decision-making. In fact, it is the *disaggregation* of value chain activities that can be augmented or automated with AI that is creating a business opportunity. Put differently, the potential for AI in business lies in the number of repetitive decisions across the value chain that can be improved by its application. When a major pharmaceutical company recently sought to optimise their advertising, they turned to AI to maximise their ROI. They started by comparing the effectiveness of different media channels: social media versus print journals. Of course, the number of decisions and their variance increased as the activity was broken down further, enabling them to differentiate among four media categories, more than 20 different social media platforms and print journals, and countless campaigns and creatives. Each level of granularity provided more opportunities to make improvements, from adjusting campaigns to meet the needs of different customer groups to enhancing creatives. By carefully and thoughtfully deconstructing the activity, the company was able to increase the number of high-quality decisions with AI that increased the company's media ROI to significant higher levels.

This example highlights that while replicating human-centered business processes with AI can create value, deconstructing these activities may unlock even greater business potential. However, the augmentation or automation of a value chain through AI and the deconstruction of activities often brings forth the challenge of obtaining accessible data that accurately reflects the underlying processes. When a process lacks digital support and its data is unavailable, a significant risk emerges. This leaves you with two options: identifying processes that are already digitised and coming with available data or concentrating on digitising processes using the appropriate technology.

The perspective of value chains is critical because it provides the value creation link of sometimes seemingly independent activities. The degree of interconnectedness of value chain activities can either pose a barrier to unlocking value creation with AI or serve as the key to discovering new business opportunities. For instance, an increased investment in quality inspections during the production of a car may reduce the need for service efforts after sales in the field, or higher media and marketing expenses may result in lower spending on sales representatives.

Consider the AI project described in Chapter 3, in which a telecommunications company aimed to enhance the effectiveness of their direct mailing campaigns. Through the utilisation of data from previous campaigns, they developed an AI algorithm that significantly increased the response rate to their mailings. However, the impact of this improvement may be rendered meaningless if not accompanied by an understanding of downstream activities in the value chain. In the case of the telecommunications company, one such downstream activity involves assessing the creditworthiness of customers to determine their eligibility for the company's services. If the direct mailing campaign targets customers who are ultimately deemed ineligible for credit approval for a phone contract, the enhanced mailing response rate fails to generate value for the company.

This highlights the significance of a comprehensive value chain perspective and a holistic view of the underlying processes – often a missing piece. Even though the AI solution is adding value, other aspects of the value chain can inadvertently be overlooked. Consequently, it may appear that your AI project isn't creating value, but it's actually the absence of integration within the broader corporate context. This is a common occurrence, underscoring the need to always adopt an end-to-end/value chain approach because the potential for failure often lies in areas outside the AI solution.

Algorithmic

The algorithmic foundation of AI's machine learning is not new. Although the cornerstone of contemporary AI and its present-day definition were established in the 1950s, through the pioneering work of visionaries such as Alan Turing and John McCarthy in the exploration of machines to mimic human cognitive functions, the history of its algorithmic foundation extends even further back (Anyoha 2017; Press 2022). In the domain of algorithmics, a strong connection exists between the algorithmics of statistics and the machine learning algorithms within AI. At the heart of both statistics and machine learning lie algorithmic principles that drive data analysis and pattern recognition. Although substantial common ground exists, it is pivotal to acknowledge significant differentiators that arise from the historical evolution and circumstances of each discipline.

In 1654, Blaise Pascal and Pierre de Fermat laid the groundwork for the field of algorithmics with their pioneering work in probability theory (Ore 1960), giving rise to the field of statistic, which has long been essential to fields such as economics, finance, pharmacological research, insurance, and manufacturing. Statistics is based on probability estimations and the inference of relationships from a smaller sample of data to make assumptions about the general population. For example, surveys of 3,000 people in the United States can be used to analyse their real estate purchase behaviour and to understand why people buy houses at different price levels, even though the survey represents a population of more than 300 million people.

Statistics-driven analytics has long relied on robust theoretical backgrounds and business- and domain-specific assumptions (hypotheses) to make sense of data that has never been readily available for an entire population and has proven to be costly to obtain. Statistical algorithms, while powerful, have been relatively simple to test and verify the assumptions made by researchers. By combining methodological rigor with theoretical foundations, the results of statistical algorithms can be used to validate outcomes and uncover statistically significant relationships between predictor variables and an outcome variable. One of the most commonly used algorithms in statistics is regression analysis.

Regression analysis could be a powerful tool, for example, to uncover the impact of age and income on a house purchase price and to predict future house prices. But it's important to consider that such statistical algorithms are based on certain methodological assumptions, such as linear relationships between predictor and outcome variables, and no correlations between predictor variables, which may not always hold true. For example, in the real world, as age increases, income usually increases, too, enabling people to purchase more expensive houses. Although age and income are not the only variables that can explain house prices, small sample data has required researchers to simplify their algorithms and select only a subset of predictors, accepting the limitations of that approach. During the statistical algorithm development process the relationships between variables must be formalised in mathematical equations. As such, the statistical algorithms must be founded on a theoretical basis, enabling the outcomes of the algorithm to be properly validated.

Statistics and machine learning are built on common mathematical and probabilistic foundations. They share concepts such as probability theory, linear algebra, optimisation, and calculus, which are essential for developing algorithms and models in both domains. However, since the new millennium, we've seen a revolution in technological advancements, upending the traditional notion of statistics and ushering in a new era of AI. Widespread data availability, cost-effective data storage, and computing power offered by cloud providers have reduced the need for probabilistic statistical methods to make assumptions about entire populations. Instead, machine learning, as the core algorithmic component of AI, has gained greater relevance in today's data-rich environment. Additionally, AI's machine learning algorithms, such as neural networks, decision trees, random forests, and gradient boosted machines, were able to overcome some of the problems of statistical algorithms, such as variable interactions and linearity assumptions. These algorithms enable far more complex decision-making processes than humans are capable of, and they are able to uncover complex patterns in large datasets.

Although statistics is grounded in theory and employs assumptions to construct mathematical formulas, the complexity of AI's algorithms has posed a significant challenge in terms of validation by humans. Consequently, the focus shifted from theoretical validation to singular metrics, such as accuracy or area under the curve (AUC) scores. Although these metrics might assist in assessing an algorithm from a high-level perspective, they mostly do not contribute to evaluating an algorithm's soundness in decision-making. However, the constantly increasing volume of data and the evolving computational capabilities enable organisations to continuously improve their AI algorithms. This enables AI algorithms to adapt and learn from new data, optimising their decision-making outcomes.

Data

Data is undoubtedly a critical component of any analytics endeavor, and when organisations set out to develop AI, data is often top of mind. However, Andrew Ng, a renowned AI visionary and the cofounder of Coursera and Google Brain, emphasises that one of the keys to success with AI lies not in data itself, but in the discipline of engineering the data needed to build a successful AI system. Unfortunately, due to a lack of insight into the data characteristics required for AI, its full potential is frequently left untapped (Kahn 2022). According to Andrew Ng, the understanding of AI's data requirements is essential in order to avoid 'lots of, let's call them $1 million to $5 million projects [. . .] that no one is really able to execute successfully' (Brown 2022).

But how exactly can organisations leverage their data for AI? Organisations have to move beyond their understanding of data requirements for traditional business intelligence and adopt an AI-centric perspective. The four major characteristics for AI-centric data are its *disaggregation level, immediacy, quality, and context specificity*.

We already discussed that AI can unlock greater business opportunities by providing enhanced decision augmentation, offering insights into causes and actions to improve decision quality. We also discussed its potential to create a business opportunity by automating decision-making at a much more granular level by identifying trends, disparities, and opportunities that might not be apparent when looking at aggregated data. For example, AI can make decisions on website design and its elements for each individual visitor optimising their user experience, rather than having a website manager define the design elements for target groups based on aggregated data. However, data must be available at the *granularity level* of AI's decision-making.

AI-centric data is also characterised by its *immediacy*: it must be available at the moment of decision-making. Historic data is used to train algorithms and identify patterns that inform decisions, but new data must be present to make new ones. For instance, company sales representatives plan their routes and strategies on Sundays for the coming week. Having data about which stores will increase or decrease in sales volume over the next two to three weeks would assist them in prioritising their efforts. To accurately predict store sales volume, the algorithm might need access to the last two weeks of sales data, sales data from two years ago, external data such as the 10-day weather forecast, or even recent sales team actions.

Another critical characteristic of AI-centric data is its *quality*. According to Gartner, insufficient data quality exacts an annual average cost of roughly $12.9 million on enterprises and IBM's assessments reveal the overall consequences of subpar data quality at a staggering

$3.1 trillion – or about 17% of the GDP of the United States in 2016 (Gartner 2021; Redman 2016). Low data quality affects many stakeholders such as decision-makers, managers, knowledge workers, and data scientists, who have to address it in their everyday work. It is time-consuming to correct and inconvenient to accommodate. However, although poor data quality might be only a nuisance for business intelligence, it diminishes business opportunities for AI because it significantly affects an AI's algorithms ability to learn patterns within low-quality data. Unlike business intelligence AI is not able to compensate for low data quality through aggregation. With an increasing data volume, the challenge of poor data quality worsens. Hence, the emphasis on data quality's significance for the application of AI cannot be overstated.

The last characteristic of AI-centric data is its *context specificity*, a requirement that has important implications for the ability to draw conclusions from it. Andrew Ng highlights an example from manufacturing for technical reasons with the need for custom AI algorithms being tailored to each individual factory's output: 'In deep visual defect inspection, every factory makes something different. And so, every factory may need a custom AI algorithm that's trained on pictures' (Brown 2022). However, context is not only determined by technical conditions; it can also be affected by business, legal, or political factors. Take, for instance, publicly available demographic data published by the census bureaus from various countries. Although there are many organisations that put trust in the accuracy of that data in the US, China's census bureau statistics has been questioned for potentially not being accurate and skewed by Beijing's 'motive and means to fudge its statistics' (Lowsen and Tiezzi 2022). Consequently, the utilisation of census data in AI algorithms may yield distinct effects on decision-making in the US and China. Another illustrative example for the context specificity is coming from the application of AI for food inspection. AI-driven vision systems are commonly employed to carry out this process and enhance food quality assessment. Due to variations in regulations in food quality across countries or the language displayed on packaging, AI solutions including AI hardware and software have to adjust to consider varying context information (B&R Industrial Automation 2023).

Stakeholder Motivation

Effective AI solutions necessitate expertise in a specific business domain, an understanding of unique data characteristics, focussed algorithmic approaches, and a profound comprehension of stakeholder motivations to navigate the challenges of AI adoption. Particularly, conflicts of interest among various stakeholders can pose a significant risk. The value perception of an AI solution is dependent on its ability to meet stakeholder needs and interests, and if there is potential for risk, stakeholders may be hesitant to embrace it. For instance, the debate surrounding the impact of AI on the job market has caused many employees to shy away from adopting AI in their work environment (Vasunandan and Annamalai 2023). If the motivation is to automate business processes through AI to reduce costs, this risk has to be addressed. Although some are concerned about the possibility of job loss resulting from AI automation, it is equally important to consider how AI might affect intrinsic work motivation. If AI augmentation or automation leads to the feeling of more external control or fewer social interactions, there may be less interest in adopting it (Kelley et al. 2023). Similarly, customers are cautious about AI technology due to concerns about AI discrimination and ethical implications of AI decision-making. It is important to recognise that AI solutions differ from other software solutions and that successful AI adoption requires a deep understanding of stakeholder motivation and the ability to mitigate potential risks.

Decades of research in psychology have revealed that there are two primary forms of motivation: extrinsic and intrinsic (Deci et al. 1999). Both types of motivation play crucial roles in driving individuals to adopt AI solutions in their professional and personal lives (Choi 2020; Vreede et al. 2021). Intrinsic motivation refers to an individual's inherent drive to seek out challenges, novelty, and opportunities for growth, exploration, and learning. This behaviour is often self-rewarding and personally fulfilling, meaning that it has a significant impact on an individual's self-perception. There are three essential needs that can either bolster or hinder intrinsic motivation: autonomy, relatedness, and competence. When these fundamental needs are met, individuals tend to exhibit higher levels of engagement, performance, well-being, and, ultimately, greater levels of motivation (Buckingham and Coffman 2005; Vreede et al. 2021).

To feel *autonomous*, rather than controlled, is a fundamental driver of human behaviour. It's the desire to determine one's own fate, to experience autonomy and freedom. But AI solutions can create a sense of being controlled and constrained in decision-making by augmenting or automating it. For example, AI's data hunger has created concerns about the extensive use of personal data used for training of its algorithms or the use of AI causing misinformation (Haan 2023). On the flip side, AI can help to establish autonomy, provide clarity and control for complex decision-making, and curate and offer insights essential for making sound business decisions.

The second fundamental motivation driving human behaviour is *relatedness* – the longing to feel connected to other people and groups. This need can be fulfilled through both physical and digital connections. Spending time together, being involved in one another's lives, and showing expressions of care are just some of the ways to nurture the need of relatedness. Especially with the recent development of generative AI, where AI showed that it is capable of taking over human conversations in for example call-center interactions, there are fears that communication and collaboration will be diminished (Kelley et al. 2023). Yet AI also has the potential to foster relatedness in the area of robotics, where AI one day might help to alleviate loneliness and elevate mental health, suggests a research report from Auckland, Duke, and Cornell Universities. Although a real companion is certainly the best solution, an artificial one might be 'a solution for the millions of isolated people who have no other solutions' (Vahaba 2023).

The desire to acquire *competence* and bolster expertise is a fundamental need in the professional context – one that can have a profound impact on job motivation (Deci et al. 2017). With the rise of AI and its potential for augmented and automated decision-making as well as AI's promise of improved business outcomes compared to its human counterpart, AI is affecting how people think about their own competence and has the potential to increase or diminish the feeling of competence. For example, AI can support the driver of a car with the ability to drive more safely or to eventually take over driving fully.

Extrinsic motivation, however, is often driven by rewards or punishments tied to payment, social status, seniority, or reputation. Fear of job loss, reduced income, and decreased power due to AI can be extrinsic inhibitors to collaborating with an AI initiative and cocreating and eventually adopting an AI solution.

Stakeholder Value Creation Through AI Solutions

Many AI initiatives focus on maximising the value derived from AI solutions by prioritising perceived usefulness and ease of use. Although the former can improve an organisation's performance, the latter is aimed at reducing employee resistance to adopting the technology (Krauth 2018; Scholkmann 2021). However, this approach overlooks the stakeholder motivation of employees or customers, which is the key factor in creating stakeholder interest in adopting an AI solution. To truly leverage the potential of AI, it is essential to harness its business opportunity for the organisation and the positive value it can bring to its customers and employees. The challenge, then, is to develop an AI solution that satisfies motivation requirements across all stakeholders involved. For example, partial automation of media campaigns via AI could present a high business opportunity. However, without careful consideration, it could undermine the intrinsic motivation of stakeholders, leading to feelings of low competence, reduced decision autonomy, decreased relatedness, and even the threat of job loss. A more effective solution could be to augment, rather than automate, media planners' decision-making, thus creating a positive business opportunity without compromising motivation. Furthermore, if the AI solution increases performance-related income, it could create extrinsic motivation for adoption. However, value creation for all stakeholders might not always be possible and a conflict of interest is inevitable (e.g. reduction of labor costs) with clear consequences that have to be addressed before the project start.

This example may suggest that automation leads to reduced stakeholder value creation. However, that is not necessarily the case. In the insurance industry, underwriters have expressed concerns about the potential negative implications of automating and augmenting the underwriting process with AI (Intelligent Insurer 2023). Nonetheless, AI can be utilised to increase intrinsic and extrinsic motivation. For example, AI can automate the underwriting process for applications that do not carry any risk, freeing up human underwriters to focus on more complex cases that demand their experience and skills. This enables them to have greater autonomy over their time, more time to work with customers, and to interact with their peers on more challenging cases.

Despite the significance of stakeholder motivation, the ease of use of an AI solution is still crucial for its successful adoption. For instance, media planners are accustomed to receiving PowerPoint presentations with performance insights and actionable suggestions from media agencies. If an AI solution does not provide this guidance, the media planning team may be hesitant to use it because it increases the risk of mistakes. Therefore, it is crucial to ensure that stakeholders feel comfortable using an AI solution.

Stakeholder Value Creation Through Cocreation of AI Solutions

An AI project can be a source of motivation for stakeholders beyond just the value delivered by the AI solution itself. Intrinsic and extrinsic motivation can be derived from the project's success and the recognition it brings. For example, the reputation of AI as an innovative technology can enhance the reputation of stakeholders who are heavily involved in the project, providing them with career advancement opportunities and recognition for their contributions.

This can be achieved by assigning a stakeholder to an AI project, empowering them to 'own and drive' the concept with the support of the AI initiative, and subsequently 'present' it to other stakeholders. This instills a sense of pride and ownership, consequently enhancing the probability of success. For example, a workshop series to showcase AI's potential for value creation could be sponsored by a specific leadership stakeholder of an organisation. With the first workshop being a resounding success and setting the gold standard for executive-level transformation tools, stakeholders who sponsored the event will get credit for its success and associate themselves with the project's forward-thinking and innovative vision. Although project success may rest on one person's shoulders, intrinsic motivation can be shared among stakeholders. AI projects can facilitate knowledge sharing, bringing together valuable knowledge from different stakeholders and building competence in the field. By fostering a sense of relatedness through collaboration, stakeholders can gain competence and career autonomy, positioning them for future job opportunities. As the intrinsic and extrinsic value of the AI project increases, successful implementation and adoption of the AI solution become more likely.

An example of an effective approach to achieve is offering cross-functional and cross-hierarchical team-based workshops that target specific areas of AI solution development. The 'cross-functional' aspect is pivotal, because it integrates input from various points within the value stream, highlighting impacts on and by different stakeholders. Simultaneously, the cross-hierarchical dimension provides insights into the day-to-day operations and challenges faced by teams on the ground, aiding leaders in understanding their perspectives. Conversely, frontline workers can glean insights and learn from the thought processes of their leaders.

Dr. Das Dasgupta, Chief Data Analytics and AI Officer at Saatchi & Saatchi

As the chief data analytics and AI officer at Saatchi & Saatchi, and with previous positions at Viacom and Amazon, my primary focus has always been the convergence of business, data, algorithms, and stakeholder motivation to create value through AI.

For me, every AI project begins with a business perspective. To identify where AI can benefit business operations, I always consider the dimensions of excellence outlined in Michael Treacy and Fred Wiersema's (1995) book, *The Discipline of Market Leaders: Product Leadership, Operational Excellence, and Customer Intimacy*, which closely aligns with the types of AI value creation discussed in this book. Viewing the world through this lens enables the identification of AI use cases. Some cases have already been proven, and others continue to evolve. For instance, companies such as UPS, FedEx, and Walmart focus on operational excellence and process optimisation, whereas companies such as Apple or Pfizer concentrate on product development and marketing. Meanwhile, companies such as Amazon, Netflix, and Meta's advertising arms focus on delivering unique

(continued)

customer experiences through recommendation engines powered by AI. However, the key to AI value creation for all these companies is not merely replicating human decision-making but speeding up and enhancing decision-making, especially at the individual customer level.

Subsequently, AI algorithms are connected to the various types of AI value creation. For instance, convolutional neural networks and graph neural networks drastically accelerate drug discovery and product creation. AI algorithms enable the ideation and launch of new products by exploring millions of product design combinations informed by engineering principles. Augmented and automated decision-making leverages AI to predict when, how much, and how willing customers are to make purchases based on their behaviour in social media, app use, website interactions, and buying habits. Last, robotic process automation, aided by process-mining tools like Skan.ai or Celonis, streamlines manual, repetitive tasks, reducing costs significantly.

The subsequent step is based on 'data'. Frequently, people begin with the wrong question – 'What do we do with all this data?' I, however, always start with the business question – 'What specific, measurable, actionable, relevant, and time-bound problem would you like to solve or opportunity do you wish to explore?' This approach ensures that the data's context, quality, availability, and timeliness align with the business's requirements. The business question then guides hypothesis generation, determining the data required for precise modeling exercises.

Stakeholder motivation plays a critical role in these exercises. The first question on stakeholders' minds is, 'What's in it for me?' The optimal response is to align their business challenges with an AI solution by fostering a sense of ownership. Throughout my career, I have consistently empowered business stakeholders to 'own' their AI projects and present the business outcomes and findings in cross-departmental meetings. This approach motivated them to collaborate, assist the AI initiative in obtaining what they needed, codesign and codevelop solutions, and ultimately celebrate the results.

AI-Centric Elements in Advertising

Now, let's explore the role of AI in the media and advertising industry. AI has already revolutionised numerous processes within the advertising industry by providing a more efficient, quicker, and cost-effective way of decision-making. We can divide the advertising process into campaign development and live campaign phases involving market research, campaign strategy, script generation, creative development, media planning, and media flighting.

For instance, extensive research is conducted when planning a product launch campaign, including consumer surveys and online behaviour analysis, segmenting the audience according to their preferences. Targeting the right audience and crafting tailored messaging now rely on proven AI techniques such as unsupervised clustering methods, for example, hierarchical clustering or K-means clustering of respondent data, supplemented by demographic, ethnographic, and psychographic data overlays.

Once the target audience is defined, the next step involves scripting a strategic message. Although advertising agencies traditionally rely on specialist copywriters for this task, contemporary generative AI tools such as ChatGPT can generate high-quality scripts. When it's time to move from scripting to the creative design phase, AI solutions such as MidJourney can be used to create visuals, and vendors such as Monet Networks and Swayable can analyse the reactions of participants to those designs by reading their facial expressions, effectively predicting the impact of creative content on the target audience.

Allocating media budgets to the appropriate channels to reach the audience is another area where AI excels, employing AI optimisation to maximise key performance indicators such as awareness, consideration, propensity, and exposure while minimising costs. AI solutions such as EDO can predict campaign success by analysing internet search activity for a product within an hour of its TV airing. Similarly, various AdTech vendors offer alternative solutions, including iSpot, Neustar, Acxiom Analytic Partners, Nielsen, and others.

However, we've encountered various challenges related to data and stakeholder motivation. Securing the right data with high-quality and contextual relevance for effective AI applications has proven to be a significant challenge. Even when we've identified relevant data within the organisation, the AI initiative often encounters hurdles in its acquisition. Moreover, it has become evident that data can be subject to inaccuracies in collection, manipulation, and misrepresentation.

(continued)

These obstacles are, to a large extent, intertwined with issues related to human motivation. Political sensitivities are an ever-present concern, and unless stakeholders have trust in the AI initiative with their data, challenges arise right from the outset. We've often found it necessary to revisit our approach and proactively address motivational and data-related obstacles to attain actionable insights for informed profitable decisions.

5

Collecting Valuable Data

Most of the time spent in school is devoted to the transmission of information and ways of obtaining it. Less time is devoted to the transmission of knowledge and ways of obtaining it (analytic thinking). Virtually no time is spent in transmitting understanding or ways of obtaining it (synthetic thinking). Furthermore, the distinction between data, information, and so on up to wisdom are seldom made in the educational process, leaving students unaware of their ignorance. They not only don't know, they don't know what they don't know.
—R. L. Ackoff (professor at the Wharton School, University of Pennsylvania)

In today's data-rich business environment, sifting through the noise to identify relevant data is paramount because the financial burden of collecting data can be significant for an organisation. Data management costs, including third-party sourcing, architecture, governance, and consumption, can account for up to 5% of a company's operating costs (Grande et al. 2020).

Especially when organisations start to scale the application of AI, the demand for AI-centric, disaggregated data invariably increases, making data optimisation a key challenge for businesses. As organisations start to recognise the financial burden that data creates, they are responding by optimising their data life cycle management, including data sourcing, data governance, data infrastructure and storage, and even archiving and deleting data. AI achievers have learned the value of focus, often restricting the scope of data management to fewer than 50 reports and 2,000 variables (Grande et al. 2020). However, in order to focus on the most valuable data, it is essential to shift the perspective from data's statistical makeup to its functional characteristics.

Data's functional characteristics are directly related to its impact on AI's decision-making. Data's functional properties are typically specific to each domain, bound tightly to the theoretical foundations that govern it. Take, for instance, behavioural economics: information about consumer attitude, satisfaction, emotions, and past behaviour is hugely helpful in predicting their future behaviour. Similarly, in the realm of medicine, knowledge of diagnostics and past patient behaviour can be incredibly useful in predicting medical outcomes, such as the future onset of a chronic condition. Its insights can help to avert the possibility of such events by prompting a shift in patient behaviour. As those examples illustrate, data's functional value and true power lies in its capacity to predict events and uncover causal relationships (Brown 2022).

A Data Value Framework

For decades, R. L. Ackoff has been lauded as a pioneering systems theorist, unifying the disparate disciplines of computer science, business, and philosophy. His groundbreaking work at the Wharton School of the University of Pennsylvania has provided insights into the functional nature of data providing a framework of how to identify valuable data (Ackoff 1989; Jennings 2020).

According to Ackoff, *data*, in and of itself, is of no value. It's unorganised and lacks context, making it difficult to interpret. However, when data is processed and shaped into a relevant form, it becomes *information*, which adds value to the perception of a subject and is the product of discrete, objective facts or observations. It's more compact and useful than data, though the difference between the two is not necessarily structural, but rather functional. In the field of analytics, the specific information available for all observations is referred to as a *variable*. For example, the age of a customer as a data point in a table with other customers is transformed into information.

Information is the building block of *knowledge*, which is the outcome of learning, from others or from experience. It is the know-how that enables us to transform information into actionable instructions. Knowledge gives us the ability to answer the why and how-to questions that enable us to increase efficiency. AI is often seen as a way to apply existing knowledge, rather than generate new knowledge. However, some AI systems are able to learn, adapt, and acquire knowledge. Although knowledge has a longer life span than information, it eventually becomes obsolete.

The highest level of Ackoff's hierarchy is wisdom. Wisdom is the highest form of content held in the human mind (see Figure 5.1). Each of these content categories builds on the one before it; for example, there can be no wisdom without understanding and no understanding without

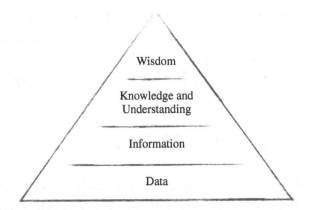

Figure 5.1 From Data to Wisdom Pyramid
Source: Adapted from Ackoff 1989.

knowledge (Ackoff 1989). Wisdom and knowledge are both essential for creating business value, albeit in different ways. According to Ackoff, it requires knowledge and its understanding to increase efficiency, whereas wisdom entails the ability to increase effectiveness. Although wisdom is an outcome of knowledge, wisdom is not just the attainment of knowledge, but rather 'a process in which an individual increases their ability and desire to satisfy their own needs and legitimate desires, as well as those of others' (Ackoff 1989). In other words, wisdom is an increase in potential, not attainment.

According to Ackoff, this is a key point to consider when looking at the capabilities of AI. AI is able to increase efficiency through knowledge and logic, but it lacks the ability to increase potential. This is why, for Ackoff, wisdom is something that machines cannot achieve. In relation to the types of value creation discussed in Part I of the book, knowledge is key to increasing the efficiency of processes, whereas wisdom can become of relevance for augmenting and automating decision-making and especially for building products and services with AI. Tracing the journey from wisdom and knowledge to create a business opportunity and downwards to data reveals the underlying value of data, which is ultimately determined by its functional significance at the bottom of the hierarchy.

Putting a Value on Data

Data has the power to open up new business opportunities by, for example, improving decision-making quality. Knowing how to utilise data to maximise AI's potential for producing more accurate decisions is essential for unlocking its full decision-making opportunities. Here's what this could mean in an example. The financial stakes for credit card companies are high when it comes to underwriting credit card applications – a credit card debt of almost $1 trillion for all Americans was recorded in 2022. Yet, despite this, default rates remain relatively low, with only approximately 2% of cardholders defaulting annually (Schulz and Shepard 2023). But even a mild decrease in these defaults could make a profound difference to a credit card company's bottom line. With the average US account holder owing an average of $7,279 in credit card debt as of December 2022, a company with 1,000,000 customer accounts would lose $146 million each year just in defaulted payments, if we apply the mentioned 2% average on this simplified example and do not consider additional expenses (Schulz and Shepard 2023). By carefully evaluating the risk of potential customers during the credit card application process, a company can create a business opportunity by avoiding the risky ones. It's important to note that about 2% of cases fall into this category using standard practices. By employing AI solutions alongside customer data, a skilled underwriter can more effectively distinguish between risky and non-risky customers. This could potentially lower the 2% rate to about 1.8%, resulting in an added contribution margin of $14.6 million. This represents a 10% reduction from the initial $146 million.

Inspired by the 2021 National Financial Capability Study that tracked over 20,000 Americans and their associated financial data points, we created the following fictitious and simplified example, in which about 17% of Americans reported difficulty paying off their credit card balances in full within the last 12 months (Lin et al. 2022). This information can serve as an indicator of which customers may be at risk for delinquency and potential default. With this knowledge, the underwriter can make more informed, higher-quality decisions and reduce the risk of bad investments.

However, let us define a baseline scenario to be able to identify the value of data. If an underwriter would not have any data about an applicant, they had to accept a random subset of all applications. As it is a random subset, its distribution would represent the overall population with a 17% share of customers struggling to pay their credit card. Figure 5.2. shows those customers.

This scenario provides a valuable baseline for decision-making and any improvement in decision quality has the potential to create a business opportunity. However, what would happen if we had information about the applicant and insights about customers with the same information?

Using information such as the age of credit card applicants, the underwriter can compare the applicant to existing customers. When breaking down the potential

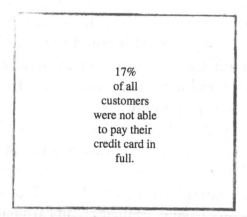

17%
of all
customers
were not able
to pay their
credit card in
full.

Figure 5.2 All Potential Customers with Percentage Unable to Pay Credit Card in Full

applicants by age, the data shows that 27% of those under 34 are unable to pay their credit cards off, compared to 17% of those between 35 and 64, and just 4% of those 65 and over. Figure 5.3. visualizes those customer segments.

Another piece of information the underwriter might be able to leverage about credit card applicants is their income. When breaking down the population by income, 22% of those with an income under $50k have difficulty making payments on time, compared to 13% of those between $50k and $300k and 15% of those making more than $300k. Figure 5.4. shows those customer segments.

Let's calculate the value of those individual data points. We know that of the 1,000,000 potential applicants who have been screened before applying standard screening methods, only 100,000 can be accepted. But of those 100,000, 2,000 of them carry a risk of $14.6 million in credit card defaults as per our example. How can we use data to identify which applicants are least likely to default? Leveraging age and income

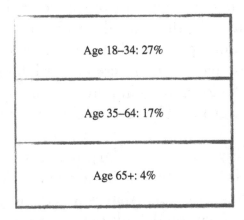

Figure 5.3 Potential Customers by Age with Percentage Unable to Pay Credit Card in Full

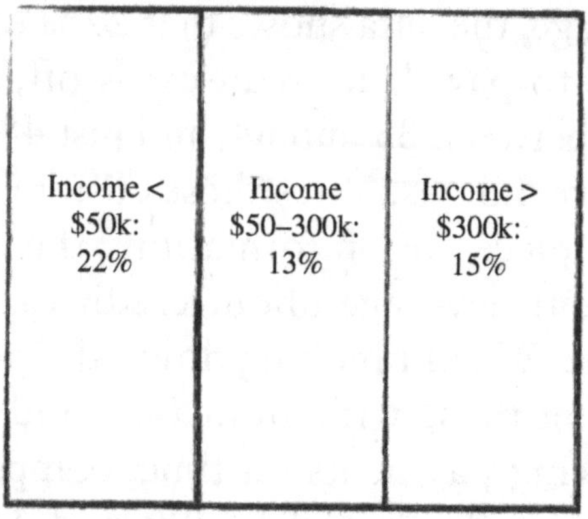

| Income <
$50k:
22% | Income
$50–300k:
13% | Income >
$300k:
15% |

Figure 5.4 Potential Customers by Income with Percentage Unable to Pay Credit Card in Full

data to select applicants can dramatically reduce overall default risk. For example, by selecting only applicants 35 years and older or those with household incomes of over $50,000, the total default risk could be reduced by up to 25% or $3.65 million.

By joining both age and income information, underwriters can unlock further insights and discover groups of people who represent an even lower risk of default. As the data reveals, those aged 35 or older and earning $50,000 or more per year have a lower, in fact 11%, chance of not paying their credit card bills – a 36% decrease and $5.26 million in potential savings if we only focus on that group. Figure 5.5. shows those customer segments.

In this very basic exemplary demonstration we see the value of data playing out in improving the quality of decision-making. Although that is a very simple example where we only focus on default risk, a decision tree–based

Age 18–34 and Income < $50k: 31%	Age 18–34 and Income $50–300k: 23%	Age 18–34 and Income > $300k: 40%
Age 35–64 and Income < $50k: 23%	Age 35–64 and Income $50–300k: 14%	Age 35–64 and Income > $300k: 12%
Age 65+ and Income < $50k: 6%	Age 65+ and Income $50–300k: 3%	Age 65+ and Income > $300k: 2%

Figure 5.5 Potential Customers by Age × Income with Percentage Unable to Pay Credit Card in Full

AI algorithm is built on the same principle. The distinction between human and AI decision-making can be found in their complexity. With access to more data beyond income and age, such as payment history or spending patterns, AI algorithms can make more complex and higher-quality decisions, separating high- and low-risk customers with greater accuracy.

Identifying the Right Data

How do we identify the correct data to capitalise on business opportunities? Ackoff's framework helps guide us on that path, which provides a visual illustration of the process of getting from business opportunity to the data it requires to be created (Ackoff 1989). The flow chart in Figure 5.6 helps to connect the dots between data and business outcome.

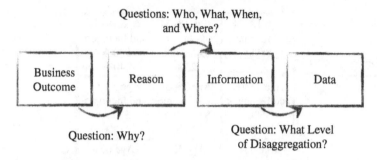

Figure 5.6 Working Backwards from Business
Outcome to Data

Business Outcome

First, we need to select the business outcome. This can be
revenue generation or cost reduction, as well as indicators that affect those, such as customer loyalty, operational
efficiency, or others. In a specific context such as default
risk, from our previous example, we are trying to reduce
costs by decreasing default of potential customers.

Reasoning for a Business Outcome

Second, it is imperative to understand why a specific outcome is occurring. In the customer default risk example, the
challenge is in understanding *why* certain customers have
difficulty handling credit and struggle to pay off their credit
card debt while others easily do so. Extending research in
the functional field of payment behaviour offers valuable
insight into the multiple causes that can explain *why* some
people are at a higher risk of not paying off their credit
card debt when compared to others. Financial education,
lifestyle, sociological background, attitudes towards debt
and credit card use, income situation, net worth and
financial ability, as well as life events can all play a role in

forming an individual's financial decision-making process with impact on default risk (Fernando and Khartit 2022). Let us focus on two of the reasons behind the challenges of credit card decision-making: financial literacy and financial ability. Both just serve as an example to explain the subsequent steps of the framework.

Information That Is Connected to Reasoning

Financial literacy is defined as the competence 'to understand and effectively use various financial skills, including personal financial management, budgeting, and investing' (Fernando and Khartit 2022). With the help of the 2021 National Financial Capability Study data we can see if the reason is valid (Lin et al. 2022). According to their data, those with a lower financial literacy rate have a higher chance of not being able to pay their credit card bills (23%) compared to those who consider themselves financially literate (14%). Although having an insight into the financial literacy of credit applicants would be beneficial for improving decision quality, the task of objectively assessing it during the credit card application process is challenging.

However, by asking who, what, where, and when questions, we can gain insight into potential applicants who may possess a low/high financial literacy. For example, we might find that financial literacy is correlated with age – younger applicants are typically less experienced with financials, and thus show more irresponsible purchase behaviour. This was confirmed by research that showed that age is indeed related to financial literacy, and that younger people consider themselves less financially literate than their older counterparts (*Citizen Tribune* 2023).

In addition, we can ask when there is a time of less financially literate/more impulsive purchase behaviour. Research has suggested that irresponsible spending patterns are often seen during the Christmas season, when people tend to spend more money than usual (Accenture 2022). We could make further assumptions about where people with lower financial literacy live. In comparison to the reasoning of financial illiteracy, which cannot be directly assessed during the credit card application process, the information leading to it might be possible to consider.

The second reason we are considering as a contributor to credit card default risk is a consumer's inability to pay credit card bills or the ability to cover day-to-day needs and still have money left over at the end of the month. Based on the 2021 National Financial Capability Study data, the risk of not being able to always pay credit card bills was 23% for individuals who never or sometimes have money left over at the end of the month, compared to 9% for those who always have money left over. This suggests that financial ability might be a crucial factor for credit card issuers to consider when assessing applications. However, it is hard to directly determine an applicant's financial capability during the credit card application process. However, a person's income can be indicative of a person's financial capability. Knowing that a minimum income level is necessary to cover living costs, it is possible to collect information about an applicant's yearly household income and overall living expenses. People with lower incomes and higher living expenses might be more likely to experience shortages at the end of the month. Assessing where people live (e.g. New York or San Francisco, where living expenses are higher) or what job they have might gain further insights into the future financial situation of a potential credit card holder.

Data/Level of Information Disaggregation

Eventually, the level of data aggregation for understanding the reasoning behind the individual credit card applicants is at the individual level. We will require information about every applicant at the time of application to apply AI for the purpose of predicting an applicant's default risk probability.

Defining the Value of a Data Portfolio

Data is often described as an asset with economic value for organisations, but its true worth is difficult to define. Accounting approaches such as the market approach, with-and-without method, and cost approach have been suggested as ways to put a hypothetical price tag on data. The market approach uses data transactions to evaluate its monetary value, the with-and-without method estimates the value of data by quantifying its impact on cash flows if they need to be replaced, and the cost approach considers the cost of replacing data as an indicator of its value (Deloitte 2020).

However, the traditional approaches to data valuation have lacked an understanding of how data can affect an organisation's business outcomes. Moreover, it has been difficult to recognise value differences of individual data assets in the existing data portfolio, making it hard to shape. The capability to assess value of data at different data aggregation levels of the data portfolio enables organisations to increase their return on investment, a measure that is known as return on data assets (RODA) (Nakai 2022). The RODA concept enables organisations to analyse how efficiently they are using their data assets for business purposes. A higher RODA indicates that the organisation is utilising their data assets more effectively.

The fundamental formula for RODA is simple (see Figure 5.7).

By breaking down the equation into income driven by data assets divided by the cost to create and maintain them, it forces a focus on both maximising the business value of data assets and finding the most cost-effective way to create, maintain, and secure them. The RODA formula can be a powerful tool for AI and data initiatives. CDOs can use the RODA formula to compare domain-specific data assets across the organisation and uncover new ways to maximise the return on their data investments. At the micro level, the RODA framework acts as a practical tool to help prioritise project-specific data assets. Although high RODA values can help to allocate resources for data governance towards data assets, low RODA values on data assets can provide an indicator to decommission them. On the macro level, it gives valuable information to allocate capital more strategically and provides insights needed to make data-related technology decisions that improve the corresponding return on investment.

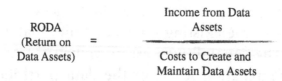

$$\text{RODA (Return on Data Assets)} = \frac{\text{Income from Data Assets}}{\text{Costs to Create and Maintain Data Assets}}$$

Figure 5.7   RODA Formula

Karan Dhawal, Enterprise Data and Transformation Strategy Leader at ZS Consulting

As the enterprise data and transformation strategy leader at ZS Consulting, I have collaborated with numerous organisations to unlock the value of their data portfolios. Understanding the significance of data and how to leverage it effectively is crucial in driving companies towards the development of internal or external data products that can lead to revenue generation through various business models.

Based on my personal experience, I have observed that data value comes from data products. A compelling example of this comes from my passion for the Milwaukee Bucks, a basketball team in Wisconsin. They launched a unique service called *Bucks Pass*, a highly personalised data product. Using customer 360 data, seat availability, demand forecasts, and profitability as input variables, they crafted a subscription offering called the *Bucks Spring Pass*, covering 10 regular season games. The catch was that seat assignments changed for each matchup, depending on availability. This innovative approach proved to be a win-win for both the Milwaukee Bucks franchise and the fans. For fans, getting 10 games for $200 was 120% cheaper than before, and the franchise saw a substantial improvement in game attendance, averaging over 62,000 more attendees per year compared to the previous five years (excluding COVID-19 years), with an average of more than 720,000 attendees per year.

Highly data-driven organisations achieve this through a foundational process of data valuation. They consolidate information across the enterprise and business lines, diligently tracking the decisions being made, their types, and the decision-makers involved. By meticulously documenting key business processes and the underlying data that supports them, these companies establish visible data value chains, highlighting the essential data elements that enhance their business processes. These identified data elements then become potential candidates for data monetisation. The data monetisation process relies on insights derived from the relationships between key business questions, outcomes, processes, and the available key data, all contributing to the decision-making along the data value chain.

6

Creating Actionable Insights

The goal is to turn data into information and information into insight.

—Carly Fiorina (former CEO of HP)

Years of experience in data-driven decision-making have made it clear to us that simply pursuing a data-driven approach will not lead to business opportunity creation. Despite today's technology offering numerous ways to leverage data for business operations, and the promise of consultancies, data, and analytics initiatives to deliver insights that bolster the bottom line, only 26% of organisations have experienced success (Bean 2022). But what is the key to success?

Crafting 'actionable insights' from data holds the key to business opportunity creation. Although the phrase *actionable insights* has become popular, its application to guide the design and development of analytics and AI solutions is not widely adopted. Despite AI practitioners often prioritising metrics such as accuracy, recall, precision, sensitivity, and specificity to optimise algorithms, the aspect of actionability is typically overlooked in their evaluation (for an overview of commonly used evaluation metrics; see Blagec et al. 2019).

However, what are effective examples of actionable insights? In the marketing arena, they could assist in determining a budget allocation, selecting a creative campaign, or setting a product's price – each aimed at driving sales. In the context of customer relationship management, actionable insights might involve assigning a customer success manager, presenting a warranty or loyalty offer, or providing discounts – all with the goal of ensuring customer retention and proactively preventing attrition. In quality management, this could entail identifying defective products. Ultimately, actionable insights play a role in guiding decision-making throughout value chains, and these insights can be translated directly into actions that yield tangible impacts on business outcomes.

Let's explore how AI can be used to facilitate actions to achieve tangible business results. AI offers two distinct strategies to inform actions: output-based selection and output adaptation. However, AI goes beyond providing insights; it can also take actions that lead to the desired business outcome. In this chapter, we will investigate the details of how to connect actionable insights with actions using these different strategies: output-based selection, output adaptation, and AI taking action.

Actionability Through Output-Based Selection

Output-based selection is an approach that utilises AI-generated prediction outputs to make informed choices from a set of options. By employing this strategy, businesses can strategically prioritise certain choices, such as choosing high-revenue customers over low-revenue ones or prioritising low-cost customers over high-cost ones out of a pool of potential customers, thus influencing a business outcome.

Although the objective of AI in this case is to provide insights that can influence actions, it is essential to ensure that the actions have an impact on the desired business outcome. For instance, in the example of insurance retention highlighted in Chapter 2, we demonstrated that it is possible to accurately predict potentially churning car insurance customers out of the whole customer pool.

Unfortunately, the actions we discussed might not prevent them from leaving and can therefore not create a business opportunity. However, a project predicting potential customers that are at risk of canceling a contract with a telecommunications provider might be able to create a business opportunity because the offer of discounts or additional services are actions that have an impact on customer loyalty (Rudin 2020).

However, even if there are actions that can influence a business outcome it is important to make sure that the insights delivered by AI enable an organisation to take those actions. Let us demonstrate using the retention example from the telecommunications industry. For a major telecommunications provider, the objective of a retention project was to identify and target customers with a high likelihood of attrition in order to proactively retain them. The key challenge was to define the output variable: what constitutes customer attrition and how can it be measured? Initially, customer attrition was defined as the cancellation of their contract. However, it became evident that this definition was not actionable. By the time a customer cancels their contract, they have typically already taken advantage of an offer from another telecommunications company. The chances of winning them back at this point are very low and leave the organisation with no further actions to take. Therefore, a more refined definition of customer attrition was needed. It was found that customer attrition should be defined as when a customer is actively considering changing their telecommunications provider and may be contemplating canceling their contract. Identifying this critical moment enabled the telecommunications company to take proactive actions and influence the customer's decision. As a result, the refined definition of attrition became 'Attrition is when customers are actively considering changing their telecommunications provider'.

Output-based selection is a powerful strategy to create actionable insights with AI, yet it is only effective if you have a sufficient number of choices, for example, if a credit card company can choose low-risk customers out of a pool of many credit card applicants. But what if you don't want to make a selection – or you can't?

Actionability Through Output Adaptation

When the selection of observations based on a predicted output/insight is not feasible, it may be necessary to adjust the output itself. To properly weigh the possible impact of various actions on a given output, AI can be a powerful tool. The difference to output-based selection is that with this strategy of input adaptation it is possible to assess actions based on the extent of their impact on the business outcome, for example, AI can help to select the most profitable actions by comparing potential returns to their associated costs.

Let's consider our example of a credit card company with 1,000,000 customers. The standard action for a credit card company in situations when existing customers might have a risk of default is to reduce the customer's credit line in order to protect the company's financial interests (Thanawala 2023). However, are there other actions that can be taken to mitigate the risk of default? For instance, could we proactively address a customer's risk of default? In Chapter 5, we examined various reasons that contribute to a credit card holder's struggles to pay off the balance of a credit card and eventual default. Those reasons included financial education, lifestyle, sociological background, attitudes towards debt and credit card use, income situation, net worth, financial ability, and life events (Fernando and Khartit 2022; Lin et al. 2022). What if we could enhance a customer's financial education and guide them towards a more financially aware lifestyle? Or provide them with protection, such as insurance for unexpected life events that may lead to default? By taking such proactive measures, we might be able to reduce a customer's default risk and positively affect their credit card payment behaviour. In addition, we might increase the loyalty of such customers as well.

Both strategies of triggering business actions, namely, output-based selection and output adaptation, can be implemented in parallel to maximise the impact on your business outcome. For instance, a credit card company can utilise output-based selection to identify customers who are at a higher risk of default, and then proactively take measures to mitigate that risk. By combining these two strategies, organisations can enhance their decision-making processes and optimise the effectiveness of their actions.

Actionability Through AI Automation

The third option for facilitating actions with the help of AI involves the combination of insights and actions. The output of AI in that case is not the insight but the action itself, which is critical for the automation of decision-making.

Tesla's self-driving AI feature is an example of AI combining insights and actions to enable autonomous driving capabilities. It is at least partially able to take action and navigate on autopilot and allows the vehicle to automatically change lanes, take highway exits, and navigate on-ramps and off-ramps with driver confirmation (Threewitt and DePietro 2023). Although the driver remains responsible for supervision, the actual execution of these actions is carried out by AI. Another illustration of AI's practicality emerges in the realm of industrial applications. In daily industrial operations, AI frequently takes action, particularly within quality control processes. For instance, in almond processing, AI plays a pivotal role in identifying and segregating undesirable almonds from conveyor belts to prevent further processing. In this case, AI not only generates insights about which almonds to remove but also actively takes action to achieve this (FANUC America 2023).

One more recent example for AI taking action is the application of generative AI. Generative AI refers to a type of AI that can produce original content, such as images, music, or text, resembling human-created content. Generative AI algorithms utilise machine learning techniques, such as deep learning, to generate new data based on patterns and examples from existing data. One notable application of generative AI is OpenAI's generative language algorithm, ChatGPT. It is a type of AI algorithm that uses deep learning techniques to generate human-like text responses in a conversational manner. ChatGPT is trained on large amounts of text data and can understand and respond to questions and statements in a conversational format. It can be used in a wide range of applications, such as virtual assistants, customer service chatbots, language translation, and more. ChatGPT is designed to understand text and take action by generating text responses that are contextually relevant and coherent, making it a powerful tool for natural language processing and conversational AI applications. In addition to the application of generative AI in conversational AI applications, it can be used for various applications, including art, music, literature, gaming, design, and more. For instance, generative AI can create realistic images, compose music, and even design new products (Gupta and Parker 2023; McKinsey 2023).

Identifying Actionable Inputs for Output Adaptation

We explored in Chapter 5 how to connect data to business outcomes. In detail, we proposed an approach to identify reasons that are causing a specific business outcome and connected measurable information to those reasons. By asking a series of questions (why, who, what, when, and where), it is possible to understand the underlying causality including related predictor variables that can increase AI's prediction relevance and accuracy of a specific prediction output. Although this is the approach to identify valuable data for output-based selection, the good news is that the approach to identify actionable information for output adaptation requires only a slight adjustment. We just have to dig a little bit deeper for the reasoning of the business outcome and pose the essential question of how to affect the business outcome by affecting a specific reason. In other words, what actions can we take to influence the reasoning of a business outcome? This question will divide our previous approach into two distinct pathways, separating actionable from non-actionable insights (see Figure 6.1).

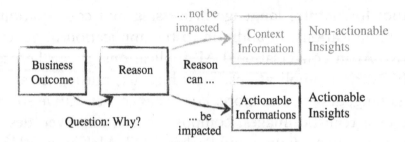

Figure 6.1   The Two Pathways of Insights

Although the non-actionable insights are invaluable in setting the stage and forming the context of a business outcome, it is the actionable insight that has the power to actually change business outcomes and, in turn, capitalise on the business opportunity. The following use case from the area of sales territory management will help to understand how to create actionability through output adaptation.

Example: Creating Actionable Insights for a Luxury Car Manufacturer

A luxury car manufacturing company has set its sights to increase the sales volume of their dealerships. They are not able to select dealerships to maximise their sales and have to apply output adaptation to exploit a business opportunity. At the core of a car dealership's success is their ability to influence the sales volume – a business outcome – in their location or region. Figure 6.2 shows the geographical distribution of the car manufacturer's dealerships across the US.

The visualisation indicates significant disparities in yearly car sales volumes between dealerships. The question is *why* do dealers differ in their sales?

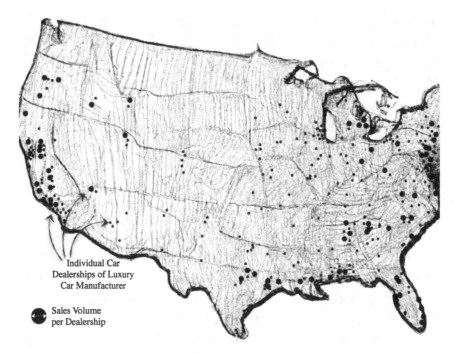

Individual Car
Dealerships of Luxury
Car Manufacturer

Sales Volume
per Dealership

Figure 6.2 Overview of Car Dealerships of Luxury Car Manufacturer across the US

Source: Visualisation based on creation from DALL·E 2 from OpenAI.

Interviews with the dealer leadership, industry experts, and dealer owners, along with secondary research, uncover a variety of reasons potentially influencing the sales volume differences between the dealerships. External conditions such as dealership accessibility, regional competition, and the size of the luxury car target group in the area; afford-ability driven by average pricing, promotional discounts, local dealership offers, and regional gas prices; preferred car availability, which is affected by the size of the car inventory; out-of-stock situations for specific models; customer care represented by the number of sales representatives related to number of customers; customer awareness, affected by regional advertising, and many more can be identified as potential reasons and predictors of sales volume (output) differences among dealerships. When asking *how* those reasons can be affected, we can split the given information into two groups: non-actionable and actionable. Although external conditions such as regional competition or dealership accessibility are mostly non-actionable, most of the others might be influenceable.

Let's focus on two exemplary dealerships: Dealer ABC in Ohio and Dealer XYZ in California, which had significantly different sales volumes last year – 500 new cars for ABC and 2,100 new cars for XYZ. As we previously discussed, our focus is on identifying the reasons, such as average pricing, out-of-stock occurrences, price promotions that contribute to this substantial disparity in sales volume between the two dealerships. The ultimate goal is to precisely understand how each of these factors influences the sales performance of a specific dealership.

By gaining precise insights into the contribution of each of those factors to sales, the leadership of each dealership can effectively influence the levers that affect their outcomes. For instance, dealer ABC's smaller size may result in customers not finding their preferred car in the dealership's inventory. Moreover, the disparity in the number of salespeople between the two dealerships could lead to customers waiting longer and ultimately choosing to visit a different dealer. Dealer XYZ's provision of additional offers and promotional discounts for specific car models may also contribute to their higher sales volume. Furthermore, the geographic location of each dealership plays a role, as dealer ABC's Ohio location may have a lower concentration of target customers for luxury cars compared to dealer XYZ's California location. Understanding the various reasons behind the sales differences can help dealerships devise effective actions to influence their sales volume positively. By leveraging AI and analysing the decision-making process involved in predicting sales volume, using the mentioned information as input, dealerships can evaluate the impact of potential actions on sales volume. Figure 6.3 provides an overview of the importance of all the various predictors on car sales volume across all dealerships.

The figure reveals that although the majority of the differences in sales volume between dealers can be attributed to non-actionable variables (from the perspective of a dealership), actionable variables still exert a significant impact. In fact, based on the estimation from Figure 6.3, actionable variables can account for up to 20% of the sales volume differences, presenting a compelling business opportunity (sales opportunity) that cannot be overlooked.

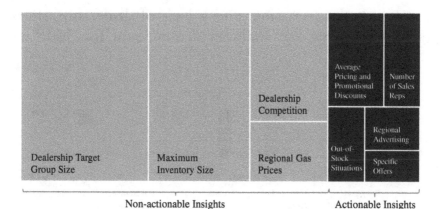

Figure 6.3 Overview of Most Important Sales Volume Predictor Importance Across All Dealers

To capitalise on this opportunity, the leadership of a car dealership takes the AI-generated insights on how both actionable and non-actionable variables can influence the sales volume at a specific location. As depicted in Figure 6.4, AI can effectively identify car sales volume optimisation opportunities for dealership ABC. This AI-driven approach empowers dealerships to make informed decisions and take targeted actions to enhance their sales performance and overall business success.

The results of dealer ABC compared to an average dealership uncover a number of distinct differences that are key to understanding the lower sales volume seen there. The smaller target group size and the smaller maximum inventory size (maximum cars on the lot) lead to 200 cars less than the average dealer. Those variables describe the local environment and conditions, which are mostly non-actionable for the dealership. That means that they are not in control of the dealership. However, there are actionable insights to be gained as well. The lack of promotional discounts and a higher average pricing, less regional advertising, and a lack of dealership offers on, for example, car maintenance account for 300 cars

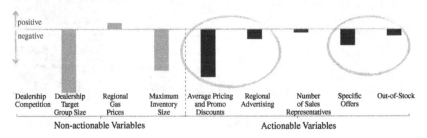

Figure 6.4 Impact of Sales Volume Predictors for Dealership ABC

below the average dealership. The car manufacturer can now take advantage of those actionable insights to support their individual dealerships to increase sales volume. Those actionable insights are the ones that eventually create a business opportunity.

Increasing Actionability Through Decision Disaggregation

In the previous example, we discussed how information can help to drive a dealership's actions to affect sales volume. However, what if the team has only very limited or inefficient actions at their disposal? Can they still take actions, and if so, how can the dealer leadership team create actionability with AI? Drawing from Porter's teachings about value chains, the key to unlocking greater actionability lies in breaking down business activities and disaggregating decision-making processes (Porter 2008).

Example: Actionability Through Disaggregation of Media Operations

One of the most common decision challenges in media management is optimising and allocating a company's media budget effectively. By using the power of media mix algorithms, organisations can gain valuable insights into the average impact of different media channels on sales volume. For example, a telecommunications company analysed two years of data and realised that it achieved 9% short-term ROI on its media campaigns, which means that for every $1 spent in media campaigns it made a return of $1.09. This was accomplished by allocating their media budget across three channels: television (50%), social media (30%), and print (20%). The average short-term ROI for each of these channels was 10% for television, 20% for social media, and −10% for print (as shown in Figure 6.5).

Media departments face the challenge of determining the best way to allocate their media budget to achieve the maximum ROI, with numerous budgetary combinations to consider. However, the impact of that activity on media ROI is limited due to our example company optimising their decisions only at an aggregated level. That means that the impact of reallocating some of the budget from TV to social media or the other way around on total media ROI is relatively low. To fully leverage the potential of media investments, making decisions at a more disaggregated media level can increase ROI through greater actionability. This involves breaking down media budget decisions and moving from choosing between different

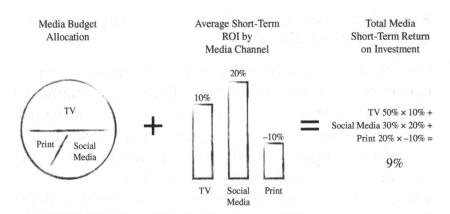

Figure 6.5 Total Short-Term Media ROI Calculation Across Media Channels

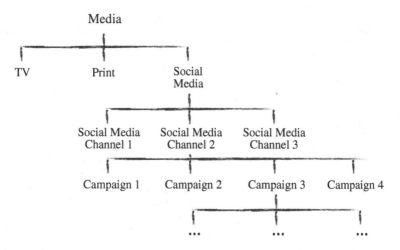

Figure 6.6 Disaggregation of Media-Related Decision Opportunities

media channels to making decisions within those channels, and even further down to individual campaign levels (as shown in Figure 6.6).

For instance, social media comprises different sub-channels, each with its own unique ROI. Over the last two years, the ROI for these sub-channels has varied significantly, ranging from −40% for social media channel 3 to +80% for social media channel 2 (as illustrated in Figure 6.7).

By reallocating the budget from social media channel 3 to 2, the media department may witness a potential rise in ROI from their social media efforts, increasing ROI from 20% to 42%. With the same social media budget, the overall media ROI could increase from 9% to 16%.

Nonetheless, media optimisation can be taken even further, with the media department breaking down decision-making to individual campaigns on social media channel 2. On average, the ROI for that channel was 80%, but certain campaigns exceeded 500% or more in

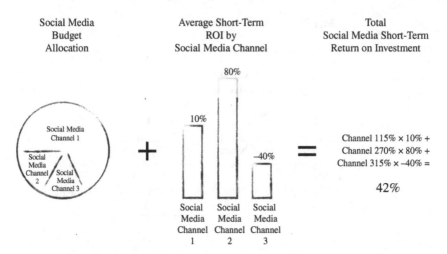

Figure 6.7 Total Short-Term Media ROI Calculation Across Social Media Channels

ROI. Why such a difference? The answer might be that some campaigns only aired TV commercials that were not optimised for the social media channel, whereas the more successful ones utilised social media influencers who engaged with their followers. By considering all decision-making levels and options, optimising ROI on a campaign level for each sub-channel and sub-channels for each media channel can raise total media ROI to 50% or more.

The capabilities of AI for decision optimisation is critical in that example because with every further disaggregation level, the complexity of decision-making increases dramatically. Although it might be possible for humans to make decisions on a high level, it will become increasingly complex on a level that considers, for example, investment decisions by combining channel, sub-channel, campaign, creative/influencer, target group, and even time of the day or day of the week. AI can help to suggest or take action to optimise investments on every level and increase ROI overall.

Increasing Actionability Through Experimentation

Sometimes a business activity cannot be broken down further for increased actionability, all available actions have been taken, are unlikely to have an impact on a specified outcome, or a lower aggregation level of decision-making cannot be supported with the data available. The only way out is to experiment with new actions that might have the ability to effect an outcome and therefore create a new business opportunity. Experimentation involves manipulating one or more actions while measuring their effect on an outcome variable, and controlling for contextual non-actionable factors.

Experimentation is deeply rooted in business practices and is widely applied in diverse sectors to drive informed decision-making and enhance business outcomes. For instance, in digital marketing and advertising, experimentation is employed to assess distinct ad versions, landing pages, email campaigns, and calls to action. In commerce and retail, particularly online retail, diverse layouts, product placements, pricing strategies, and checkout processes are tested to elevate user experiences, boost sales, and heighten customer loyalty. Similarly, in product development, experimentation serves to evaluate new features, product variations, and enhancements. A commonly employed experimentation technique is A/B testing, which involves comparing various choices of a specific action to identify the choice that achieves a better business outcome (Gallo 2017).

Experiments hold a pivotal role for AI value creation. They can be applied to substantiate the business impact of AI algorithms by comparing AI-driven outcomes with control scenarios lacking AI, or by testing actions for implementation within AI optimisation. For instance, the video streaming provider Netflix employs A/B testing and experimentation to constantly test their innovations, such as new AI recommendation algorithms to evaluating actions supporting AI with choices. For example, Netflix is optimising its content recommendations or promotion tactics to elevate user experiences, amplify customer engagement, and increase customer loyalty (Netflix Research 2023; Urban et al. 2016).

Example: Increasing Actionability Through Experimentation in HR

From large-scale job losses to the 'Great Resignation' following the COVID-19 pandemic, many companies had to rethink their approach to employee retention (Fuller and Kerr 2022). In the following example, a car manufacturing company was seeking ways to retain its employees. Analysing the reasons why people were leaving their job, the company uncovered a mix – from overall burnout represented by many years in a profession, reduced spare time because of a long commute due to the distance they had to travel, to missing competitive compensation with a lower salary.

The key to retain the talent is to take action and address the reasons for why the employees are leaving the organisation. For example, an employee in the marketing department might show signs of departure and AI provides insights to the cause related to the employee's long commuting distance and their current salary. But what can the manager do to prevent the employee from leaving? The manager is not able to act and change where the employee is living in relation to their job location, yet the manager might have the opportunity to alter the employee's salary. Unfortunately, in that case, the organisation holds extremely tight restrictions when it comes to payment ranges, meaning the worker is already receiving a top tier salary for their role. This would leave the manager without any actions to take.

However, the manager realises that the employee in question has a long commute to work, which presents an opportunity to act: allow the key talent to work from home. After reviewing the situation, the manager discoveres that 30% of the marketing department's employees have a lengthy journey to work. Although the HR department has to approve this action for the marketing department, the manager can experiment with that action to understand its impact on employee retention.

Paul Hurlocker, CTO at Spring Oaks Capital

As the chief technology officer at Spring Oaks Capital and former VP of machine learning at Capital One, my primary focus has always been driving impactful technological advancements. However, the true value of technology, particularly AI, lies in its ability to support and drive business actions, which serve as the bedrock for creating business opportunities. Among the various methods of evaluating and driving these actions, experimentation stands out prominently.

A common thread among successful organisations that derive value from AI is a robust culture of experimentation. Establishing this culture entails dedicating time to define and measure business outcomes within the context of experiments. When this approach is scaled across the entire organisation, experiments accumulate, yielding data-driven insights and actionable conclusions. This continuous learning agenda nurtures exceptional product experiences, optimised

(continued)

financial outcomes, and the agility required to maintain a competitive edge. Cultivating this culture starts with the unwavering commitment of leadership to make experimentation a fundamental element of value creation. To ensure experiments are aligned with business objectives, leaders must set measurable enterprise-level goals. Teams then focus on projects that drive these goals forward. Whenever feasible, executing these projects as A/B tests ensures precise effectiveness measurements. A/B tests are particularly valuable for evaluating the performance of AI algorithms and providing them with new actions within diverse contexts. Alongside this strategic framework, leaders should invest in processes, roles, teams, platforms, and tools to facilitate rapid experimentation on a larger scale.

For instance, within the financial services sector, we successfully implemented an AI-optimised multichannel engagement platform. The core differentiators and growth targets of the business were translated into business objectives and key results, forming the foundation for the product road map. One specific objective aimed to enhance consumer engagement through AI across communication channels. Key results were established to elevate right party contacts over the phone and enhance click-through rates for emails and text messages. AI algorithms were developed to deliver actionable insights on optimal moments and methods for engaging consumers through various channels. Experiments were conducted to compare randomly scheduled communications in the control group with those selected by AI in the test group. The efficacy of experimentation was evident from the outset.

In summary, the creation of business opportunities is intrinsically tied to fostering a culture of experimentation that is in alignment with business objectives. This approach perpetuates continuous learning, yields exceptional outcomes, and bestows a competitive advantage.

7

Building Stakeholder Trust

A lot of times, the failings are not in AI. They're human failings, and we're not willing to address the fact that there isn't a lot of diversity in the teams building the systems in the first place. . . . And you realise, if you're not thinking about the human problem, then AI isn't going to solve it for you.

—Vivienne Ming (executive chair and cofounder of Socos Labs)

One of the most significant challenges for AI initiatives has been building stakeholder trust. Trust plays a crucial role in creating value through AI because stakeholders are more likely to adopt and not resist an AI solution if they trust that it will deliver the promised benefits and does not create negative side effects (e.g. discrimination of customer groups that might lead to a lawsuit). But establishing trust is not a one-dimensional task. To achieve success, AI initiatives must establish trust with all stakeholders, including the organisational leaders, employees, customers, as well as other groups of interest, such as regulators or investors.

However, the challenge of creating trust for technology adoption that AI is facing is not new. Since before the new millennium, enterprises have been undergoing digital transformation, yet the adoption of a data-driven culture in most enterprises remains elusive. This is evidenced by the adoption challenges of dashboard technology, which, since the early 2000s, has been hailed as a platform for business intelligence, promising to visualise data and share valuable business insights across an enterprise. However, the adoption rate of dashboards remains stagnant at about 30% (ThoughtSpot, 2021).

Technical issues, such as design, user experience, and real-time availability, have been cited as causes of non-adoption. Yet, despite common user complaints about their experience, lack of security, and challenges in processing and visualising large data volumes, Microsoft Excel has been adopted by more than 1 billion people (Carstens et al. 2021). This demonstrates that technical issues cannot be the only reason for the rejection of dashboard technology. The real reasons go much deeper – they are rooted in the very foundations of the intentions of organisations to leverage data and analytics. A study conducted by Deloitte in 2019 revealed 67% of executives do not feel comfortable accessing or using data from their organisation's tools or resources. Even at companies with strong data-driven cultures, a significant 37% of respondents still express discomfort, indicating a profound lack of trust in their enterprises' business intelligence initiatives (Smith et al. 2019).

With the growing adoption of AI for its advanced data-driven capabilities, building trust in the technology and its providers has become crucial for businesses. Creating stakeholder trust is therefore a critical factor in overcoming the challenge of AI value creation. In this chapter, we will delve deeper into the ways to earn trust among stakeholders in AI.

Creating Trust

To earn the trust of stakeholders, an AI initiative must demonstrate its ability to deliver value and meet stakeholder expectations. Once trust is established, it serves as the driving force that motivates stakeholders to fully embrace and leverage AI-enabled solutions.

The topic of trust in the space of AI is often addressed from a technical perspective, such as AI transparency, explainability, and the potential for bias in decision-making. Although this is an important consideration, it can be short-sighted if not paired with an understanding of the motivations behind its application. AI solutions can be trusted to make high-quality, unbiased decisions, but they may not be applied in a way that benefits all stakeholders. To ensure that AI solutions are embraced by all stakeholders, trust in the AI initiative and the AI solution must be established. The experience of AI achievers and psychology research has shown that *benevolence, ability, and integrity* are the essential dimensions for creating trust in AI and its initiative (Svare et al. 2019).

Benevolence is seen as a belief that one party is focussed on the well-being and best interests of another party, beyond any profit motive. It can signal that an AI initiative has positive intentions and that an AI solution is unlikely to harm a stakeholder, that an AI initiative is trustworthy because they are not motivated solely by self-interest, and that it can create a sense of connection to the stakeholder. Most important, it can create a sense of obligation to reciprocate that behaviour.

Ability is the capacity to wield influence within a particular domain and bring an AI opportunity to fruition. It involves the skills, competencies, and characteristics necessary to construct a viable AI solution and one that will create value for its stakeholders. When the AI initiative has a track record of success or demonstrates consistent performance, it can create a sense of predictability and reliability.

Integrity is the perception that an AI initiative adheres to a set of principles that stakeholders deem acceptable, that an AI initiative's actions and communications and an AI solution's decisions are transparent, consistent, and ethical. When the AI initiative honours prior agreements and an AI solution makes decisions in accordance with established standards of justice, it is said to possess integrity.

Although all of the trust dimensions are relevant, not all of them are equally important in building a trustful relationship between an AI initiative and its stakeholders. Research has proven a conditional structure of the three dimensions related to the order in which they become relevant. Ability is a key factor in forming ties, but only once benevolence and integrity have been established (Shazi et al. 2015). Especially when the goals of the different stakeholders (from the enterprise and its management/ shareholders to its employees and customers) have a potential to be misaligned and a conflict of interest might arise in which the adoption of an AI solution could have negative consequences for one of them, benevolence and integrity are critical.

Establishing Trust in an AI Initiative

For years, AI achievers have been striving to build trust in their AI initiatives. From John Deere, Commonwealth Bank of Australia, IBM, and Google, organisations have proved that their AI initiative can offer value and show benevolent behaviour, improve lives and have a positive impact on society. We will show how those organisations created trust in their ability to use AI responsibly through sharing their expertise and knowledge. Furthermore, by upholding integrity through transparency and accountability in their actions, these organisations created trust among their stakeholders and cultivated an environment of trust for the application of AI.

Establishing a Benevolent AI Initiative

Over the past several years, AI achievers have launched various AI projects to show benevolent behaviour by demonstrating their commitment to employee and consumer welfare. For instance, IBM established the Green Horizons initiative in 2014 to tackle air quality issues through predictive analytics based on data collected from connected sensors in Beijing (Javerbaum and Houghton 2020). Meanwhile, Google is investing $8.5 million+ in funding to 31 NGOs and academic groups who are using AI and data analytics to tackle the pandemic, such as monitoring and forecasting disease spread, improving health equity, and supporting health care workers (Javerbaum and Houghton 2020). Commonwealth Bank of Australia is a prominent example in fostering collaboration and promoting knowledge sharing. In this way, it has been able to make a real impact in creating trust in their AI initiatives (Commonwealth Bank of Australia 2023).

The concept of *collaboration* for driving innovation is not new – it has been around for decades (Christensen 2013). Collaboration is an outcome of trustworthy behaviour, such as performing to promise, dealing honestly and equitably with each other, sharing resources and responsibilities, and to act with the partner's interests in mind. Let's explore a few ways to jumpstart the collaboration between an AI initiative and its stakeholders. One way to facilitate benevolence through collaboration and to understand the interest of different partners is through active listening. Listening can have many forms, such as brainstorming sessions and workshops, in-depth interviews, or casual engagements and conversations. The intention behind listening is to show interest in the stakeholders' motivation and to find out how to create value for them. It also helps to identify business opportunities and to find and evaluate stakeholder risks. Personal conversations, interviews, and small-group conversations are methods that are appropriate for that purpose. However, although it is possible to listen to a small group of employees, listening to a larger population of employees or consumers to understand their needs and motives can be more challenging. This lack of listening and observation skills in today's technology education and industry has created opportunities for a new type of expert in addition to the technical ones, resulting in a surge of anthropologists joining the ranks of technology giants. As anthropologists have long been captivated by the richness of human cultures, customs, and their interrelationships, Intel and Xerox have been quietly tapping into their knowledge and skills to get a deeper understanding of their customers and to inform product design. Now, more tech companies such as Uber, Facebook, Spotify, and Google have begun to do the same (Tett 2019). Good listening requires asking the right questions to gain an accurate understanding of the other person's point of view. It's essential to avoid assumptions based on our own knowledge and experience and to create trust by talking to stakeholders.

In addition to listening, timely and honest communication is crucial for collaboration. Communication is especially critical when it comes to showing transparency and to provide clear project expectations. However, unrealistic expectations towards AI are often set before an AI initiative is even underway. Consulting and accounting firms, AI industry partners, and the media contribute to the hype of AI by generalising selected business outcomes and making claims that are more aspirational than realistic. To avoid disappointment and ensure success, AI initiatives, perhaps even more so than other organisational initiatives, have the burden to keep expectations grounded in reality. Unrealistic expectations are one of the reasons why many organisations and stakeholders are feeling let down by the technology's capabilities to create business value. However, transparency is critical not just when it comes to unrealistic expectations. It's essential to provide information about the rationale behind the decisions made by AI. For instance, illustrating why a consumer receives a specific credit score and how they can influence it is necessary to build trust in it. For example, Experian, the multinational data analytics and consumer credit reporting company, explains the influencing factors of their credit score to their customers and provides individual insights to their customers on actions to improve it (Experian 2023). Likewise, outlining how a business outcome and potential opportunity is generated from AI's decision-making is essential to instill trust in the results.

In many cases, stakeholders may not know what they want or need because they're unaware of what's possible (Aten 2021). This is why *knowledge* sharing is important, especially at the beginning of AI projects. This reciprocal process of exchanging information between an AI initiative and its stakeholders is a critical component to identify business opportunities, make predictions, and take action. Knowledge sharing can be enabled through a variety of methods, including in-person workshops, online courses and classes, handbooks, and other tools. The Commonwealth Bank of Australia has crafted an innovative foresight webinar series to enable its business customers to confidently chart their path into the future with

AI (Commonwealth Bank of Australia, 2023). Intel's AI Academy offers an incredible resource of knowledge for developers, data scientists, students, and professors, and Google's AI resource center is home to a groundbreaking 15-hour AI crash course to equip employees and spark interest in emerging technologies (Intel® AI Academy 2022). Sharing knowledge has been demonstrated to be the catalyst for building trust and fostering successful innovation efforts not just in the area of AI (Todtling et al. 2013).

Showing an AI Initiative's Ability to Create Value

Since the 2010s, many organisations have invested heavily in AI initiatives and sought to hire the brightest tech talent from the biggest tech firms and those with PhD and master degrees in computer science, engineering, and mathematics. Yet, translating this expertise across industries to create value has proven to be difficult and is often not enough. Therefore, many AI initiatives have relied on providing a proof of their potential to create value. One of the approaches to do that has been a so-called proof of concept (POC). Although a POC can demonstrate that a solution meets stakeholder requirements for a specific business case and that it is technically feasible, it often fails to capture the potential of business value creation for the organisation showing an AI solution's real-world application. A proof of value (POV), however, goes one step further. It focusses not only on technical feasibility but also on the practical business value that a solution can deliver. A POV is more concerned with demonstrating that a proposed solution addresses a specific business problem or opportunity effectively and provides tangible benefits.

As such, a POV has the power to be a beacon of success, a *north star project* that can inspire a whole organisation. Amazon and Netflix have been leveraging POVs to experiment and prove the benefit of AI solutions to its stakeholders. Netflix, for example, has a long-standing tradition of experimentation, which dates back to the 1990s. The company is applying the same approach to AI, and is experimenting with ever-increasing velocity to prove the value of their ideas. This has led to the development of Netflix XP, an experimentation platform that makes data collection, statistical analysis, and visualisation of results easy and accessible (Netflix Techblog 2022). Amazon is also leveraging POVs to test and experiment with AI solutions. Before scaling an AI-powered recommendation system, which analyses customer data and preferences to suggest products that customers are likely to buy, its impact is evaluated. According to Amazon's enterprise strategist, Mark Schwartz, 'We agreed that current best practices suggest conducting rapid experiments to test ideas, and that such small, low-risk experiments should become part of everyday IT practices' (Schwartz 2018). The proof of value eventually ended in the implementation of its recommendation engine, leading to a 35% increase in sales for Amazon (MacKinzie et al. 2013). Such examples demonstrate the immense potential of POVs for successful AI value creation.

POVs are useful to assess the return on investment of time, money, and effort before taking a full-scale approach. The advantage of demonstrating the capacity to produce value with small-scale experiments is that only a small investment is necessary to establish trust in the initiatives' ability to deliver value.

Showing the Integrity of an AI Initiative

A few AI leaders and AI initiatives have demonstrated their integrity towards internal and external stakeholders by taking a responsible approach to their actions, communication, and decisions related to AI.

The nonprofit research organisation OpenAI has launched multiple language algorithms incorporating the latest and greatest in supervised and reinforcement learning techniques with the goal of creating an AI chatbot that in conversations feels as natural as talking to a real person. Just recently, the company partnered closely with Microsoft, which supported its endeavor with a multiyear, multibillion-dollar investment (Capoot 2023). However, at a StrictlyVC event in 2019, Sam Altman, CEO of OpenAI, was asked how OpenAI planned to make a profit. His honest and transparent answer? 'We have no idea'. Despite never having made any revenue, Altman was adamant that OpenAI had 'no current plans to make revenue'. Instead, he stated, 'We have no idea how we may one day generate revenue. We've made a soft promise to investors that, "Once we build a generally intelligent system, that basically we will ask it to figure out a way to make an investment return for you". As laughter echoed through the room, Altman made it clear he was serious: 'You can laugh. It's all right. But it really is what I actually believe' (Loizos 2019). In contrast to many AI start-ups, consultancies, and initiatives, Altman did not create unrealistic expectations about OpenAI's business outcomes.

Another example comes from Google's AI research firm DeepMind, which built an AI algorithm to predict the future likelihood of a patient developing acute kidney injury, a life-threatening condition. According to the research letter in the journal *Nature*, the organisation intended to predict the condition up to 48 hours in advance. However, instead of only providing the project's positive outcomes, the team openly discusses its flaws and highlights its racial and gender bias. This example demonstrates DeepMind's commitment to fairness and non-discrimination. Similarly, when Microsoft's AI chatbot Tay quickly became racist and offensive, the team shut it down and took responsibility for the issue, showing their commitment to ethical decision-making and accountability (Lee 2016). IBM's AI team developed a tool to help businesses detect and address bias in their recruitment processes. They were transparent about its capabilities and limitations, and worked with clients to ensure the tool was being used ethically and responsibly (Rayome 2018). By doing so, they showed their commitment to transparency, respect for privacy, and ethical decision-making.

Establishing Trust in an AI Solution

Although building trust in an *AI initiative* is essential for an AI project's success, it isn't only the trust in the initiative that matters. A stakeholder's trust that the AI solution will deliver on its value creation promises and make sound decisions on behalf of all stakeholders will eventually ensure its adoption. Trust in an AI solution generally refers to the level of confidence and reliance that stakeholders have in the fairness (or benevolence), quality (or ability), and reliability (or integrity) of an AI solution's decision-making.

Showing the Fairness/Benevolence of an AI Solution

The *benevolence of the AI solution* is closely linked to the concept of AI fairness. A fair AI refers to creating and deploying AI solutions with genuine intentions to treat employees and customers without bias. This is particularly significant when it comes to sensitive areas such as hiring, criminal justice, or health care. Despite good intentions and avoiding any sensitive data that could lead to prejudice during algorithm development, an algorithm, similar to a human, can still end up being inequitable. For example, the *Washington Post* recently highlighted a case when an AI-powered medical algorithm favored white patients over sicker black patients for emergency care. Despite being designed to be sensitive to race, the algorithm used the metric of medical costs that was not as race neutral as expected. The result was that black patients incurred $1,800 less in medical costs than white patients each year, leading to the algorithm scoring white patients at a higher risk than their black counterparts (Johnson and Johnson 2019). This isn't the first time that a decision-making algorithm is accused of discrimination. One of the first known cases traces back to 1988, when the UK Commission for Racial Equality found that a British medical school was guilty of bias against women and applicants with non-European names (Lowry and Macpherson 1988).

Ensuring the fairness of AI solutions is a complex problem. For example, to ensure impartiality, algorithms must be trained on a diverse dataset that includes data from multiple groups and communities, so underrepresentation and bias are avoided. To prove AI's fair decision-making, AI solutions can be evaluated by comparing their performance across different groups, and specific explainability techniques can be used to reveal any biases in the system's decision-making process.

In order to ensure and prove the fairness of AI algorithms, AI achievers have developed and leveraged several methods. For instance, Facebook has developed a tool called Fairness Flow to detect and mitigate bias in their algorithms (Kloumann, 2021). This tool examines data and forecasts the potential outcomes of AI's decisions for various groups. Facebook has provided evidence of the effectiveness of this tool by publishing research on it. Google has crafted an unbiased learning framework designed to reduce bias in AI algorithms by identifying and measuring different types of bias (Wang et al. 2018). Google offers instructions for adjusting algorithms to make them more equitable and have published several scholarly articles on this framework. IBM and Microsoft each have created an AI ethics board that reviews products and features to make sure they meet ethical standards, and also provides guidance on ethical AI practices. Additionally, IBM has developed the AI Fairness 360 Toolkit, an open source library of tools to detect and reduce bias in AI algorithms (IBM 2023b). The toolkit includes metrics for measuring fairness and can operate with a variety of AI frameworks (Perez 2021).

Showing the Ability/Decision-Making Quality of an AI Solution

How do you assess the ability/quality of AI's decision-making? Quality usually gets associated with how well an algorithm can predict a specific output, which can be shown and proven through various methods, such as evaluating the algorithm's performance on a test dataset, comparing its predictions to ground truth labels, analysing its confusion matrix, calculating its precision and recall scores, conducting A/B testing with different algorithms, and monitoring its performance over time with real-world data.

Although methods related to the evaluation of decision-based quality measures on unseen data can certainly show the accuracy of an algorithm, its value creation ability can only be shown through a demonstration or proof of value experiments. For example, the decision-making quality of Google's AlphaGo algorithm, developed by DeepMind, was demonstrated publishing several research papers detailing the performance of their algorithms, including AlphaGo Zero and AlphaZero, which achieved state-of-the-art results on several game-playing benchmarks. However, the understanding of its ability to create value came when the team showed that its AI solution was able to defeat the world champion at the game of Go (Silver et al. 2017). IBM's Watson AI team demonstrated the decision-making quality of their AI solution by performing well on several natural language processing and AI benchmarks. However, to show its real ability to create value, the Watson team collaborated with industry partners to apply their system in practical scenarios, such as health care and finance, and conducted user studies to evaluate the value creation ability of their AI solution (UNC Lineberger Cancer Center 2015).

Showing the Integrity/Reliability of an AI Solution

Integrity and reliability are key for demonstrating the trustworthiness of an AI solution to stakeholders. OpenAI,

Google, IBM, and Microsoft are all examples of AI achievers who have successfully employed various strategies, including transparent and explainable AI, robustness and security, independent verification and validation, and human oversight and accountability. These measures can help build confidence in the algorithm's performance, consistency, and decision quality.

Reliability of AI solutions is proven through transparency and explainability. OpenAI's language algorithm stands out as an example of an AI solution in which the AI initiative has gone the extra mile in this area. By providing detailed documentation of its architecture, datasets, algorithms, and decision-making process, OpenAI has made the algorithm as transparent and explainable as possible – enabling stakeholders to understand not only how the algorithm works but also how it arrives at its results. By inspecting the algorithms' intermediate outputs and attention weights, they can gain visibility into the thought process of the algorithm. This level of transparency and explainability is setting the standard for reliable AI algorithms (OpenAI 2023). However, as AI solutions get more and more complex, this challenge will be even more important in the future.

A good example of an AI solution's integrity is Google's TensorFlow solution. To demonstrate the robustness of this solution and safeguard it against potential adversarial attacks, Google has tested it against a variety of inputs and datasets while also implementing security measures such as differential privacy and federated learning (TensorFlow 2023b). This has enabled them to prove that the TensorFlow framework can handle large-scale data processing without compromising the security of user data (TensorFlow 2022). IBM is another example.

They have had their IBM Watson independently verified and validated by third-party experts. This has included rigorous testing and evaluation of the solution's performance and accuracy, providing an unbiased assessment. As a result of these efforts, IBM has established a reputation for delivering an AI solution that is reliable and trustworthy, evidenced by the numerous research papers that document its performance and accuracy in various domains. Microsoft's Xiaoice, a conversational AI chatbot used in China, offers another successful example of integrity in part through human oversight and accountability in the decision-making process. The company has trained human moderators to review the algorithm's conversations and ensure that they are consistent with ethical and legal standards (Zhou et al. 2020).

The Requirement of AI Transparency Beyond Building Trust

The importance of AI transparency, or the ability to explain AI's decisions in a way that is understandable to humans, is paramount for building trust in AI-based decision-making. However, Megan T. Stevenson and Christopher Slobogin, two prominent professors of law from esteemed universities, show that transparency is not only desirable but also essential in avoiding serious negative implications for decision quality, fairness, and reliability (Stevenson and Slobogin 2018).

In their article about algorithmic risk assessment of defendants, they discuss the impact of missing AI decision-making transparency in augmenting judges and parole boards in their decision-making. They examine one of the leading AI solutions at this time, the COMPASS Violent Recidivism Risk Score, which does not provide information about the reasoning of its decisions and only produces a risk score predicting a defendant's risk of future violent behaviour. In their investigation, the authors found that 60% of the score, indicating a possible future violent behaviour, was attributed to age. Eighteen-year-old defendants, they observed, had risk scores that were, on average, twice as high as 40-year-old defendants. This is not a surprising finding, because criminal rates and age are closely correlated and criminal behaviour is known to peak between the ages of 16 and 21. Therefore, a judge relying on his own judgement may consider youth partially excusing, due to the reduced culpability of youth. But if that same offender is denominated 'high-risk' and the judge, unaware that this label is heavily influenced by the defendant's youthful age, interprets it as a statement of bad character, then youthfulness unwittingly contributes simultaneously to moral condemnation (Stevenson and Slobogin 2018). In other words, if a judge is unaware that AI's risk score is mostly influenced by age, as an outcome of the algorithm's missing transparency, they may interpret it as a statement of bad character and may 'unknowingly and unintentionally use youth as a blame-aggravator', which the authors deem 'illogical and unacceptable' (Stevenson and Slobogin 2018).

This example illuminates how a lack of transparency can lead to unfair and substandard decisions, and how an absence of contextual information for understanding the outcomes can prevent sound judgement from taking place.

Scott Brooker, Business Architecture Director at Premier Tech

Being a long-time practitioner and leader in the field of business analytics, I firmly believe that nothing holds greater importance for the success of a project than the trust of its stakeholders. But trust is not a given, irrespective of one's professional titles; rather, it is something that must be earned over time. Trust is meticulously constructed through a consistent commitment to delivering on promises, manifesting integrity, dependability, and transparency in both our words and actions when engaging with stakeholders.

The following example stems from one of my previous engagements. A few years ago, we embarked on the ambitious task of piloting an AI solution, a project strategically positioned to be among the pioneering initiatives shaping our leadership team's perspective on AI. However, on launching the project, we found ourselves in a precarious situation where sponsors and potential end users were struggling with uncertainty about what to expect from the final AI solution, coupled with reservations regarding its alignment with their day-to-day business operations. In the face of budget constraints and looming deadlines, we made the resolute decision to press forward, with the intention of showcasing the project's value towards the end of it.

As the project team made progress, however, it became evident that we needed our stakeholders to invest further resources and to provide data in order to complete the project. Without their confidence in our ability to ultimately deliver relevant business outcomes, it would be impossible to complete the project and to demonstrate the solution's tangible impact and value.

Despite not being explicitly asked, we began a practice of consistently reporting the project team's progress towards the final goal. Week after week, we reported key metrics, actions taken, and the steps we were taking to get to the final solution. In the initial weeks, we received no responses – no comments or feedback. However, by the fourth week, stakeholders began to show involvement and provide feedback. Through our reports, we not only displayed integrity through transparent communication, benevolence by seeking their input, but also established confidence in our ability to create an AI solution.

Gradually, we earned the trust of our stakeholders, eventually securing the data and resources needed to complete the project. Although the project took longer than initially anticipated, our weekly reporting on the project's status saved us from project failure. That experience proved that trust plays a pivotal role in value creation by not just facilitating solution adoption but also stakeholder involvement throughout projects.

8

Managing AI's Decision-Making

I'm just a scientist who suddenly realised that these things are getting smarter than us.

—Geoffrey Hinton (cognitive psychologist and computer scientist)

The use of AI for making faster and more accurate decisions compared to humans is critical for creating added value with AI. However, the pursuit of new AI innovations in the past year has prompted various AI leaders and researchers to issue an open letter urging AI labs to pause their work for six months. In their letter, they state that the latest advancements in AI could represent a profound change in the history of life on Earth and should be 'planned for and managed with commensurate care and resources' (Rash 2023). The consequences of not providing such care and planning can be dire as these 'powerful digital minds' may become impossible to understand, predict, or reliably control, even by their creators (Future of Life Institute 2023). Prominent AI leaders who signed the letter include Yoshua Bengio, founder and scientific director at Mila and professor at the University of Montreal; Bart Selman, professor of computer science at Cornell and past president of AAAI; Elon Musk, CEO of SpaceX, Tesla, and X (formerly Twitter); and Steve Wozniak, cofounder of Apple. That concern was shared by researchers from Max Planck Institute in a recent academic publication. In their publication they are arguing that humankind might not be able to control a super-intelligent AI because it is 'potentially incomprehensible to humans, let alone controllable' (Alfonseca et al. 2016).

However, it is not just the threat of recent advancements in AI to the future of humanity that is of concern. Although AI is powerful in terms of decision-making

Identifying causality is a complex challenge. For example, missing variables or the correlation between input variables can make it difficult to make assumptions about causality. For instance, consider a media mix optimisation algorithm used by a car manufacturing company to estimate the impact of various media channels on sales, including TV, radio, and print. Based on its calculations, an AI algorithm might suggest that radio has a higher ROI than TV or social media, estimating a ROI of 10% for TV, 45% for social media, and more than 10,000% for radio. However, the ROI for radio is way too high to be realistic. It could be the case that the high ROI for radio was due to the fact that the company was a major sponsor of the Super Bowl, the annual final game of the National Football League, and radio was the primary media channel used during the event. The information about the event was not taken into account in the algorithm, which caused the extreme overestimation. However, even taking into account the information about the event might heavily affect the attribution of sales to the radio channel because both events are perfectly correlated. This illustrates the complexity of identifying causality, even with the ability to explain an algorithm's decision-making process.

In the realm of AI, there has been a growing emphasis on causality and its role in understanding and interpreting algorithmic outputs. This focus on causality serves a twofold purpose: it helps prevent erroneous conclusions drawn from algorithmic explainability, and it can also enhance the simplicity and efficacy of an algorithm. When the variables chosen to build an algorithm reflect the causes behind a phenomenon, fewer variables may be required to achieve the desired level of accuracy. Furthermore, these chosen variables may include actionable components that can be quality, understanding the limitations of those 'black box' algorithms will determine its positive or negative impact on business value creation. Studies by McKinsey have shown that the effective management of AI's decision-making can have a significant impact on business value creation, with practices in place to help stakeholders understand the reasoning behind the technology's decision-making (Grennan et al. 2022). However, failure to comprehend AI's limitations can pose significant risks to organisations. This chapter outlines some of the major pitfalls in AI decision-making and provides best practices in managing it.

Explaining AI's Decision-Making

Algorithms, similar to decision trees and neural networks, form the foundation of AI's decision-making capabilities. Neural networks simulate the cognitive networks of the brain and can replicate human intelligence and its mysterious nature. Due to their intricate structure and ability to consider a vast amount of information, most AI algorithms are referred to as *black boxes*, which means that they are difficult for humans to comprehend. Although these black box algorithms are powerful in terms of decision-making quality, their closed-off nature makes it challenging to understand how they arrive at their answers. However, as Roman V. Yampolskiy, a professor of computer science at the University of Louisville, warns, if we become accustomed to accepting AI's answers without an explanation, we may not be able to tell if it starts providing incorrect or manipulative answers, essentially treating it as an Oracle system (Yampolskiy 2019). Therefore, it is essential to examine AI's decision-making explainability, because the absence or dependence on inaccurate explanations of AI's decision-making processes can lead to erroneous conclusions and counterproductive actions.

Finding the Right Explanation for AI's Decision-Making

The ability to explain AI's decision-making remains one of the most difficult challenges in the field of AI. To tackle this issue, various methods have been developed, each offering a different perspective on the problem and reaching its conclusions. The key challenge lies in identifying the method that reveals the ground truth.

To gain a deeper understanding of the challenge, let us examine two commonly used methods for explaining AI decision-making. Consider the example of a school using AI to determine which students are sick and should stay home. Two popular methods that can be employed to explain AI decision-making in this context are Shapley values and information gain–based explanation methods. Both methods are commonly used to explain AI decision-making. The goal of both methods is to show the importance of the various input variables on the output of AI. The key differences between Shapley value and information gain–based explanation methods lie in their theoretical underpinnings and their approach to attributing importance to input variables. Although the Shapley value approach comes from cooperative game theory and is used to fairly distribute importance across input variables, information gain–based methods focus on how much each input variable contributes to reducing the uncertainty in predictions. Both explanation approaches are reasonable to explain the individual importance of an input variable on an algorithm's output.

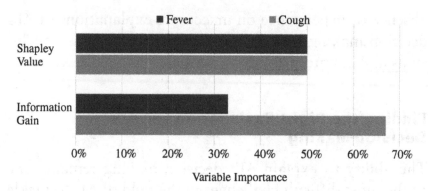

Figure 8.1 Comparison of Variable Importance Between Two Methods

Source: Adapted from Lundberg et al. (2019).

Figure 8.1 illustrates the attribution of two symptoms, fever and cough, in predicting the risk of sickness using the two different explanation methods. Although the Shapley value method assigns similar importance to both symptoms, the information gain–based method assigns different levels of importance to each symptom. The crucial question that arises is which explanation is more accurate.

One possible way to approach this question is to compare the methods to our human decision-making experience. In the case of the student sickness use case, the Shapley value method may be the closest to replicating human decision-making. A study by Lundberg et al. (2019) asked participants how they would apportion the influence of cough and fever on the risk of illness and found that their answers closely aligned with the ones provided by Shapley values.

Ultimately, it is crucial to discover a suitable approach for explaining AI's decision-making within a particular context. Regrettably, there isn't a simple, direct resolution, but the effort to provide an explanation is essential. The two methods mentioned could serve as a foundational starting point.

Choosing the Right Perspective for AI's Decision-Making

As mentioned, accurate explanations for AI's decision-making are crucial to improve outcomes and business results. However, even when choosing one explanation method to represent the ground truth, its explanations can significantly vary depending on the perspective taken or the framing of the decision-making problem during AI algorithm training.

A fictitious example from a pharmaceutical company illustrates how different perspectives during AI training can dramatically affect the conclusions drawn. The company faced the challenge of an increase in employee attrition, resulting in setbacks for the whole organisation. To address this issue, the organisation decided to leverage AI to predict which employees were most likely to leave in order to take proactive actions to retain high-performing talent. To achieve this, the management needed to understand the underlying causes of employee turnover in each department, as studies show that employees leave organisations for various reasons such as long working hours, a low monthly income, and dissatisfaction with the organisational environment. To gain a deeper understanding of these underlying causes, the AI initiative developed an algorithm using data from the human resources, research, and sales departments.

The results of the importance of variables (representing the reasons for attrition) from two different perspectives are shown in Figure 8.2.

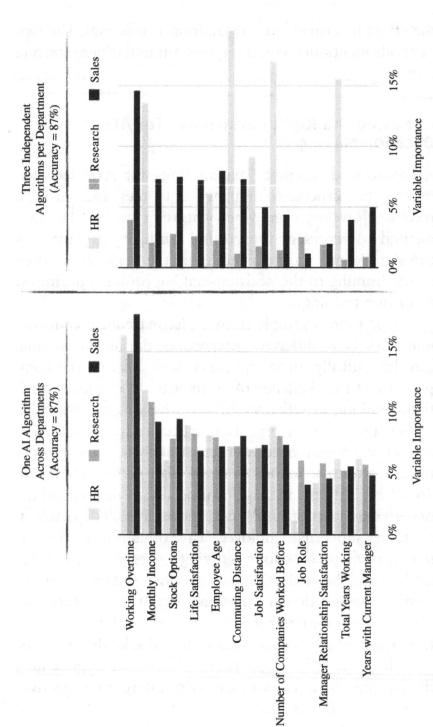

Figure 8.2 Comparison of Variable Importance Between Two Perspectives

In one perspective, the algorithm was trained using data that represented all three departments combined, and in the other perspective, three separate algorithms were built using data from each department separately. In other words, the data was the same, but separated for training three different algorithms in the second scenario. In both scenarios, the accuracy of correctly predicting employee attrition was comparable, with an accuracy rate of 87%.

The left-hand side of Figure 8.2 shows the results when only one algorithm was trained for all three departments and displays the relative importance of variables representing various causes for employee attrition, such as working overtime, monthly income, and stock options being the top reasons for leaving the organisation, and years with the current manager, total working years, and manager relationship satisfaction being the least influential factors in employee attrition. The figure also suggests that the reasons for employee attrition are somewhat similar across all three departments. However, someone with a deeper understanding of the company and its departments may have a different perspective. One could argue that the importance of underlying causes for leaving may vary across departments due to differences in job duties and work environments. This led to the training of three different algorithms, one for each department.

When separate department-specific AI algorithms were built, the results regarding the AI's decision-making process were different, as seen in the figure. The explanations for employee attrition vary significantly across departments. For example, the HR department may be more sensitive to monthly salary as a cause for attrition compared to the research department. Working overtime may be a more important reason for attrition in the sales department compared to the HR department.

The actions that would be initiated to minimise attrition for each of the departments would vary significantly based on the chosen perspective during the training of the AI algorithm. Although the accuracy was comparable in both scenarios, the explanations of AI's decision-making were significantly different. This example emphasises the importance of comprehending AI's decision-making beyond its mathematical foundation and to understand a business problem's theoretical background to validate AI's outcomes.

The Limitations of AI's Decision-Making

As just described, AI's decision-making is complex and presents challenges when it comes to its explanation. Particularly, the tendency to idealise and anthropomorphise AI's decision-making capabilities by imagining that AI is 'thinking' or 'coming to conclusions' similar to humans can be misleading and potentially risky (Fernandez 2022). Acknowledging its limitations can greatly diminish the feasibility and adoption risks associated with its application. Three of those limitations of AI's decision-making is its generalisability, consistency, and decision scope.

Generalisability of AI's Decision-Making

Generalisability of an AI algorithm refers to its ability to perform well on new, unseen data that it hasn't been trained on. It describes how effectively an AI algorithm can apply the patterns it learned from the training data to make accurate predictions or decisions on previously unseen data. When an AI algorithm demonstrates good generalisability, it means that it has successfully captured the underlying patterns and relationships in the training data without merely memorising it. As a result, the algorithm can make reliable predictions on new data that comes from the same distribution as the training data. Poor generalisability, however, indicates that the algorithm has essentially memorised the training data and is unable to adapt to new situations or data that are even slightly different from what it has seen before. This phenomenon is known as overfitting, where the algorithm fits the training data so closely that it fails to generalise to new data points.

The application of AI for decision automation at Zillow serves as an example of the importance of generalisability. Zillow is a US real estate marketplace company founded in 2006 that provides an online platform bringing homebuyers and sellers together. Over many years the organisation collected lots of data from monitoring US real estate transactions and leveraged this vast amount to predict a price for every house on and off the market, called Zestimate. This estimation is usually pretty accurate with a nationwide median error rate for on-market homes of about 2.4% and off-market homes of 7.49%, according to Zillow (Zillow 2023). In 2019 Zillow made a move that dramatically changed the face of their business. With the help of their vast amount of data, they entered the home-flipping market by leveraging AI for decision-making, creating a profit from buying, fixing, and selling homes. However, just two years after launching its new AI-driven business model, on November 3, 2021, Zillow's CEO Rich Barton announced in a CNBC interview the decision to shut down Zillow's home selling operations resulting in a 25% decrease of their workforce and a substantial decline in stock value from February to November 2021 (Levy 2021). This strategic move was prompted by Zillow's considerable loss in the fiscal year 2021, which was predominantly attributed to their home-flipping activities (Zillow Group 2022). The reason behind this turn of events? When Zillow turned to AI for decision-making, the company encountered a challenge. Barton explained it as follows: AI had 'unintentionally purchased homes at higher prices than our current estimates of future selling prices' (Zillow Group 2021), which left Zillow facing a significant challenge of holding underwater assets (Levy 2021). In fact, during the third quarter of 2021, CNBC reported that about two-thirds of the homes Zillow acquired were listed below their purchase price (Levy 2021). Market Watch, a Dow Jones company, further highlighted the gravity of the situation by reporting that during the third quarter, Zillow 'bought 9,680 homes and sold 3,032 of them, with the sales producing an average loss in gross terms of more than $80,000 per house' (Swartz 2021).

The reason for that outcome seemed to be that the AI algorithm used to predict house prices was not able to adapt and make accurate predictions for the unexpected change in the underlying assumptions of the real-estate market as the COVID-19 pandemic hit. KB Home CEO and tenured real estate expert Jeffrey Mezger explains the history of events in the housing market during the pandemic. 'If you go back to 2019 and leading into the pandemic in January 2020, our business was very good, and then it stopped [during the lockdowns], and you navigate that and then buyers came back with a vengeance that summer . . . and then the Fed decides [in 2022] they're going to stop housing and jacks up [interest] rates, and it [housing] stops again. Those were really dramatic shifts in a really short period of time. Normally it is a slower shift in trend that takes months, and in this case it was days' (Lambert 2023).

However, although a human decision-maker might understand that patterns learned from before the pandemic might not hold true anymore, AI seemed to have problems adjusting to the new situation to act accordingly. According to Zillow CEO Barton, the company was with the help of AI 'unable to accurately forecast future home prices at different times in both directions by much more than they modeled as possible' (Zillow Group 2021).

But not just Zillow has faced problems with AI's ability to generalise decision-making. Amazon faced a challenge when it attempted to build an AI-based solution to help recruit top talent in the tech industry: they had trained their algorithms on data collected over a 10-year period in which the vast majority of candidates were male, creating an algorithm that disadvantaged female applicants. Despite the company's attempts to make the program gender-neutral, the AI algorithm still gave higher priority to male résumés, and lower scores to résumés that included activities associated with women, even when the names were anonymised. Amazon eventually shut down the AI algorithm because it was not able to generalise from the data it got trained on (Dastin 2018). Therefore, it is critical to understand the limitations of AI to make decisions in situations it was not trained on.

AI's Decision-Making Consistency

We are mostly aware that our own human decision-making is not without flaws. And even experts often make decisions that differ significantly from one another. Research has shown that when it comes to tasks such as valuing stocks, appraising real estate, sentencing criminals, and more, the judgements made by different people are highly variable. But confronted with the same problem at different times, even the same people can change their judgement drastically. For example, when software developers were asked to estimate the completion time for a given task on two separate days, their projected hours differed by an average of 71%. Pathologists' assessments of the severity of biopsy results had a correlation of only .61 (out of a perfect 1.0), indicating that their diagnoses were inconsistent (Kahneman et al. 2016). The problem with inconsistent decision outcomes is that they certainly do not create trust in those experts' decision-making.

Although we are not consistent when it comes to decision-making, we often expect decision-making consistency from AI. But this expectation towards AI is as unrealistic as it is towards humans. Various AI algorithms can come to different conclusions, every additional datapoint in the training dataset can influence an algorithm's decision-making, and even every retraining of an AI algorithm will result in varying outputs.

But this is not a flaw; it is a feature and was designed that way! One reason for the success of AI algorithms such as neural networks, random forests, and gradient boosted machines is their intended randomness during algorithm training. Although the approach of a neural network optimises with random parameters, random forests and gradient boosted machines employ random samples of data and variables to draw their conclusions. The randomness is part of the design of those sophisticated algorithms to make them more generalisable. By randomly selecting data and input variables during algorithm training, their decision-making process becomes more robust. It's like asking a 1,000 human experts about their opinion on a specific problem, and then averaging the answers. However, that also means that the outcomes and explanations can differ each time an AI algorithm is retrained, posing a challenge to judge their consistency, especially when there are a lot of variables and a low number of observations to work with.

AI's Limited Decision Scope

In spite of the remarkable progress that AI has made in the realm of decision-making, one characteristic that still distinguishes it from humans is its single-objective optimisation. AI algorithms are usually designed to optimise a single outcome, yet human decision-making is capable of taking into account multiple outcomes and ramifications of a particular decision. The classic 'trolley problem' illustrates the dilemma: do you choose to switch the course of a runaway streetcar, putting one child at risk instead of several adults? Is the only goal to optimise towards the lowest number of casualties or towards the type as well? In the business world, maximising the revenue impact of a decision is only one objective – but what are the cost implications? What are the ethical implications? What is the strategic impact of a decision? And what type of risks should be considered?

Formulating all possible decision objectives is a challenging task – even more so when weighing them against each other. When the objectives are harmoniously aligned, the decision-making process is relatively straightforward. But when objectives come into conflict, it can be a vexing conundrum to decide which outcome is more important. Is there a middle ground? In the world of business, there are various examples that could benefit from multi-objective optimisation. The credit card business is a prime example of how to accurately predict default risk while mitigating discrimination and bias towards any particular group. Similarly, technology companies struggle with multi-objective optimisation when planning features for software updates, striving to keep customers happy while minimising costs. Although many business problems could benefit from that approach, the field of research in multi-objective optimisation is still in its infancy.

Controlling AI's Decision-Making

AI achievers seeking to overcome the limitations and mitigate the risks in AI's decision-making usually focus on three key steps: simplifying AI's decision-making process, aligning human and AI objectives, and focussing on causality rather than explainability of algorithms.

The Simplicity of AI's Algorithms

Since the early 2010s, the advancement of AI algorithms has surged at an unprecedented pace, yielding increasingly accurate algorithms. Yet, a crucial factor has frequently been neglected: simplicity. Although the objective of accuracy is often attributed to more complex algorithms, the significance of simpler ones – such as linear regression and decision trees – is frequently underestimated. However, these simple algorithms offer advantages in terms of interpretability, fostering ease in validation, enhancing decision-making generalisability, and consistency. Moreover, simpler algorithms typically demand less training data, require less time for training and inference, and need less storage space.

Despite the common belief that accuracy is directly proportional to algorithm complexity, that does not hold necessarily true (Gosiewska et al. 2021; Rudin 2019). Researchers have explored AI algorithms ranging from linear regression to deep learning neural networks and proven 'that a trade-off between accuracy and interpretability is a myth and improved interpretability is not necessarily followed by reduced model performance' (Gosiewska et al. 2021). Therefore, AI experts should aim for the lowest level of complexity to achieve the highest accuracy combined with interpretability.

Although simplifying algorithmics can lead to reduced complexity, increasing simplicity can also result from using less data. The prevailing approach and belief are that greater data volumes are necessary for achieving a high accuracy. However, this notion is only partially accurate. Additional information incorporated into an algorithm tends to have a marginal impact. This is especially the case when a new variable is correlated with others; its incremental impact is often minimal and may even undermine the algorithm's interpretability and performance. Frequently, only a small set of variables play a pivotal role in predicting the majority of the output variable's variance, which is essential for achieving accurate predictions (Miao and Niu 2016). Figure 8.3 illustrates typical outcomes from an algorithm aimed at predicting, for instance, sales volume using about 60 variables. On the left, the contribution

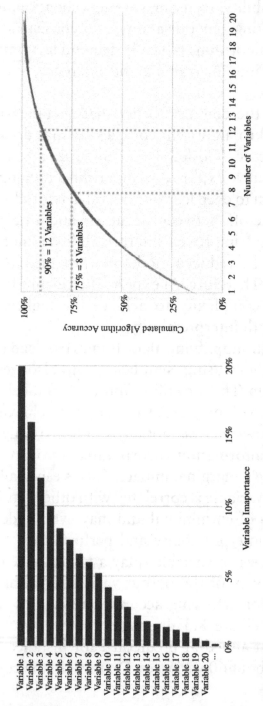

Figure 8.3 Individual and Cumulated Variable Importance

of the first 20 variables is displayed, and the right side demonstrates the cumulative explanatory power of each additional variable on the algorithm's accuracy.

Interestingly, the top 20 variables among the 60 appear to encompass roughly 99% of the output variable's variance. Nonetheless, 99% accuracy might not even be necessary. In our example, an algorithm trained on merely 12 variables could attain a 90% accuracy rate, while one based on 8 variables could still yield a reasonably accurate result of 75% compared to utilising the complete set of variables. However, it is not the quantity of variables that holds significance, but rather how these variables capture the underlying reasons for the desired business outcome. For instance, in the context of sales volume, pivotal variables might include those linked to consumer awareness, product accessibility, and pricing.

Years of AI experience have shown us that often less is more in terms of algorithms and data. Employing simpler algorithms trained on meticulously chosen variables frequently enables organisations to derive more value than those opting for more intricate algorithms trained on extensive datasets.

Aligning AI's Decision-Making to Business Objectives

Although a higher AI decision quality, characterised by greater accuracy, is often linked to more significant business opportunities, a perfect 100% accurate AI algorithm remains elusive. In reality, an algorithm with an accuracy of about 80% is way more common. However, simply relying on an algorithm's accuracy percentage to determine its potential impact on a business is a shortsighted approach and an algorithm with lower accuracy might be equally qualified to create a business opportunity.

Consider a hypothetical example of a hospital or health care provider who has developed an AI algorithm to forecast the likelihood of a heart disease for patients using medical records. With the correct prediction of the AI algorithm, the hospital can intervene and potentially save a patient's life. Conversely, an incorrect prediction could result in a missed opportunity to intervene, putting the patient's life at risk.

To understand the intricacies of AI's decision-making processes, we must first delve into a concept used to evaluate decision-making quality in AI. The concept is called a *confusion matrix*, which is a two-dimensional representation of an AI algorithm's predictive accuracy, divided into reality and prediction. The confusion matrix consists of four distinct quadrants, each representing a different outcome (see Figure 8.4).

In the first quadrant (top left), AI accurately predicts the occurrence of a heart disease, resulting in true positives. By contrast, the opposite quadrant in the bottom

Figure 8.4 Confusion
Matrix Concept

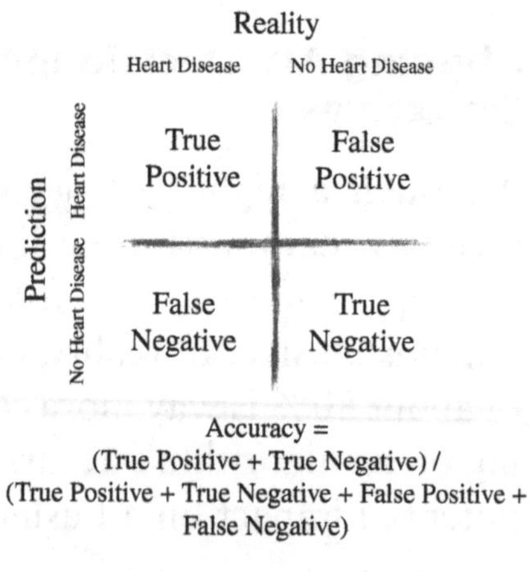

Reality

	Heart Disease	No Heart Disease
Prediction — Heart Disease	True Positive	False Positive
Prediction — No Heart Disease	False Negative	True Negative

Accuracy =
(True Positive + True Negative) /
(True Positive + True Negative + False Positive +
False Negative)

right represents true negatives, where the AI correctly predicts no heart disease. The top-right quadrant, false positives, occurs when the AI predicts a heart disease when none exists, and the bottom-left quadrant, false negatives, results from the AI failing to predict a heart disease when one exists. Understanding the implications of each quadrant is crucial in evaluating AI's decision-making quality accurately. Although true positives and true negatives indicate a high level of predictive accuracy, false positives and false negatives can be catastrophic in certain contexts. For instance, in our example, a false negative prediction for a heart disease could result in life-threatening consequences for a patient.

AI's accuracy is a measure that refers to the percentage of correct predictions made by an algorithm over the total number of predictions it executes. In the context of a heart disease prediction, accuracy is crucial because it enables timely intervention. Of course, we all aspire to develop algorithms that are 100% accurate in identifying potential heart disease. However, the reality is often far from this ideal, and it is not uncommon to achieve an accuracy rate of 80% or lower (Rescue One 2023). In other words, such algorithms are bound to make mistakes in 20% of cases, either by predicting a heart disease when there is none, or worse yet, failing to identify a real risk.

Nonetheless, not all inaccuracies are valued equal. Indeed, the costs of falsely alerting patients to a nonexistent risk are relatively low, especially when compared to the catastrophic consequences of failing to notify those at genuine risk. In other words, it is a minor inconvenience to have a few patients alerted unnecessarily, but it is an outright tragedy if even a single person dies due to a missed warning.

Thus, the imperative lies in optimising AI's decision-making processes towards this outcome. Even with an algorithm that boasts an accuracy rate of only 80%, we can choose to have the error on the side of caution and alert all patients or to avoid any false prediction of a heart disease. In doing so, we can ensure that everyone at risk of heart disease is made aware of the danger, and we minimise the chances of any fatalities occurring or, as depicted in Figure 8.5, we can reduce false alarms with the consequence of up to 20% fatalities.

As we can observe in the figure, the left confusion matrix depicts the dire outcome of AI's inability to predict correctly in 20% of cases, resulting in a high-risk situation for all 20% of patients. Conversely, the right confusion matrix indicates no patient risk despite the same 80% accuracy rate. This illustrates the importance of not only examining overall accuracy but also the consequences of errors for business outcomes.

The repercussions of mistakes can be far-reaching, as we saw in the Zillow use case we discussed previously in this chapter. The errors in the algorithm's future house

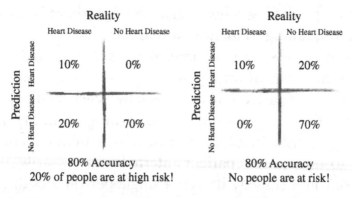

Figure 8.5 Two Confusion Matrix Examples

price prediction led to significant losses. It is crucial to recognise that the impact of overestimating and underestimating future house prices is not symmetrical. Underestimating can benefit an organisation, and overestimating can result in loss. As such, it is imperative to consider the potential costs and benefits of inaccurate predictions and adjust the algorithm's parameters accordingly.

Focussing on Causality, Not Explainability

In the business world, human decision-making is usually based on the assumption that decision reasoning and decision explanations are aligned with each other. When making a prediction or decision such as why a customer might buy a product, a salesperson, for example, may cite relevant information such as the customer's interest in the product, the suitability of the product to the customer, and the customer's financial standing. All of those variables do not just explain but also reflect the causes for their prediction. However, when it comes to AI, that assumption might not be true.

Despite the growing demand for explainable AI, it is important to understand that explainability and causality are not the same (Gade et al. 2019; Grennan et al. 2022). Although explainability methods such as Shapley values can help us understand how an algorithm makes its decisions, they may not necessarily reveal the underlying causes behind the decision phenomenon. For example, an algorithm that predicts an increase in sales volume may attribute its prediction to factors such as the sales trend over the past year or seasonal effects, but it may not be able to explain the economic reasons behind those factors.

manipulated to influence the output. As a result, although it is essential to prioritise transparency and explainability in AI, it is equally crucial to acknowledge the limitations of these methods when it comes to uncovering causality.

Dr. Ambar Sengupta, Professor in Mathematics and Department Head at University of Connecticut

Artificial intelligence, a significant field of study and development for decades, has experienced a rapid surge in interest in recent years. The foundational components of this subject intertwine computer science, mathematics, and statistics. Having served as a mathematics professor and department head at the University of Connecticut, I've had the privilege of delving into the fundamental mathematical concepts underpinning AI.

In the realm of mathematics, progress is being made in AI's ability to comprehend and handle abstract mathematics. One such endeavor is the Lean Theorem Prover, an open-source project initially launched at Microsoft. The long-term implications, extending beyond the intricate realms of mathematics, of AI executing highly sophisticated processes of reasoning and identifying logical patterns, can only be speculated on at this juncture.

In the broader context of applying AI to the understanding and reasoning of humans, a pivotal moment occurred in late 2022, marked by the breakthrough in generative AI, prominently demonstrated by ChatGPT – an innovation from OpenAI's research lab. Across academic circles and various domains, the response to this advancement has been a blend of enthusiasm and caution. Educators are proactively exploring ways to integrate AI into their teaching strategies, while also contemplating scenarios where AI might replace human instructors. On an operational level, generative AI already contributes to shaping course designs and syllabi. However, not limited to education, in workplaces worldwide, generative AI has become an everyday tool, assisting in drafting business correspondence, formulating job

(continued)

descriptions, and even generating initial iterations of programming code. Its potential is vast, arising from the fusion of knowledge to give rise to novel creations. Those who have interacted with ChatGPT can attest to the wonder of witnessing fresh ideas taking shape, whether through eloquent essays or expressive poems.

Nevertheless, the management of generative AI's decision-making process poses a notable challenge, and concerns about its explainability and generalisability persist. For example, ChatGPT's outputs heavily depend on context and require specific instructions. The system generates a variety of outputs, occasionally producing fabricated information and citations. Although generative AI's results closely resemble human-like outcomes, discernible distinctions remain. ChatGPT operates by selecting the most suitable words following the preceding text, whereas human writing originates from conceptual thought, employing word choice as a means of articulating ideas.

As efforts continue to unveil AI's ramifications for human culture, finance, and the expansive realm of business – where the possibilities seem limitless – it remains crucial to acknowledge its limitations and potential consequences.

Part III

Enterprise Integration

The integration of AI within an organisation is crucial for the sustainable creation of value using this innovative technology. The integration starts by aligning on how AI can contribute to achieving the organisation's goals and objectives, defining the organisation's interaction with AI initiatives, and addressing how AI will reshape the organisation's values, beliefs, norms, customs, behaviours, and practices.

In detail, we will explore how to craft an executable AI strategy that aligns with a business's overall strategy, lead successful AI projects that overcome the challenges of AI value creation, and drive AI adoption across the enterprise and especially at leadership level through facilitating an AI-friendly culture.

We outline practical frameworks for scaling AI across an enterprise, drawing from the insights shared throughout this book. We provide case studies of other organisations we have worked with, offering guidance and inspiring ideas on how to tailor these frameworks to your own organisation.

9

Crafting an AI Strategy

Strategy without tactics is the slowest route to victory.
Tactics without strategy is the noise before defeat.
                    —Sun Tsu (military general, strategist,
                                philosopher, and writer)

The implementation of AI in various business operations has been on the rise across organisations around the globe. However, most organisations lack a well-defined strategy for AI implementation (*Business Wire* 2019; IBM 2022b). Although many start with tactical approaches and use cases, these often fail to create sustainable value. A disconnect between the AI strategy and enterprise strategy can lead to misalignment, organisational challenges, unrealistic expectations, and adoption problems at the executive level. Various AI achievers who have successfully created value with AI have demonstrated the importance of aligning their AI strategy with the broader enterprise strategy (Chui et al. 2022). However, this holds not just true for AI but also for the alignment of the overall digital and enterprise strategy (Ismail et al. 2017).

An effective AI strategy is designed to simplify the complexity of organisational operations for AI and to achieve alignment across the organisation. A well-crafted AI strategy offers clear vision and direction for the use of AI, aligns it with the company's business operations, and provides a framework for planning, transparency, and knowledge-sharing to create value. Last but not least, it is critical to identify the necessary value-driving capabilities and establish a support system. By offering a road map for an organisation's AI journey, a sound strategy serves as an invaluable guide for achieving lasting success and navigating an organisation through the highs and lows along the path of implementation.

Delivering an Executable AI Strategy

Although an AI strategy offers numerous benefits, the most significant is its ability to provide focus. To determine where this focus should be directed, we will rely on the strategy framework presented by Lafley and Martin (2013). A. G. Lafley, the former CEO of Procter & Gamble (P&G), and Roger L. Martin, the dean of the Rotman School of Management, outlined this framework. Established in 1837, the multinational consumer goods company P&G has a long history of successfully implementing innovations in a wide range of products including cleaning agents, personal care products, beauty and grooming items, health and wellness products, and more. P&G's brands include well-known names such as Tide, Pampers, Gillette, Crest, Pantene, and many others.

As per Lafley and Martin, strategy is defined as 'a coordinated and integrated set of five choices: a winning aspiration, where to play, how to win, core capabilities, and management systems' (Lafley and Martin 2013, 3). This framework has also been found applicable to the challenges of integrating AI into enterprises. The Deloitte Center for Government Insights, recognised for its pioneering research that informs US public officials, has found this model to be valuable in shaping AI strategies for US government agencies, including the Department of Defense and the Department of Energy (Eggers et al. 2019).

In their strategy framework, Lafley and Martin propose the following choices, which we applied to the field of AI:

1. **Aspiration:** *What is the role of AI within an organisation and what is the level of AI ambition?* A description

of what AI is intended to accomplish for an enterprise and its stakeholders, and what AI is not intended to do.

2. **Focus:** *What are the focus areas of an AI initiative?* The focus on business opportunities in specific business areas (e.g. business verticals, geographic areas, or organisational challenges within and across its industry).

3. **Value creation:** *How is AI going to create value?* The definition of how to address those business opportunities with specific ideas on types of AI value creation and strategies to overcome AI's value creation challenges.

4. **Capabilities:** *What is needed to create value with AI?* The definition of capabilities, such as talent, partners, data, and technical requirements to create value out of identified business opportunities and to reduce adoption and feasibility risk.

5. **Management systems:** *What system will support AI's integration and its management?* The identification and definition of organisational systems that support, foster, and manage the AI initiative's strategy.

All of those strategy choices are hierarchical in nature. Choices at the top of the hierarchy shape the context for those below, and lower-level choices reinforce the higher-level ones (see Figure 9.1).

For example, the focus (choice 2) is affecting the way AI is supposed to create value (choice 3), but if value creation is not feasible, the AI initiative must shift its focus (choice 2). This aspect of Lafley and Martin's approach is pivotal because it ensures that the aspiration and focus adopted are executable.

Another advantage of Lafley and Martin's approach to strategy is the ability to align AI strategy choices with those at the enterprise level. In their cascade model, every

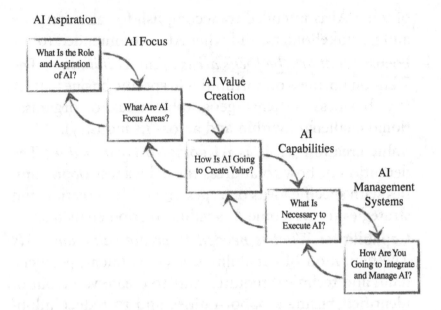

Figure 9.1   AI Strategy Choices

Source: Adapted from Alan G et al. (2013)\Harvard Business Review Press.

AI strategy choice is driven by and linked to the top-level enterprise strategy. For example, when taking the cascade from business to AI strategy and the dependencies within the AI strategy into account, the AI focus (AI choice 2) will be affected by the AI's aspirations (AI choice 1) and the overarching enterprise strategy focus (enterprise choice 2; see Figure 9.2).

Lafley and Martin's strategy approach is remarkably adaptable. It can be employed at the enterprise level and flexibly tailored to various divisions and business units, contingent on the organisational structure of the AI initiative. For instance, in cases where a company opts for a hybrid or decentralised AI initiative, individual divisions can formulate AI strategies tailored to their unique business units, all while ensuring alignment with the overarching

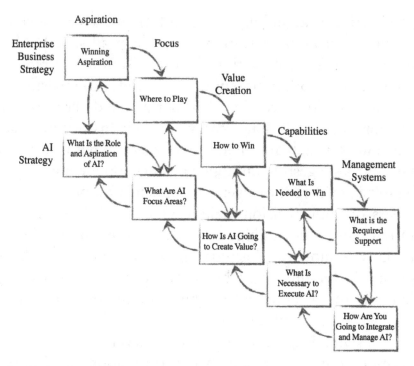

Figure 9.2 AI and Business Strategy Choice Alignment

Source: Adapted from Alan G et al. (2013)\Harvard Business Review Press.

initiative. The clear identification of dependencies among AI strategy choices and between enterprise and AI strategy cascades make that approach highly adjustable. It's crucial to bear in mind that, akin to any business strategy, an AI strategy requires evolution as AI technology and business requirements progress.

Aspiration

An AI strategy starts with an ambitious aspiration for AI, setting the stage for all other choices. A clear and concise aspiration statement conveys a vivid vision and overarching goal, acting as a guiding star for all AI endeavors. Such an explicit AI aspiration statement can help all stakeholders in grasping AI's role within the organisation and reduces uncertainty about its intentions. It's useful to envision AI as a new senior executive. Without a role description for this newcomer, all that's known is their history of creating value through automation elsewhere. What if this new hire starts suggesting untapped business opportunities you hadn't considered, or even recommends automating segments of your decision-making process? A lack of aspiration can breed ambiguity and concerns about the AI initiative's motives. Formulating an aspiration for AI is pivotal in building trust by showcasing benevolence and integrity to all stakeholders, thus building the foundation for successful AI adoption.

Drawing inspiration from AI achievers, here are some exemplary aspiration statements from Google's AI initiative, Tesla, and Microsoft:

> Google's mission has always been to organize the world's information and make it universally accessible and useful. We're excited about the transformational power of AI and the helpful new ways it can be applied. From research that expands what's possible, to product integrations designed to make everyday things easier, and applying AI to make a difference in the lives of those who need it most – we're committed to responsible innovation and technologies that benefit all of humanity.
>
> —Google (Google AI 2023)

> We develop and deploy autonomy at scale in vehicles, robots and more. We believe that an approach based on advanced AI for vision and planning, supported by efficient use of inference hardware, is the only way to achieve a general solution for full self-driving and beyond.
>
> —Tesla (Tesla 2023)

Microsoft's stated commitment to AI is even reflected in its corporate vision; the technology is so integral to the enterprise that it has been included in the company's vision statement showing that AI represents an essential element in Microsoft's plans for future business operations:

> Microsoft is a technology company whose mission is to empower every person and every organization on the planet to achieve more. We strive to create local opportunity, growth, and impact in every country around the world. Our strategy is to build best-in-class platforms and productivity services for an intelligent cloud and an intelligent edge infused with artificial intelligence ('AI').
> —Microsoft (Levy 2017)

Although Microsoft has taken steps to integrate their enterprise and AI visions, many other organisations are not as advanced in their AI journey to seamlessly blend the two. However, Tesla and Google's AI strategies are closely aligned with their enterprise aspirations. Let's consider another example that illustrates how a corporate vision can influence AI aspirations.

The Mexican food restaurant chain Chipotle has more recently begun its journey with AI. With more than 3,000 locations and more than 100,000 employees in the US, Canada, and Europe, the complexity of the business has grown exponentially (Chipotle 2023).

Chipotle describes their enterprise aspirations: 'We strive to cultivate a better world by serving responsibly sourced, classically cooked, real food with wholesome ingredients and without artificial colors, flavors or preservatives. We are passionate about providing a great guest experience and making our food more accessible to everyone while continuing to be a brand with a demonstrated purpose' (Chipotle 2021).

In line with their enterprise aspirations, Chipotle CEO Brian Niccol describes the aspiration of its AI initiative the following way: 'Machine learning and automation is going to be a big disrupter because it just allows you to do processes that people didn't love doing before. As a result, they [will be able to] do them with great accuracy or great consistency. That [will marry] with analytics so you can better forecast, better prep, [and have] better execution. Companies that invest in these areas will end up with hopefully better work for our employees and better outcomes for our customers' (Abril 2022).

In Chipotle's AI aspiration, we witness the intended role of AI within the enterprise's operations. It contributes to cultivating an improved work environment for employees and enhancing the customer experience, while optimising business processes through enhanced forecasting, preparation, and execution. These aspects are fundamental to Chipotle's enterprise vision of delivering exceptional guest experiences and ensuring food accessibility for all (Chipotle 2018).

Focus and Value Creation

Determining where AI should be applied to and how to create value with it has been shown to be key to securing AI's long-term business impact (Burns 2018). But, where to start? Considering the link between AI and corporate strategy, by understanding the strategic choices at enterprise level, AI initiatives will have a solid foundation to identify areas for the application of AI.

Let's go back to the enterprise strategy level. After the choice of enterprise aspiration, the next step is to define where to play, which is intertwined with the subsequent step, how to win. Although the enterprise aspiration serves as the foundation for the enterprise's scope of activities, it is where to play and how to win that define the specifics. Where to play is crucial in selecting the playing field, establishing regions, categories, channels, and consumers to focus on in order to narrow the competitive playing field of the organisation. Questions to ask when evaluating a company's competitive standing include What markets is the company targeting? Who are its customers and consumers? Through what channels is it selling? What product categories is it offering? At which vertical stages of the industry is the company competing? Choosing how to win is key to gaining a competitive edge on the where to play battlefield. This entails making specific choices that have the ability to create a unique value to generate and maintain a competitive advantage over industry rivals. How to play is a set of choices connected to each playing field selected on the where to play step (Lafley and Martin 2013).

The focus of AI's application is directly linked to where to play decisions. The question then becomes Can AI provide a competitive advantage in the playing field? Is there a business opportunity to be found through AI-based actionability? Having the answers to these questions is essential in determining the next steps: the details on how to create value for each possible set of where to play choices. Is the business opportunity feasible and possible for the AI initiative to create the opportunity, and eventually what are the risks of it not getting adopted?

Chipotle's goal to achieve its aspirations has been narrowed down to crucial where to play areas. By focussing on key areas, the company identified the following opportunities and challenges it must address:

- *Becoming a more culturally relevant and engaging brand to grow love and loyalty;*
- *Digitizing and modernizing the restaurant experience to be more convenient and enjoyable for customers;*
- *Running great restaurants with great hospitality and throughput;*
- *Being disciplined and focused to enhance the company's powerful economic model; and*
- *Building a great supporting culture as Chipotle innovates and executes across digital, access, menu and the restaurant experience. (Chipotle 2018)*

Chipotle focuses on disciplined execution to solidify their economic model. Their operations are facing adverse results as ingredient and operating costs have risen. AI is being deployed to optimise both cost categories.

The company is using AI to address the challenge of rising ingredient costs. By learning how much of an item is required for food preparation on different days and times, they can minimise waste and ensure customer satisfaction. Chipotle CEO Brian Niccol remarked, the 'way it works currently is, [workers] just don't really realise that they went through more guacamole until they get to dinner. Then it's 7 o'clock when they run out, and then we disappoint customers' (Abril 2022).

The second cost driver is operation costs, largely driven by human resources. Chipotle is turning to AI to help manage business operations, from predicting consumer demand to optimising food preparation. This frees up time for management to focus on other areas of the business, such as building a great customer experience and enhancing company growth. AI offers higher accuracy and consistency, standardising and optimising processes that can improve employee satisfaction by taking over tedious tasks. Additionally, in the highly competitive, volatile, and unpredictable restaurant industry, Chipotle is using AI to stay ahead of the game and protect their employees during the COVID-19 pandemic. By predicting food preparation time and adjusting the amount of digital orders in real time, they are able to ensure their employees don't burn out as well as an optimal customer experience. Those AI-generated insights feed into various focus areas of Chipotle's strategy: running great restaurants with great throughput, remaining disciplined and focussed, and offering a fantastic customer experience – all while maintaining profitable and sustainable growth.

Capabilities

AI capabilities can profoundly influence the success of an AI initiative and follow the strategic choices about where to focus AI's application. It is the choice of AI capabilities that are required to create value out of the focussed business opportunities. The capabilities necessary can be broken down into the main area of AI technology, the right AI talent, data management, and their respective processes.

The strategic decision-making process when selecting AI technology is complex. Many companies attempt to face the challenge by building their own solutions to retain intellectual property and keep costs low at the beginning of their AI journey. However, considering all the tasks related to building an AI pipeline, including AI algorithm development and deployment, makes the process daunting. As a result of the level of complexity, AI achievers often use the strategy of augmenting their technology stack with ready-to-go solutions to meet all the various demands. Chipotle has taken that step with its partnership with Miso Robotics to create Chippy, an autonomous kitchen assistant that cooks and seasons their signature tortilla chips. Using AI, the robot can replicate Chipotle's exact recipe, cooking and seasoning with exacting precision. According to Nevielle Panthaky, Chipotle's VP of culinary, Chippy achieves 'subtle variations in flavor' that customers expect (Beckett 2022). The robot is trained to use corn masa flour, water, and sunflower oil to cook the chips, and then tops them off with a dusting of salt and a hint of lime juice. This isn't Chipotle's first foray into AI-powered innovation; they also partner with the digital food management platform PreciTaste. With PreciTaste, cooks are notified about the ingredients they need for any dish and the platform automatically helps plan for what is needed, leveraging AI and image recognition (Ajao 2022).

The right AI talent is key for successful AI initiatives. But what sets apart the ideal talent pool for such an initiative? In the last part of this book, we will further explore the individual tasks necessary for AI value creation to define the various skills and competencies required to create value with AI. Those skills and competencies can then be translated to various roles, which can differ between organisations across the stages of their AI journey. The necessary skills and competencies reach from technical to nontechnical as well as soft skills. At Chipotle, AI talent is multifaceted, fulfilling a variety of tasks in product management, software development, data analytics, cybersecurity, infrastructure, and enterprise project management teams (Dol 2021). Although those roles are technical in nature, they require a blend of technical and nontechnical skills and competencies to enable effective decision-making and drive growth, innovation, and operational excellence at Chipotle.

Data has become a strategic asset in any organisation, and managing it properly is key to maximising its AI value-creation potential. To realise the full benefits of this asset, the proper management of data at the right level is critical – a key factor in sustaining its value. Chipotle has implemented the Microsoft Dynamics 365 Customer Insights platform, organising and analysing their customer info to deliver marketing initiatives on a much finer scale. With multiple sources of customer data – such as a loyalty program boasting more than 17 million members, POS data, a customer care center, and digital platforms – Chipotle is now able to harness the power of data and apply AI's decision-making on a customer level (Berthiaume 2021).

Management System

An AI management system encompasses the definition and review of an AI strategy with a guiding and supporting coalition, communicating the AI strategy effectively, creating the core capabilities, and continuously measuring to ensure the strategy is on track. Without such a management system, even the best strategy is likely to fail.

An AI initiative requires organisational support from various areas. The best way of gaining that support is by creating a guiding coalition that can contribute in creating and reviewing an AI strategy. That AI strategy is supposed to be an evolving document that allows for understanding of value creation gaps, builds trust, and inspires enterprise commitment. It should capture the learnings from failures and successes on the AI journey, and be crafted with the input of key coalition members from, for instance, IT, data management, HR, and finance, who together provide the capabilities, knowledge, and experience to support the AI strategy's objectives.

The *communication of an AI strategy* requires a two-way dialogue: internally to the organisation and externally to the customers. Internally, it is essential to provide stakeholders with knowledge transfer, while also building trust and demonstrating how their job relates to the value AI provides and the goals of the enterprise. Externally, AI aspirations and value should be communicated to all stakeholders, including the enterprise (board and management), employees, and customers.

Every AI initiative necessitates support to *facilitate the development and upkeep of its AI capabilities*. The task is to identify what resources are necessary and create them in alignment with the core components of the AI strategy. For instance, a financial sponsor for the AI investment is needed, with the initial costs typically covered by the budgets for digital transformation, IT, or business intelligence. Securing the appropriate funding is key, because it grants the initiative the power and resources to hire and retain AI talent, a task for which HR must be consulted to understand their incentives, demands, and salary expectations. However, resources and support cannot only be gathered internally; in many cases external partners might be a wise choice for building and sustaining the core capabilities of and supporting the AI initiative.

Last, it is essential to measure and show the progress of the AI initiative. Measurement plays a critical role in providing focus, feedback, learning, and incentives. According to Lafley and Martin, the key is to measure the progress towards a future outcome when it comes to innovation. For measures to be effective, they emphasise the importance of prespecifying the expected outcomes. In the context of AI, the definition of an expected outcome and its assessment has to be done in alignment with the business stakeholder.

But determining the right metrics to measure can become a challenge in an innovation area such as AI, where the project failure rate is high, and business outcomes might take a while to realise or are dependent on success factors that are not in control of the AI initiative. Thus, it is essential to measure progress by tracking actions taken and gauging their success/failure.

In such an innovative field, it is all too easy to overlook the reality of outcomes, attributing positive results to the actions taken and any negatives to external factors beyond our control. To ensure maximum success, it is of paramount importance to employ careful assessment and analysis of processes and results.

Dr. Marcell Vollmer, Start-Up Investor, CEO, and Former Partner at Boston Consulting Group (BCG)

Throughout my career as start-up investor, CEO, and former partner at BCG, I have had the privilege of advising and collaborating closely with numerous C-level executive teams from global firms, guiding them in crafting their digital strategies, which often incorporate AI technologies. Drawing from my experience with these organisations,

(*continued*)

I have learned certain best practices that have consistently resulted in successful AI value creation.

First and foremost, sustainable AI value creation hinges on an AI strategy that aligns closely with the overall enterprise strategy, effectively connecting the capabilities of AI to the specific needs of the organisation. However, it is not necessary to begin with an all-encompassing strategy covering the entire enterprise. A more effective approach is to start small, with a focus on the customer. For instance, it is advisable not to attempt to implement AI across the entire supply chain all at once. Instead, commence with a small pilot project that targets customer-centric improvements, allowing stakeholders to witness how AI can work for the organisation. An illustrative case is one of my clients who managed to save $1 million in the first year through AI implementation, particularly by enhancing their supply chain operations. By automating the process of entering purchase orders, the company freed up employees to concentrate on negotiating better prices with suppliers. This successful pilot project laid the groundwork for a broader AI roll-out across multiple supply chain business operations, leading to further savings and efficiencies.

Second, an effective AI strategy should consider not only the business opportunities but also the feasibility and adoption risks associated with implementation. It is essential to address the value creation across all stakeholders, including employees, customers, partners, and suppliers, ensuring that they understand the benefits of AI and are willing to embrace the transformative change.

Additionally, organisational capabilities must align with the challenges posed by the chosen use cases. This may require investing in technology based on a solid business case and fostering the right data and technical expertise within the organisation. For instance, in the context of supply chain optimisation, this might involve leveraging AI-supported technology and knowledge, such as Internet of Things devices for data collection on product conditions or radio-frequency identifiers to track their movement.

Last, it is crucial to recognise that a strategy is not a static document but rather a dynamic one that must adapt to the ever-changing environment it was designed for. To implement such changes, it is necessary to continuously monitor and update the underlying assumptions while evaluating the progress of strategic decisions. This flexibility and responsiveness enable the strategy to remain relevant and effective as the business landscape evolves.

10

Leading Successful Projects

You've got to start with the customer experience and work back toward the technology – not the other way around.
—Steve Jobs (former CEO of Apple)

Nearly half of IT projects exceed their budget, 7% exceed their time frame, and typically deliver 56% less value than initially expected (Bloch et al. 2012). However, it's important to note that an AI project is not just any IT project; software projects carry the highest risk of cost and schedule overruns, and AI projects tend to underdeliver even more frequently (Gartner 2018).

To mitigate the risk of project failure, classic project management techniques prove to be invaluable. In most cases, effective project management is based on mastering the fundamentals and ensuring that essential aspects are diligently executed. For instance, AI projects frequently fail because they have missing or wrong outcome expectations, miss stakeholder involvement at the initiation of a project, lack proper planning of resources and capabilities, or fail to understand the full business problem and therefore fail to anticipate how an AI solution will ultimately be integrated into business processes (Nunez 2021; Schmelzer 2022). For instance, we frequently see that AI projects miss an accurate value estimation and project scope, that a project is missing or not following a predefined life cycle, that committed and assured resources are missing when they are required, financial resources are not planned and allocated correctly, and that an IT solution gets built but not a business solution. Getting these fundamentals right requires the application of a project management framework. Although a mature project management framework will address those challenges for project management, the challenges specific to AI projects must be understood as well. However, these challenges are not always immediately apparent and can be quite elusive. For instance, the AI landscape is complex and fast-moving, unfamiliar to many, and its potential applications are not always easy to comprehend. Consequently, individuals often use heuristics to simplify this technology and make it more relatable. This explains why AI is frequently described as a magical wand (Thomas 2019). This perception is encouraged by AI product companies such as Alphabet, who label their latest generative AI developments as a 'magic wand' for their popular Google Docs software. This software, thanks to AI, can draft content like marketing blogs, training plans, or any other text in the user's preferred tone (Dastin 2023). Although this 'magic wand' perception fuels the hype around AI, it conceals the complexity of its value creation and results in a misguided understanding of AI's capabilities, its potential for value creation, and the challenges it presents.

Another challenge often overlooked is understanding the complexity of integrating a planned AI project into an existing corporate environment. This uncertainty can lead to project durations ranging from 3 to 26 months, dependent on factors such as data readiness, solution complexity, and the experience of the AI talent involved. On average, AI projects take about 12 months to complete (Deloitte and Google Cloud 2017). However, larger projects are more likely to fall behind schedule, exceed budgets, and miss critical features compared to smaller ones. They are also over 10 times more likely to face abandonment due to shifting business priorities (Project Management Works [PMI] 2021). Therefore, newer project management approaches and incremental value creation can be critical. Additionally, AI projects don't typically end with the completion of an AI solution. AI algorithms need continuous monitoring and potential retraining (Walch 2022).

Furthermore, AI project stakeholders may not have a complete understanding of the potential outcomes of an AI solution when they commit to a project, especially when conflicts arise between personal and organisational interests. Although these scenarios are common and are often explained through the lens of principal-agent theory, it's essential to acknowledge this issue due to its far-reaching implications on the adoption of an AI solution (*Wikipedia* 2023). For example, a business stakeholder may embrace the idea of an AI solution that could increase the team's ROI by 400%, but they may not anticipate the possibility that their own accomplishments could be overshadowed by the AI initiative until they see the first test results towards the end of the project. This could lead to a hidden rejection caused by the conflict of interest, usually represented by various feedback loops, multiple requests for solution adjustments, and other creative ways to delay the solution's launch.

Do any of those AI project challenges sound familiar? Many AI initiatives have encountered these challenges and have explored various approaches to address them. In this chapter, we'll offer general insights into project management for AI projects and discuss different AI project management approaches for your organisation. Moreover, we will address the challenges of creating trust and stakeholder value by focussing on leading change within AI projects.

AI Project Management

The main objective of AI projects is to produce AI products, services, or analytical outcomes that add value, such as facilitating transformative shifts towards AI-driven decision-making and enhancing operational efficiency. Typically, these projects encompass the configuration, development, implementation, and utilisation of AI solutions and require the management of various project activities and functions.

As per the Project Management Institute (PMI), a globally recognised professional association specialising in project management, *project management* is defined as the 'application of knowledge, skills, tools, and techniques to project activities to meet project requirements' (PMI 2021, 4). In this chapter, our emphasis will be on PMI's project management framework, with the objective of creating value through AI. We have chosen to focus on PMI due to its widespread adoption in the field of AI, its central role as a resource hub for project management professionals, and our belief that it can be a valuable asset for your AI project management endeavours as well. PMI offers resources, certifications, standards, research, and networking opportunities within the field of project management. A more comprehensive understanding of this topic can be obtained by referring to the *Project Management Body of Knowledge* (*PMBOK*) book, a comprehensive guide published by PMI that outlines industry-standard practices in project management. However, it's worth noting that your company may already have an established corporate project management framework in place.

AI Project Functions

The creation of value in AI projects is most of the time the result of collective efforts from a diverse team of contributors. These team members fulfill various roles that affect project planning and execution, encompassing functions such as overseeing operations, coordinating activities, delivering feedback, facilitating and supporting the project team, executing tasks, providing valuable insights, applying specialised expertise, ensuring governance, and offering strategic direction and resource allocation.

In the context of AI projects, project managers typically shoulder the responsibilities of oversight, coordination, and feedback delivery. They play a central role in ensuring that AI projects adhere to predefined schedules and budgets. Their duties involve orchestrating the collaborative efforts of data scientists, engineers, domain experts, stakeholders, and other contributors. Additionally, they provide invaluable feedback on the project's progress, ensuring that it remains aligned with the overarching organisational objectives.

To illustrate the importance of facilitating and supporting the project team, consider the role of a data engineer within the context of AI projects. Data engineers are instrumental in supporting project teams by managing data pipelines, thus guaranteeing high data quality and availability, which are crucial for AI project success. When it comes to executing the project tasks and contributing insights, data scientists typically take the lead. They are at the forefront of designing and developing AI algorithms and solutions that drive the project forward. To ensure compliance with regulations and ethical considerations in AI projects, legal counsel must provide their specialised expertise. They work diligently to ensure that AI initiatives adhere to relevant regulations and standards, minimising the risk of bias and discrimination as well as to ensure compliance with different jurisdictions.

For the purpose of providing business direction and allocating resources, business stakeholders and domain experts play a pivotal role. They must collaborate closely in defining the objectives of AI projects, aligning them with the broader business goals. Furthermore, they must actively participate in securing the necessary budget and resources for AI projects, offering invaluable guidance on how AI can effectively address specific business challenges.

AI Project Environment

The value created by AI projects is a result of the interplay between the internal and external project environments (e.g. organisational influences, market and industry impacts). A profound understanding and effective management of these environments are paramount for achieving value with AI projects. Several internal factors can significantly affect AI projects, including organisational culture, resource availability, data quality, and data accessibility, among others.

Organisational culture within an organisation can exert a profound influence on the trajectory of AI projects. If an organisation fosters a culture characterised by data-driven and analytical thinking, a culture that encourages innovation and experimentation, and one that promotes collaboration and trust, AI solutions are more likely to be embraced, and AI projects are more likely to succeed (Fountaine et al. 2019). Resource availability and allocation, which encompass budget, skilled personnel, data, and computing infrastructure, play a direct and pivotal role in determining the feasibility and execution of AI projects. A shortage of these essential resources can lead to project delays, compromise project quality, or even result in project failure. The quality, availability, and accessibility of data constitute fundamental cornerstones for AI projects. Subpar data quality or the presence of data silos can undermine the accuracy and effectiveness of AI solutions, underscoring the critical importance of addressing data-related challenges in AI initiatives.

Shifting our focus to external factors, AI projects are subject to various external elements, including market dynamics, industry regulations, and technological trends. Market conditions, which encompass factors such as competition and evolving customer demands, can exert a significant influence on the business objectives of AI projects. For instance, if a new competitor enters the market with a disruptive AI-driven product or service, it may necessitate adjustments to an existing AI project's strategy or objectives to remain competitive. Industry-specific regulations, as observed in sectors such as health care or finance, may impose unique constraints and requirements on AI projects, necessitating adherence and adaptability. For example, in the health care sector, AI projects must adhere to strict patient privacy laws in the United States. These regulations will affect the design and implementation of AI solutions.

Furthermore, the evolving landscape of AI technology can have a considerable impact on project planning and execution. Remaining on top of these technological trends is of paramount importance to ensure that AI projects remain relevant and effective in the face of rapidly advancing AI capabilities.

AI Project Life Cycle and Project Development

Every project follows a life cycle, defining a series of phases from value scoping to completion. The approach employed to create value with AI within this life cycle is known as the project development approach.

Life Cycle

Depending on its nature, a project can be split into several broad phases within its life cycle. This life cycle serves as a road map for managing a project, helping project managers, stakeholders, and the AI initiative to plan, execute, monitor, and control all aspects of a project's development. Inspired by the PMI project management framework, we can separate the following phases:

Planning-related phases:

1. **Value scoping:** define the business case, understand its business opportunity, assess adoption risks and evaluate its feasibility, by mapping the organisation's capabilities to deliver the intended project outcomes. Definition of project scope is the sum of all the products, services, and results provided and defines the project's deliverables and their acceptance criteria. It can be defined up front or evolve over time.

2. **Design:** develop the project's deliverables. These deliverables are related to the AI solution that can create the value outlined in phase 1. This phase encompasses project requirements and the quality of the deliverables of a solution. Requirements focus on clear, concise, verifiable, consistent, complete, and traceable project specifications.

Delivery-related phases:

3. **Development:** refers to the development of the deliverables and the construction of the final solution. This phase entails in addition to data collection, data preparation, and algorithm development the integration of a solution in current business processes. Moreover, it includes quality assurance, which entails validating regulatory compliance or addressing decision bias in AI algorithms.

4. **Testing:** test the solution and its various features built in the previous stage. Stakeholder quality reviews are conducted to verify that the solution functions as intended. It includes a detailed inspection of the quality of various deliverables that meet all solution requirements.

5. **Deployment:** involves integrating the solution into the production environment including data management infrastructure and IT architecture, and making it available to the intended end user population. It also includes measuring the realisation of the solution's benefits and conducting training sessions to educate users on effective solution usage.

6. **(Un)-completion:** marks the project's closure. Knowledge, learnings, and artifacts must be documented and archived, the project team released, and contracts closed. However, an AI project doesn't conclude with the delivery of an AI solution. Continuous monitoring of the AI solution's performance and optimisations based on new data and user feedback are essential ongoing activities. That means that the solution might need to be adjusted after its deployment. Additionally, change management activities need to be implemented to reinforce the adoption of the solution addressing the unique needs and concerns of different stakeholders.

In most projects, gate reviews are conducted at each phase to ensure that the transition to the next phase meets specific prescribed conditions.

Project Development

The project development refers to the approach that is used to create or evolve an AI solution during the project life cycle. Although there are different approaches to how projects can develop, they range from highly predictive to highly adaptive.

The predictive project development approach has been a popular and successful method for tackling projects of all scales. It has been a successful approach in various functional areas and industries. Its predictability, well-defined requirements, and boundaries make it especially valuable, following a step-by-step sequencing, also known as the waterfall approach. This approach is commonly used when there is a high level of risk or a significant investment involved in a project. A predictive development approach reduces uncertainty early in the project because the scope, schedule, costs, resources, and risks are defined in the early planning phases of the project life cycle. User feedback, however, is usually given towards the end of a project. When it comes to AI projects, predictive project development would be the ideal approach. With a clearly defined outcome and requirements in place, it enables defining the business opportunity and risk factor assessments to calculate a project's ROI, plan capabilities, and precise deliverables (see Figure 10.1).

This rigid approach can be used only if the project environment and required capabilities are relatively stable.

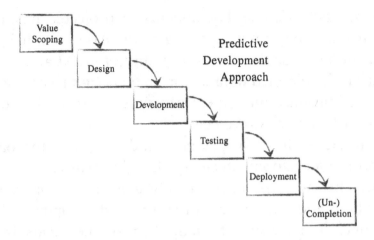

Figure 10.1 Predictive Project Development Approach
Source: Adapted from "PMBOK® Guide" (PMI 2022).

However, in today's fast economic environment and rapid developments in the area of data and AI, the technical capabilities and the context can be completely different, once a project is finished. For example, the innovation of generative AI and the technological advancement of large language models has dominated and changed the field of natural language processing significantly within only six months after its introduction in 2022 (Edelman and Abraham 2023). A predictive development approach also assumes that there is limited learning taking place during a project and that all stakeholders and project team members are fully informed at its inception. However, that can become complicated if, due to disconnected stakeholders during project planning, AI and data-inexperienced stakeholders, or inadequate stakeholder guidance at the outset, missing data and domain knowledge on the side of the AI initiative, it becomes evident during the course of an AI project that changes must be made to hit a desired or modified outcome. For instance, a projected business opportunity might not be as big as the AI-driven insights are actionable or the decision quality of an AI algorithm built on the planned data is not high enough to create an intended business outcome. Unfortunately, those are common problems of AI projects.

In the early 1990s, a new and adaptive approach to project development emerged: agile project management. This new approach quickly gained traction in the IT sphere and particularly in software development, but its principles have since been applied to other fields, from automotive engineering and sales to marketing and logistics (Denning 2016; Rigby et al. 2016). The term *agile* encapsulates the idea that project management must be dynamic to respond to changing project requirements and conditions. In contrast to predictive project management, it is offering project adaptability for usually lengthy, highly uncertain and volatile development initiatives.

Although a clear vision of a solution is guiding a project from its inception, the initial project requirements are refined, detailed, or changed during its life cycle based on short feedback loops. The project is developed through incremental steps (iterations), where each iteration's scope is based on a project's backlog (a prioritised list of work items or tasks that need to be completed during the project) and the feedback from the last iteration. Figure 10.2. shows a more adaptive project development approach.

More adaptive project management calls for more comprehensive communication among the team of project stakeholders and members. Development cycles can be rapid and iterative (one to two weeks), requiring the proactive integration of stakeholders to gather feedback quickly.

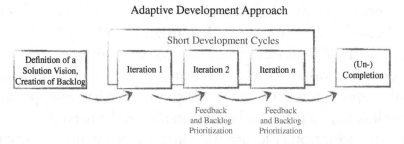

Figure 10.2 Adaptive Project Development Approach
Source: Adapted from "PMBOK® Guide" (PMI 2022).

The whole project team is usually very engaged during planning steps, determining the scope and estimating the work involved for each iteration. When it comes to AI projects, a more adaptive project development approach can support handling a project's uncertainty and enable continuous learning of all project stakeholders and members. However, agile and very adaptive project development also has its pitfalls.

The more adaptive the project management, stakeholders and team members have to cooperate more closely and communicate more frequently. Moreover, the time investment in testing and approving the deliverable to meet stakeholder expectations at the end of each phase can be significant and any lack of stakeholder participation will affect the potential feasibility and adoption risk of the final AI solution (Fridman 2016). Additionally, a highly adaptively managed project can fall off track more easily. Especially if the approach does not require much planning at the initiation of a project, constantly changing stakeholder needs and expectations and unclear stakeholder feedback and communication can lead to focus on the wrong development areas, cycles of trial-and-error, and lengthening the project duration and increase project budget to achieve a desired project outcome (Fridman, 2016).

A hybrid development approach combines the elements of both, predictive and adaptive. That means that this approach is more adaptive than a predictive approach but less than a purely adaptive one. It can be used if feasibility and adoption risks are not clear, to tackle uncertainty in projects, and if deliverables can be modularised. A hybrid approach often leverages an iterative or incremental project development. Both approaches focus on the development and delivery of a project in small, manageable segments rather than completing the entire project in a single phase. In an iterative approach, the project is divided into smaller iterations. Each iteration represents a mini-project within the larger project. During each iteration, a subset of the project's features or requirements is developed, tested, and delivered. This iterative process continues until the project is complete. Suppose the AI initiative is developing an AI solution for sentiment analysis in customer reviews. In the iterative approach, they could start by building a basic sentiment analysis model during the first iteration. The initial AI solution may have limited accuracy but provides a starting point. Subsequent iterations can then focus on improving the algorithm's accuracy by incorporating more data, experimenting with different algorithms, and fine-tuning parameters. Each iteration results in a more accurate and effective sentiment analysis solution.

The iterative approach is common and essential for AI projects but dependent on the project requirements and its environment. Usual stages of AI include POC (proof of concept), POV (proof of value), pilot, MVS (minimum viable solution), and final solution, which are interconnected in a sequential progression for the development and deployment of an AI solution. The journey typically begins with a POC to assess technical feasibility, followed by a POV to validate its business value proposition. Upon successful validation, a pilot phase is initiated, testing the AI solution in a controlled real-world setting. After piloting, the project advances to the MVS stage, where it evolves into a more comprehensive solution with essential features. Finally, the journey ends in the final solution, representing a fully matured AI system that incorporates user feedback and continuous improvements. Although the sequence generally flows from POC to POV to pilot to MVS to the final solution, it's essential to remain flexible and iterate as needed to ensure the project's success and alignment with evolving requirements.

In incremental development, a big solution is built with each increment adding new functionality or features to it. Unlike iterations, increments are additive, meaning that they build on the work completed in previous increments. Each increment is a complete, tested portion of the project. Imagine a project to create an AI chatbot for customer support. In the incremental approach, the team might start with a basic version of the chatbot that can answer frequently asked questions. This initial increment provides basic functionality and can be deployed to interact with customers. Subsequent increments can add more advanced features, such as natural language understanding, the ability to handle more complex inquiries, and integration with backend systems. Each increment enhances the chatbot's capabilities, making it more valuable to users over time.

Both approaches are well suited for AI projects where requirements and risks are not fully known up front, where there is a need for flexibility and adaptability, and where customer involvement and feedback are crucial. In both examples, the iterative and incremental approach enables AI projects to make progress while continuously incorporating feedback, addressing limitations, and delivering value to users in stages.

Selecting the Right Development Approach

In recent years, there has been a growing trend in organisations to adopt adaptive project development approaches, particularly in the area of AI (Schmelzer 2022). For instance, IBM stands out as a strong advocate for the adoption of an adaptive development approach in AI projects. The company has even published a book titled *Agile AI* and offers a training program focussed on agile project management for AI (Appugliese 2020). Similarly, John Deere has implemented an agile project development approach known as Scrum for all its IT projects. Remarkably, within a span of just two years from initiation, the company managed to increase the number of features delivered per iteration by a remarkable factor of 10 (Scrum Inc 2023). However, the choice of the most suitable approach remains context-dependent and is influenced by various factors falling into three main categories: AI solution considerations, project-specific factors, and organisational characteristics (PMI 2021).

The nature of the final AI solution and its associated deliverables is a fundamental factor in determining the appropriate development approach. If all the deliverables are well established and known up front, a predictive approach tends to be the most appropriate choice. However, when dealing with innovative products, services, or features that are less defined at the project's outset, an adaptive approach becomes more favorable. Similarly, projects with clear and stable requirements are better suited for predictive methodologies, whereas those involving uncertain, complex, and evolving requirements are more compatible with adaptive approaches. AI projects can encompass both scenarios. For instance, highly customised AI solutions tailored to an organisation's specific needs or those relying on nonstandard data sources may lean towards adaptability. Conversely, well-established AI concepts with clearly defined requirements may warrant a more predictive approach. In cases of high-risk AI projects, substantial up-front planning may still be advantageous.

Several project-related factors can significantly influence the choice of a development approach. The level of stakeholder involvement is pivotal, with adaptive approaches requiring ongoing engagement throughout the project's life cycle. Shorter project time lines can substantially increase the likelihood of success in AI projects, making adaptive and iterative approaches more appealing. Furthermore, projects with uncertainties surrounding funding can benefit from adaptive methodologies. These factors can vary widely from one AI project to another.

Organisational traits and culture play a pivotal role in shaping the preferred project development approach. Organisations characterised by hierarchical and directive structures with numerous levels tend to favor predictive approaches. By contrast, flatter, self-managed organisations are typically more open to adaptive methodologies. Additionally, larger project teams spread across multiple geographical locations, such as different offices, sites, or countries, may find predictive management approaches valuable for organising their tasks efficiently. Conversely, smaller, locally based teams thrive with adaptive approaches due to their higher demands for communication and coordination (Thesing and Feldman 2021).

Project Planning Components

The aim of project planning is to formulate an approach for creating project deliverables that steer the project towards its intended outcomes. The planning phase might be the most crucial stage in AI projects. Accurate planning plays a pivotal role in ensuring the success of AI projects, helping to steer clear of the common pitfalls and challenges mentioned at the beginning of this chapter. It enables you to precisely define the potential value of a project and set realistic expectations for project time lines, budgets, and outcomes. Realism is essential for managing stakeholder expectations and reducing the risk of disappointment or undue pressure on the project team.

Accurate planning also recognises the inherent complexity of AI projects. It provides a comprehensive understanding of technical challenges, resource requirements, and potential bottlenecks, enabling teams to proactively address complexities during project execution. Moreover, it helps identify potential feasibility and adoption risks early on, enabling the development of mitigation strategies and contingency plans to reduce the likelihood of unexpected setbacks. Involving stakeholders at this phase ensures alignment with project goals, stakeholder motivation, and organisational objectives, reducing the risk of misalignment later in the project.

The extent of planning and when it occurs during the project's life cycle should be determined by the specific circumstances. One variable that can influence the extent, timing, and methodology of planning is the chosen project development approach. In a more predictive development approach, planning and project organisation occur early in the project life cycle. Conversely, more adaptive approaches necessitate some initial planning but also require planning at the outset of each iteration. Other variables that can affect planning include project-specific deliverables, organisational prerequisites, prevailing market conditions, and legal or regulatory constraints.

There are various planning areas that should be addressed, including but not limited to the estimation of business value, development schedules, required capabilities, communication strategies with stakeholders, and result monitoring.

Business Value Estimation

The initiation of the planning process typically begins with a deep dive into the business case. This serves as the foundational step to uncover the underlying business opportunity. This involves estimating the potential business impact of an AI solution minus the budget required to bring this solution to fruition. The budget estimation should encompass all the necessary capabilities needed to complete the project, including post-completion maintenance, adjustments, and ongoing monitoring. Importantly, if the exact business opportunity remains uncertain, the estimate might manifest as a range, subject to refinement during the project's life cycle. Furthermore, when dealing with uncertainty surrounding the feasibility of delivering an AI solution capable of realising the envisioned business opportunity, you could deduct a portion of the business opportunity value based on perceived risks. Assessing this feasibility risk relies on a detailed understanding of how the solution will translate into a business outcome, accounting for factors such as required data and algorithmic intricacies. Additionally, adoption risks, which could negatively affect the value estimation, should also be considered. These adoption risks depend on how many individuals will be affected by the AI solution and how it will alter their current workflows.

The business case not only outlines the scope of the solution but also establishes the boundaries of the project. Although the scope of the solution is determined by its features and functionalities, the project scope defines the entire body of work necessary to deliver it. In predictive planning, this involves breaking down all project deliverables into a finer level of detail up front. By contrast, a more adaptive approach might commence with high-level themes or a vision, subsequently decomposed into backlog items. It's a common practice to prioritise deliverables that are novel, high-risk, or pioneering in nature to swiftly mitigate uncertainties concerning the project scope, especially before substantial investments are committed.

In case of uncertainty at the initiation of a project, budget estimates can evolve during its life cycle. In such cases, establishing a contingency reserve fund is a prudent move, serving as a risk response.

Schedules

A project schedule serves as a structured time line or plan, outlining the specific tasks, activities, milestones, and deadlines necessary to complete a project. In predictive development, the process typically involves breaking down the project scope into specific activities (so-called work breakdown structure), defining their sequence, and estimating the effort, duration, and required capabilities based on resource availability. If the schedule doesn't align with the desired time line and outcomes, adjustments to the sequence, estimates, and resources are necessary.

Conversely, more adaptive schedules require incremental planning, often based on iterations and releases (a specific version of an AI solution that is made available to its users). Although a high-level release plan outlines basic features and functionality, each release can comprise various iterations. The adaptive approach frequently employs time boxes (fixed periods), based on a prioritised backlog. The project team determines the amount of work that can be accomplished in a time box and self-manages the work. At the end of each time box, outcomes are demonstrated and feedback is collected. The remaining backlog, work estimates, and feedback from the last iteration inform schedule updates.

Capabilities

Planning the delivery of project components will be based on the necessary capabilities. Capabilities serve as the fundamental building blocks, forming the basis for value streams that support a given project objective. In AI projects, these capabilities encompass a spectrum ranging from essential AI talent and technology to data and its management.

The composition of an AI project team is intricately tied to identifying the diverse tasks required for project completion. These tasks span technical and nontechnical domains, encompassing activities such as project management, data engineering, and AI algorithm development. This task-based approach assists in determining the requisite skills and, in turn, defining the necessary roles within the AI project. These roles can be fulfilled by either internal team members or external talent acquisition.

In addition to human resources, AI projects necessitate essential technology resources, including hardware and software. Strategic planning for acquiring these capabilities, especially when they are not readily available at the project's outset, is vital. Data, being another critical resource in AI projects, must also be factored into the planning process. Furthermore, the management of those data assets, which is often overlooked but essential, needs to be meticulously planned for success.

From our experience, one of the most significant challenges lies in the absence of these foundational capabilities. For example, if there is a lack of maturity in data management and especially data governance, data quality may fall short of requirements.

Communication and Stakeholder Involvement

Effective planning of stakeholder communication and involvement is critical for the successful adoption of an AI project. It starts by identifying all project stakeholders and analysing their interests and expectations. This includes defining clear communication objectives and creating a comprehensive communication plan specifying the target audience, tailored messages, channels, frequency, senders, and feedback mechanisms.

Additionally, it involves developing an engagement strategy to involve stakeholders in decision-making and feedback sessions, addressing their concerns, and providing regular updates to maintain transparency. It's also important to keep records and have a crisis communication plan in place to address unexpected challenges swiftly.

Monitoring Progress

The link among planning, delivering, and measuring results throughout a project is achieved through metrics. These metrics are crucial for assessing work performance and whether specific deliverables meet expected quality standards. It's essential to plan which metrics to use and how often to measure progress. In addition to metrics related to the final solution, there are others related to scheduling and budgeting for evaluating project progress.

For example, in an AI project focussed on natural language processing (NLP) for sentiment analysis of customer reviews, various quality, scheduling, and budgetary metrics can be employed to monitor progress. Quality metrics could include algorithm accuracy, a key measure for NLP sentiment analysis. User feedback can also inform iterative improvements. To assess schedule adherence, task completion rate can be used to track the status of individual project tasks and activities. Budget variance, comparing planned and actual project expenses, serves as a budget metric. Positive variance indicates cost savings, whereas negative variance suggests cost overruns.

Leading Change in AI Projects

AI projects are usually innovations projects and depending on the AI maturity of stakeholders require some degree of change management. The ADKAR model, developed by

Jeff Hiatt, is a valuable framework for managing change in AI projects because it provides a structured approach to understanding and facilitating change at the individual level (Hiatt 2006). The ADKAR model is particularly beneficial when dealing with individual projects. For more extensive change initiatives, refer to Chapter 11.

The model consists of five key elements: awareness, desire, knowledge, ability, and reinforcement. The following sections detail how the ADKAR model is important for individual change in AI projects and how each element can be implemented.

Awareness

This is the first step in the ADKAR model. It involves making individuals aware of the need for change. In AI projects, it's crucial to create awareness about why the project is being undertaken, what benefits it will bring to the organisation, and how it will affect individuals' roles and responsibilities.

It includes communicating the purpose and objectives of the AI project clearly to all stakeholders, highlighting the potential benefits of AI, such as increased efficiency, improved decision-making, and enhanced competitiveness and addressing any misconceptions or concerns about AI to ensure a clear understanding.

Desire

Once individuals are aware of the change, they need to develop a desire or motivation to support it. In AI projects, desire can be fostered by showing how AI can align with individual and organisational goals, involving employees in the planning and decision-making process, allowing them to have a say in how AI will be implemented, and providing intrinsic and extrinsic incentives (e.g. recognition) for those who actively support and engage with the AI initiative.

Knowledge

Knowledge refers to the understanding of how to change. In the context of AI projects, that can be done by offering training and resources to build the necessary skills and expertise in AI; providing access to educational materials, workshops, and hands-on training sessions; and ensuring that employees have the information and tools needed to adapt to AI-driven processes.

Ability

Knowledge alone is not sufficient; individuals must have the ability to implement the change effectively. AI projects can be done by offering ongoing support and coaching to help individuals apply their knowledge in real-world scenarios, creating a conducive environment for experimentation and learning, and encouraging collaboration and knowledge-sharing among team members to enhance collective abilities.

Reinforcement

Finally, reinforcement is essential to sustain the change. This step involves recognising and celebrating successes and achievements related to AI adoption, providing continuous feedback and addressing any challenges or setbacks promptly, and incorporating AI-related metrics to measure the impact and benefits of the technology.

Implementing the ADKAR model in an AI project involves a systematic approach that focuses on the individual's journey through these five elements. It can be used to tailor communication, training, and support to address the unique needs and concerns of different stakeholders. A critical factor for the success of individual change in AI projects is the creation of trust. Building trust in the AI initiative is essential in the desire phase. Stakeholders need to trust that the intentions of the AI initiative are genuine and benevolent, that it has integrity, and that they have the ability to successfully complete the project. Trust is also critical in the reinforcement phase. Stakeholders will assess whether the AI project delivers on its promises and creates value for all stakeholders. If they see positive outcomes, their trust in the change will be reinforced. The AI initiative should regularly communicate the achievements and benefits of AI adoption to maintain and strengthen trust.

Phanii Pydimarri, Head of Strategic Planning and Partnerships at HCSC

In my role as the head of strategic planning and partnerships at HCSC, and having previously served as the head of commercial products for Stanley Black & Decker and chief analytics officer for Bose Corporation, I have accrued 18 years of experience in overseeing data, analytics, and AI projects. Although project management, in its contemporary form, began taking shape in the 1960s, it has undergone several adaptations to accommodate diverse project delivery approaches. The choice of delivery method depends on an organisation's context and especially on a project's characteristics.

AI projects demand a meticulous focus on domain expertise for tasks such as AI value scoping, data preparation and quality validation, problem-specific algorithmic solutions, and effective stakeholder change management. However, even with detailed planning, AI projects often struggle with a substantial degree of uncertainty. In my extensive experience with AI projects, I have found that project delivery must therefore be adaptive. An iterative approach to projects aligns with the experimental nature of tasks like algorithm selection, feature engineering, and model tuning. To foster trust and ensure ethical decision-making, model interpretability and explainability take on paramount importance. Transparency in the project's execution and AI's decision-making is therefore critical.

AI-Driven Projects for Product Engineering

In the core operations of a prominent manufacturing company, we embarked on an AI transformation initiative. We started a strategic journey to revamp our product engineering processes with the application of AI. Amidst our daily operations and machinery, we started a pretty forward-thinking project.

This undertaking was guided by project management best practices, commencing with a rigorous focus on value scoping as a foundational step. Our collaborative efforts with domain experts enriched our AI-driven insights, ensuring alignment with specific business expectations. Additionally, extensive efforts in data preparation and quality validation were required to make sure the final solution would align with stakeholder expectations.

We adopted an iterative approach, providing room for experimentation and research, ultimately leading to the refinement of algorithms, models, and parameters.

Transparency and ethical considerations were integral aspects of this project, with our AI algorithms designed for interpretability and compliance. We took proactive measures to address biases and privacy concerns, guaranteeing that our AI-based decisions adhered to ethical standards. We established mechanisms for continuous

(continued)

algorithm retraining and enhancement to maintain performance over time.

A user-centric approach remained central throughout, with AI-powered features tailored to meet user requirements and improve their experience. The effectiveness of our AI approaches was validated through a proof of value, which effectively managed risks while demonstrating value to our stakeholders. Our cross-functional collaboration leveraged diverse expertise, resulting in the delivery of a comprehensive solution.

By adhering to best practices in project management and adjusting it to the requirements of AI, our AI-powered product engineering led to a groundbreaking product, showcasing innovation, and triggering positive change throughout our organisation.

11

Cultivating an AI-Friendly Culture

Revitalizing people has a lot less to do with changing people and has a lot more to do with changing the context that companies, that senior managers [. . .] create around their people. Context, some manager called it 'the smell of the place', it's a hard thing to describe.
—Sumantra Ghoshal (Harvard and MIT professor)

There is a fascinating legend about Nobel Prize–winning physicist Neils Bohr often cited by renowned European philosopher Slavoj Zizek (Belinski 2016). According to the story, Bohr hung a horseshoe over the entrance of his country house, a practice believed to bring luck in many cultures around the world. When his friend asked him if he too believed in the horseshoe magic, he famously replied, 'Of course I don't believe in it. But I have it there because I was told that it works even if you don't believe in it!' (Belinski 2016). Bohr's paradoxical statement shows the power of culture. Even when he said he did not believe, his action betrayed his unconscious, deeply held superstition. Let's play a little game to see if you are influenced by the culture you grew up in. Take a look at this sequence of numbers and see if you can guess what number comes up next:

$$8, 14, 20, 26, 32$$

Did you guess 38? Most would say yes. But the truth is, any number could be the next in the sequence. Our years of educational experience led us to believe that the sequence had a *reasoning*. But nothing says they all have to be 6 apart – that just came up in our mind due to our hidden assumption (culture) that 'a number sequence like that always has a reasoning behind it'.

Similarly, culture affects our thoughts about AI. Media is one critical driver of that culture, exposing a whole population to a specific way of thinking. With newspaper headlines like *The Guardian's* 'US experts warn AI likely to disrupt jobs – and increase wealth inequality' (Greenhouse 2023) or the *Washington Post's* 'The AI we should be cautious about is already here' (Acemoglu 2021), the tone is evident. However, it's not limited to newspapers; movies such as *The Terminator*, *iRobot*, and *The Matrix* have vividly portrayed a potential future of AI that significantly affects our thoughts about this technology.

If you now find yourself concerned about the implications of AI, you're not alone. More than 90% of Americans express apprehension about AI and believe it will have a negative impact on our society (Leswing 2023). It's no surprise that business executives worldwide have identified their corporate culture as the primary obstacle to widespread AI adoption (Deloitte 2019).

The Threat of AI to the Status Quo of Corporate Culture

According to Edgar Schein, renowned culture researcher and professor at the MIT Sloan School of Management, 'Culture is not only all around us but within us' (National Defense University 2020). In other words, our culture is shaping our individual and collective identities (Schein 2010). It shapes who we are and what we stand for. That is why AI is a threat to the status quo of our culture because it has the potential to significantly influence the very perception of who we are! Consider, for instance, the case of a taxi driver who spent 30 years in their job. Self-driving cars could not only take away their livelihood, but in the process they also pose a threat to a core part of the driver's personal identity. The question arises: what becomes of the taxi driver's sense of identity if they are no longer a taxi driver?

Culture as a Framework for Corporate Identity

Within an organisation, culture serves as a framework that functions as collective memory and organisational identity. It helps to 'align effort, engender shared sensemaking, increase predictability, and encode organizational lessons about what does and doesn't work' (Keswin 2021). As we discussed in the first part of this book, AI has the potential to transform business operations and even change business priorities with impact on resource allocation and power dynamics across an organisation. With that, AI has a far-reaching impact on its culture by altering its collective identity. Although the fear of breaking the status quo can be a hurdle in AI adoption, the results of a recent MIT Sloan and BCG study underscore the positive impact it can have. Executives reported improved shared learning (87%), improved morale (79%), improved collaboration (78%), and clarity of roles (65%). In other words, AI adoption enabled teams and individuals to find their identity and greater meaning in their work (Ransbotham 2021).

The Depth of an Organisation's Culture

Culture is a complex and often hard-to-define concept, but understanding it is vital for successful change. According to Edgar Schein (2010), culture can be broken down into three distinct layers of visibility: *artifacts, espoused beliefs and values, and tacit assumptions*. Although the top layer of culture – artifacts – is visible to everyone, the other layers below are less and less visible. Schein's metaphor of a lily pond offers a helpful way to conceptualise the three layers of organisational culture (see Figure 11.1).

Figure 11.1   The Layers of Culture

Source: Visualization by DALL·E 2 from OpenAI based on the Lily Pond given in book Culture and Leadership by Edgar Schein.

The blossoms and leaves visible on the water's surface symbolise the organisation's artifacts, which are observable through its external appearance. The farmer's statement about what the lily pond represents signifies the organisation's espoused beliefs and values. Below the surface, hidden from view, lie the roots and seeds, symbolising the tacit assumptions ingrained within the culture.

The most visible of these cultural layers are *artifacts*. From office buildings and product logos to technology, decor, language, and dress code – all of these elements communicate an organisation's culture. But there's more to it than tangible signs. Stories and myths, often repeated in conversations, rituals, and even how people interact, are all important, yet possibly deceptive indicators. It's important to be aware of our own preconceived notions and biases when it comes to interpreting behaviour. Take, for example, an engineer in a technology company wearing shorts to a meeting. This action may be accepted in one culture, while in another, it would be seen as unprofessional. In Schein's lily pond metaphor, the blossoms atop the pond reflect the artifact level of corporate culture.

At the next level of culture are the *espoused beliefs and values*, which can be found in mission statements, annual reports, and the ideals of leaders. These are the values and beliefs that are either spoken or observed in conversations and meetings. For example, a corporate leader might say, 'We want to give employees a work life balance' or 'Leaving employees should be treated with respect'. When these values and beliefs become widely accepted, they become an undisputed norm and go underground.

The deepest, yet often most influential layer of culture lies in the hidden beliefs, values, and assumptions that members may not even be aware of – *tacit assumptions*. Although not explicitly discussed, these assumptions are shared among members over the years and thus have immense power. For example, in a culture where there is a hidden assumption that 'one has to be assertive' to be considered competent, employees who fail to speak up might not be considered for a managerial position. Similarly, in cultures where adhering to a formal dress code is synonymous with showing respect, individuals who don't conform to these standards may be perceived as lacking manners. In the culture where there are tacit assumptions such as 'AI will take away jobs', people may strongly resist any proposed AI projects, and efforts of persuasion might be difficult. Culture is strongly resistant to anything that contradicts its tacit assumptions. These are generally so strong, members feel anxious when they visibly violate the tacit or espoused values (Schein 2010).

The AI-Friendly Culture of AI Achievers

Mike Bechtel, chief futurist at Deloitte, has emphasised that the foremost strategic capability for future-oriented organisations is their adaptability and capacity for change (Bechtel 2023). However, the question arises: what kind of culture should organisations transition to in order to effectively harness the benefits of AI and facilitate AI adoption?

Drawing on the experiences of successful AI adopters such as Amazon, Boeing, Coca-Cola, Google, IBM, John Deere, and PepsiCo, we identified certain core cultural artifacts, values, and tacit assumptions, which can lay the groundwork for successful AI adoption. AI friendly culture has three critical characteristics: *a data-driven and analytical thinking, curiosity represented in innovation and experimentation, and collaboration and trust.*

In Chapter 1 about the journey of AI achievers, we illustrated the first milestone – *data-driven decision-making* – which also becomes a cultural characteristic of the enterprise. A data-driven approach – compared to regular intuition and heuristic based decision – has bias for collecting data for business problems and applying analytics to make decisions. Jeff Bezos, former CEO of Amazon, wrote in his 2016 shareholder letter, 'most decisions should probably be made with somewhere around 70 percent of the information you wish you had. If you wait for 90 percent, in most cases, you're probably being slow' (Amazon 2017). Boeing's CIO Ted Colbert echoed this sentiment, noting that 'when people begin to believe in the data, it's a game-changer: They begin to change their behaviours, based on a new understanding of all the richness trapped beneath the surface of our systems and processes' (Díaz and Saleh 2018).

Coca-Cola is an example of an AI-friendly culture, with *curiosity as a core value supported by an atmosphere of experimentation and innovation.* CEO James Quincey is a vocal believer, urging managers to act without fear of failure. He insists, 'If we're not making mistakes, we're not trying hard enough' (Taylor 2017). This espoused value can be seen in the company's actions, from the early days of image recognition for brand building to the countless innovations and experiments Coca-Cola has undertaken over the years. This isn't just talk – it speaks volumes about the company's tacit assumptions about the value of risk-taking and exploration (Taylor 2017). Likewise, PepsiCo is an AI achiever, committing to a culture of innovation and experimentation that extends beyond its product to its internal operations. As Colin Lenaghan, global senior VP of net revenue management, outlines, 'PepsiCo is very much an organisation and a culture that learns by doing. To further elevate the AI capability, we are making a considerable investment in broadening the analytics literacy of senior management and enhancing the culture in the process' (MIT Sloan Podcast 2021).

Collaboration and trust are the cornerstones of Google's culture today. But why are they so crucial for Google? In response to varying levels of performance and morale among its various teams, the organisation started on a journey to understand the differences between them in 2012. Google's extensive research revealed that effective collaboration is a core component of exceptional performance and that collaboration has one critical requirement – 'psychological safety' (Duhigg 2016). Consequently, the organisation actively cultivates an environment that fosters psychological safety, placing an emphasis on empathy, equitable communication, and trust in the benevolence of fellow team members (Richardson 2016). Sundar Pichai, Google's CEO, articulated this cultural goal in an official message to the organisation, declaring that 'we have a timeless mission, enduring values, and a culture of collaboration and exploration that makes it exciting to come to work every day' (Google Blogs 2019). To further foster collaboration and trust, the company conducts a regular employee survey, called *Googlegeist*, where employees anonymously share how they feel about compensation, teams, and leadership (Elias 2022). However, Google is not the sole AI achiever emphasising collaboration among its employees. Organisations such as IBM, Coca-Cola, and John Deere have also shifted their attention from siloed work environments to fostering interdisciplinary collaboration across their diverse teams (The Coca-Cola Company 2023b; IBM 2023a; John Deere 2022b).

Breaking Down a Corporate Culture

Although the organisational culture is more or less a unified entity, the artifacts and even values can vary widely depending on the level of hierarchy and function. For example, artifacts and values in the C-suite are unlike those of frontline employees. And even within the same hierarchy level, the culture of the sales team will likely be distinct from the marketing and advertising teams, with the former tending to adopt a more conservative dress code. To effectively change the culture, efforts have to be tailored to each level of culture and hierarchy. To illustrate, AI webinars for senior executives will differ in content and format from those intended for frontline customer service executives. As such, it's imperative to consider culture on multiple hierarchical levels when striving to create an AI-friendly atmosphere. For this purpose, we can divide the organisation into *frontline workers, middle management, and executive management.*

The Subculture of Frontline Workers

The frontline of most organisations is populated by operations personnel, forming the base layer of the organisational hierarchy. These individuals are typically independent contributors, such as sales personnel, software developers, or marketing planners. Frontline employees are largely responsible for their own work and are given a task, which they are expected to be carried out to the best of their abilities. In his book *Culture and Leadership*, Edgar Schein (2010) outlines some of the assumptions and beliefs among the frontline workforce. According to Schein, people believe that the success of an organisation is based on the actions of their team. They are a critical resource because their knowledge, skills, and commitment are required for business operations but especially to deal with unpredictable contingencies. They value human interaction and consider teamwork as critical for success. Although there is an appreciation of operating procedures, their culture frequently is based on how work is actually done and on operational success (Schein 2010).

Given that the frontline workforce is likely to experience the most significant impact from the introduction of AI within an organisation, effecting a successful cultural shift must encompass more than just concerns about job displacement. It necessitates a focus on addressing the underlying assumptions. This includes preparing for potential skill and knowledge replacements, considering the ramifications of AI on human interactions, and addressing any potential erosion of the sense of purpose that may result from AI's influence on operational success.

The Subculture of Middle Management

Middle managers play a pivotal role within an organisation, tasked with leading teams engaged in diverse functions such as sales, software development, and media operations. Their responsibilities encompass guiding, motivating, role clarification, process adherence, and conflict resolution to ensure team objectives are met (Drucker 1974). Typically, middle managers begin their careers closer to the front line, which gives them a deep understanding of the challenges faced by frontline teams, fostering empathy and cultural alignment (Davis 2023). However, as middle managers progress up the organisational hierarchy, a notable shift often occurs. Their leadership style may evolve from being more 'personal' and empathetic to one that increasingly aligns with the perspectives and worldviews of executive management. With an increasing team size their shift usually includes a stronger focus on capability planning and processes to manage their subordinates' actions (Schein 2010).

Because the cultures of frontline workers and executive management tend to differ (Schein 2010), middle management plays a critical role as a facilitator. Successful managers in this context excel at aligning individuals from various hierarchical levels (Jaser 2021). Consequently, they become essential change agents within the organisation. Failures in implementing change initiatives are frequently linked to challenges faced by middle management in adapting to new organisational expectations. Therefore, managers must possess a deep understanding of the changes facilitated by AI to offer their subordinates clarity and effectively respond to their emotional responses (Luscher and Lewis 2008).

The Subculture of Executive Management

At the executive management level, the primary concern is to maintain the financial health of an organisation, which means a constant focus on its survival and growth. According to Schein, this level is underpinned by certain assumptions, such as financial survival and growth is the only way to provide returns to shareholders, financial success is a battle against competitors, the economic environment is competitive and you cannot trust anyone, subordinates tell you what they think you might want to hear, and an organisation does not require people, only the activities they are providing (Schein 2010). With that said, people tend to be considered a resource like any other resource, but one that creates problems rather than solutions. According to Schein, that is an outcome of their distance to operations, which requires thinking in terms of control and routines to observe and influence basic work (Schein 2010).

Executive management might exhibit a greater openness to AI due to its potential for positively influencing an organisation's financial health and the rationalisation of its impact on its workforce. Nevertheless, their trust in the benevolence, integrity, and value-generating ability of an AI initiative remains crucial. Ensuring the seamless continuity of operations is of paramount importance.

Methods for Cultivating an AI-Friendly Culture

Now that we have identified the potential challenges of the various subcultures, let's explore a few methods that have proven effective in cultivating an AI-friendly culture. Although some of these approaches are specific to stakeholder groups, many are universally applicable but should be tailored to align with the diverse stakeholders within an organisation.

AI Webinars

The webinar format is helpful to foster communication across widespread organisations. Not merely prerecorded on-demand courses, but live, digitally streamed programs conducted by experts, these dynamic virtual events can reach a wide range of stakeholders in a short period of time—typically ranging from one to two hours. They can be partially interactive and provide a great opportunity for knowledge exchange.

The Commonwealth Bank of Australia, for example, has crafted a foresight webinar series to help its business customers successfully steer their way through their future with AI. By bringing together leading experts, this series provides an opportunity to explore the forces that are reshaping business strategies and consumer behaviour (Commbank 2023). Demonstrating the capabilities of AI to the bank's business customers can be a powerful message to create trust in their own AI efforts.

Webinars can be an effective method for broadcasting to a variety of stakeholders and developing an AI-friendly culture. However, for maximum impact, webinars should be segmented according to the audience. Middle management webinars can focus on the performance advantages of AI and its practical application, and frontline staff members can be empowered through webinars that address their concerns and discuss how to leverage AI to achieve operational excellence. Senior management, however, can explore the impact of AI on a company's financial health and strategy.

By creating targeted content designed for each group, webinars can be an invaluable tool for creating an AI-friendly work environment. However, not just the content is important but also their communicators. To address credibility issues concerning the organisation's AI capabilities, webinars featuring external AI experts can be helpful. By highlighting successful AI projects and their experimental nature, an organisation can be encouraged to conduct more AI experiments to capitalise on their potential.

AI Newsletter and Magazine

A knowledge platform, either in house or semipublic, can be a powerful asset for fostering a new organisational culture. Many of today's AI achievers have their own digital or printed newsletters and journals, such as *McKinsey Quarterly*, *Coca-Cola Journey*, *Think* by IBM, *Caring* from Johnson & Johnson, *The Dell Magazine*, *iQ* from Intel, and *The Boeing Frontiers*.

IBM's magazine *Think*, which dates back to 1935, has long been a source of articles on topics ranging from education and science to art and international relations. Originally distributed freely to an external audience, it merged with IBM's internal magazine *Business Machines* in 1971, becoming an employee-only magazine. Despite the shift in audience, *Think* continued to carry articles about topics outside of the organisation, as it had done for many years. Now, *Think* provides its audience with stories about the organisation, products, events, and new technologies such as AI (IBM 2022a, 2023a).

The essence of an in-house AI magazine is to serve as a thought leader platform that evangelises about AI. It provides knowledge about the value of AI, best practices, and can help to create trust by introducing the AI talent to the organisation. Moreover, being featured or associated with a project within an in-house magazine is considered highly valuable for a lot of people. It can help to add a deeper layer of meaning to people's work by creating social value, making it part of their identity.

AI Academy

Organisations looking to provide knowledge transfer about AI can benefit from the array of courses available from platforms such as Coursera and Udemy. These courses draw from the example of classes from top universities, such as Harvard and Wharton, which provide comprehensive, three- to six-month long courses delivered via webinars. But for a more tailored experience, a few AI achievers have developed their own AI academies and curricula to offer competencies and skills necessary for successful AI implementation. Such initiatives can also serve as valuable tools for upskilling frontline workers and middle managers.

For example, Intel and Google provide their own AI Academy for their workforce and potential or current customers (Intel® AI Academy 2022; Rayome 2018). Intel's AI Academy is created as a knowledge source for developers, data scientists, students, and professors. With a range of self-paced courses, live workshops, and webinars, this academy provides the latest knowledge and best practices on topics from general AI to deep learning. Google has launched a free 15-hour AI crash course as part of its AI resource center, designed to train employees and provide an entry point for those curious about emerging technologies. This comprehensive resource is open to everyone, from AI experts to developers to those with no experience. It includes free lessons, tutorials, and hands-on exercises tailored to all levels of experience, allowing stakeholders to develop their competencies and advance their projects (Rayome 2018).

AI Workshops

In our experience, AI workshops provide a valuable opportunity to engage with executive management in a meaningful manner. These workshops facilitate knowledge transfer and ideation, enabling organisations to develop a comprehensive understanding of how AI can create value and address specific challenges. Although there are various ways to structure AI workshops, a straightforward two-part format has proven effective for achieving those objectives.

The first part of the workshop focuses on knowledge transfer. It aims to showcase the capabilities of AI in the context of the organisation's needs and demonstrate the realm of possibilities. This external inspiration is essential because, without it, participants often tend to stick to their knowledge about AI's application, limiting out-of-the-box thinking. In the second part of the workshop, stakeholders engage in brainstorming sessions to explore potential business opportunities and establish a priority list of challenges they would like AI to address. By facilitating this dialogue between executive management and AI experts, AI workshops provide a practical means of harnessing AI's potential to solve business problems.

AI workshops function as more than just a conduit for knowledge transfer; they also serve as a platform to involve executive management stakeholders and alleviate potential challenges to AI adoption on the executive level. The goal is to establish trust with executive management, and identify executive individuals who are prepared to support the AI initiative. This format has proven highly effective in elevating an organisation's AI maturity.

Lunch and Learns

Lunch and learns have become an increasingly popular tool in the modern workplace. For teams and departments that wish to promote professional growth, these events provide a unique opportunity to interact and learn at the same time. Whether in person or virtual, lunch and learns are a chance to bring in an expert to provide knowledge transfer, and then facilitate dialogue about various topics such as AI. They are targeted to different groups of stakeholders and provide a good team-building exercise. The intimate atmosphere of a lunch and learn encourages employees to learn from each other and discuss topics in a more meaningful way than traditional one-way methods. For example, IBM has lunch and learns about various topics including the implementation challenges for AI (IBM 2022c). Lunch and learns can be especially beneficial for addressing and interacting with middle management and even frontline workers.

AI Coaching

Eric Schmidt, former CEO of Google, once highlighted the power of executive coaching in developing leadership capabilities (Bates 2011). He personally experienced the benefits of working with a coach during his tenure at Google. Executive coaching typically involves one-on-one sessions with a coach to provide guidance, support, and feedback to the executive. An AI coach can provide invaluable insights from an outside perspective, helping craft the vision and strategy behind AI while educating executives about the technology's business potential and its challenges.

An AI coach may meet with a business, analytics, or technology executive for regular or even intermittent sessions helping them facing new or challenging tasks, such as taking on a new role with AI, learning about new AI technologies and their application, and adapting leadership styles when integrating AI in business operations. But AI coaching is not just for senior executives. Coaches can help organisations at an operational level understand the barriers of integrating AI in an enterprise. By recognising the value of AI coaching, companies can gain a competitive edge needed to succeed in today's fast-changing AI landscape.

Internal AI Solutions = Internal AI Products

The complexity of building AI solutions can be hard to comprehend, leading many AI achievers to create internal AI products that give stakeholders a tangible understanding of it. Take Facebook's 'DeepText' – a natural language processing system. It was designed to understand and interpret the user content shared on its social media platform. DeepText aims to analyse and comprehend the context, sentiment, and meaning of the text in user posts, comments, and messages. Internally, this tool helps Facebook more accurately target content and advertising to its users, increasing engagement and revenue. Although this AI product isn't available to its customers, it provides significant value for the company.

This example illustrates how AI achievers use internal products to bridge the gap between AI algorithms and stakeholders, and maximise the value of AI for their businesses (Abdulkader et al. 2016). Those internal products can either be created internally or partnerships and acquisitions can be used to bring those capabilities into an organisation.

Best Practices for Cultivating an AI Enterprise Culture

To effectively nurture an AI culture, we can leverage the insights of the esteemed former Harvard Business School professor John Kotter, widely recognised for his expertise in organisational change. According to Kotter, the most common reasons for people resisting change are 'a desire not to lose something of value, a misunderstanding of the change and its implications, a belief that the change does not make sense for the organisation, and a low tolerance for change' (Kotter and Schlesinger 2013), all reasons why most digital transformation initiatives failed to provide the value expected (McKinsey 2018a; Reichert et al. 2020). However, Kotter's eight-step model provides a practical guideline for orchestrating cultural change on an enterprise level (Kotter 1995), complementing Schein's cultural framework and the diverse methodologies we've previously discussed. Kotter's framework played a pivotal role in driving transformations within renowned organisations, including Ford, General Motors, British Airways, and Eastern Airlines (Kotter 2012).

1. **Create a sense of urgency:** Implementing change, especially cultural change, is a challenging task. It requires groups or organisations to step out of their comfort zones. This can only be accomplished if the organisation and its people understand the underlying reasons for change (Kotter and Schlesinger 2013). Therefore, creating a sense of urgency is crucial. This urgency can stem from factors such as competition's use of AI, the potential impact of AI on the industry, or untapped business opportunities associated with AI. To illustrate, Tesla's pioneering efforts in self-driving car technology motivated traditional automakers to make substantial investments in AI to enhance their products (Rothfeder 2017). In the context of organisational change, the process typically begins with the executive, followed by the middle

management, because they must convince the rest of the organisation that maintaining the status quo is riskier than embracing the uncertainty associated with the consequences of the enterprise integration of AI (Field et al. 2023).

2. **Form a powerful guiding coalition:** Kotter emphasises that lasting change in large enterprises necessitates the formation of a coalition comprising voluntary leaders from across the organisation. In our previous discussion on an AI strategy, we highlighted this group as part of the AI management system. The coalition consists of leaders who support and drive the required cultural change. Although this leadership coalition will expand over time, it is crucial to identify individuals who share the commitment to drive cultural change. This coalition should include influential figures within the organisation, such as executive managers, board members, and major customers (Kotter 1995). Starting with a small number of those influential individuals, it can grow over time.

3. **Create a compelling vision:** Defining a clear vision for AI within the organisation is a vital component of cultural change and AI strategy. An AI vision helps articulate the role AI will play in the organisation. From a cultural perspective, it is essential to envision what the change will look like. The AI vision should encapsulate the desired AI-friendly culture that permeates the entire organisation. The AI vision serves as the guiding star for value creation within the organisation as shown by the vision statements from Google, Tesla, Microsoft, and Chipotle in Chapter 9.

4. **Communicate the vision:** Communication of the vision is as important as creating it. Consistently reiterating

the vision through various communication channels is critical for emphasising its relevance and credibility. People will embrace and engage with AI initiatives only if they trust in the value it creates throughout the organisation. Overcommunicating the vision is a helpful tool in achieving this trust through, for instance, the sustainability report from Chipotle, highlighting the importance of AI for their effort to improve human experience (Chipotle 2022).

5. **Remove barriers:** Obstacles, subjective and objective, are a reality in the process of cultural change. For instance, an organisation may aim to encourage more experimentation but could face challenges due to a performance management framework that restricts such endeavors. In this context, Google introduced their '20 Percent Time' philosophy, granting engineers one day a week to explore and work on new projects that benefit the company (Clark 2021). Similarly, a company striving to foster employee acceptance of AI may encounter difficulties rooted in cultural barriers. Encouraging experimentation with AI and providing knowledge transfer on the topic can be as helpful as Google's approach, which involves offering AI training to their employees (Rayome 2018).

6. **Create short-term wins:** Organisational change is like running a marathon – it demands sustained effort over time. However, people are more likely to stay committed to the journey when they experience small wins along the way. As we saw in Chapter 1, creating value at different stages along your AI journey is crucial. So, it's important to plan for and celebrate these wins throughout the process. Take Tesla, for instance – they make a

point of publicly celebrating every new and improved version of their self-driving car feature (Isaacson 2023).

7. **Consolidate improvements and create further change:** Kotter stresses the need to steer clear of premature declarations of victory, because they can potentially hinder progress. It's important to note that a successful AI project doesn't automatically transform an organisation into an AI achiever. Declaring victory too soon might reduce the sense of urgency, leading to a slowdown in investments, a halt in hiring essential AI talent, or a lack of ongoing efforts to drive and communicate cultural change. That might be one of the reasons why James Quincey, the CEO of AI achiever Coca-Cola, openly shares their achievements with generative AI but underscores that 'this is just the beginning' (Eckert 2023).

8. **Institutionalise the new approaches:** In the final phase, an AI initiative must embed new behaviours into the organisational culture, connecting them with artifacts, values, beliefs, and tacit assumptions. Communication efforts should include stories of AI success, highlighting how stakeholder teams embrace the collaboration across the organisation to develop successful AI-based features and services. By continually reinforcing the connections among the new culture, beliefs, behaviours, and organisational achievements, the AI initiative becomes ingrained in the fabric of the organisation. Kotter's framework requires regularly reviewing progress and making adjustments based on feedback to ensure that the change effort stays on track.

Scott Hallworth, Chief Data and Analytics Officer at HP

As the chief data and analytics officer at HP and former chief digital officer of Fannie Mae, I've dedicated more than 25 years to leading data and AI initiatives. Throughout my career, I've been committed to fostering a culture of experimentation and exploration, trust and transparency, as well as enablement and collaboration—a culture that ignites value creation.

In pursuit of this culture, one impactful strategy I've implemented across multiple companies involves recognising successes and 'lessons learned'. This entails leaders openly discussing instances when notable mistakes were made or insightful takeaways were gained. This practice serves as a catalyst, motivating colleagues to embrace change and to take calculated risks. Beyond avoiding repetition of errors, it encourages sharing experiences, nurturing a spirit in which individuals confidently express thoughts, voice concerns, and make informed decisions.

To facilitate this culture of experimentation and calculated risk-taking, I initiated the creation of secure, internal sandboxes to experiment with AI (e.g. generative AI) behind company firewalls. These sandboxes offer a safe space for employees to explore AI applications using company data. A well-defined intake process ensures that proposed AI projects align with company goals and come with necessary support. This process also enables a systematic evaluation, determining which ideas progress through development, production, and lastly scaling and monitoring. This approach has numerous advantages. It alleviates the pressure associated with experimentation, enabling employees to test ideas without undue fear of failure. It also cultivates a deeper understanding of AI's practical applications, moving beyond media hype. This strategy has effectively nurtured an AI-friendly culture, empowering employees to drive innovation.

In an era of rapid change and intricate challenges, an open and transparent culture is pivotal. Such a culture provides the foundation for scalable value creation with AI.

Part IV

Required Capabilities

According to a 2020 study about the best practices and AI investments from 1,200 firms conducted by ESI ThoughtLab, sponsored by Cognizant, Deloitte, Appen, Dataiku, DataRobot, and others, found that enterprises allocated an average of $38 million per year for their investments in AI with a strong intention to increase those over the following years (Celi and Miles 2020).

However, this figure is heavily dependent on an organisation's stage in their AI journey, their size, and industry. On average, AI journey starters invested $13 million, and highly mature AI achievers invested $99 million and more per year. However, organisations with more than $20 billion in revenue invested $87.5 billion on average per year, compared with $7.1 million for those with less than $1 billion in revenue (Celi and Miles 2020). The study also showed that the AI budget of an organisation is heavily dependent on their industry. Although automotive companies invested on average $59.4 million and health care organisations $54.1 million, organisations in media only spent $24.7 million for AI. The study also reveals that organisations surpassing others in terms of AI return on investment excel in cultivating robust capabilities, investing more than twice as much. Those AI achievers have dedicated substantial efforts to implementing the appropriate technology, have progressed further in data management, and are proactive in cultivating and recruiting suitable talent.

In the upcoming chapters, we explore the capabilities for creating value through AI in depth and strive to provide additional insights on how AI funds can be optimally distributed across technology, data management, and talent to maximise the returns on AI investments.

12

Technology

We provide machines with an end, and they provide us with the means.
　　　　　—Iain Banks (science fiction author)

AI technology is composed of hardware and software capabilities used to develop, implement, and operate AI solutions. Computers, servers, storage, and networking equipment are all hardware resources for these systems, used to store and process vast amounts of data required for AI applications and to train and run AI algorithms. For example, graphics processing units (GPUs) are preferred for training deep learning algorithms due to their speed and efficiency.

On the software side, specialised tools for machine learning, natural language processing, computer vision, and other AI applications enable organisations to build, train, and deploy AI solutions that are able to learn, reason, and make decisions with data. Examples of such software tools include TensorFlow and PyTorch for deep learning, spaCy and NLTK for natural language processing, and OpenCV for computer vision. This chapter addresses which technology capabilities are required to create value with AI.

The financial investment in AI technology capabilities vary along an organisation's AI journey. When companies start out, they usually invest more than 50% of their AI budget on technology, and those further down the journey usually reduce it below that threshold (Celi and Miles 2020).

In recent years, many AI initiatives have turned to cloud services to reduce the cost and complexity of investing in AI technology. Offering scalability, cost-effectiveness, and ease of use, cloud services have made it possible for AI initiatives to train and deploy AI algorithms without the need for expensive hardware, software, or infrastructure.

Leading the way in cloud-based AI services are Amazon Web Services (AWS), Google Cloud Platform (GCP), and Microsoft Azure. These platforms offer a comprehensive suite of tools and services, including prebuilt AI algorithms, AI frameworks, and data storage and processing capabilities. Perhaps most important, they enable AI initiatives to scale up or down computing resources on demand, providing a flexible and cost-effective solution for AI operations. Beyond the scalability and cost-effectiveness of cloud services, they also provide a range of tools and frameworks for training and deploying AI algorithms. Among these tools are popular frameworks such as TensorFlow, PyTorch, and Keras, which make it easy for developers and data scientists to build and test AI algorithms without the need for complex coding skills.

To better understand the individual hardware and software requirements of AI value creation, we will explore the essential components of an AI pipeline: a network of interlocking steps that enable AI algorithms to be applied.

The Technology Requirements for an AI Pipeline

The software and hardware requirements can vary significantly across the various stages of an AI pipeline. To better understand how AI technology is connected across its various steps, we break down the AI pipeline in five major stages, separated in two phases: the development and production of AI-based applications (see Figure 12.1).

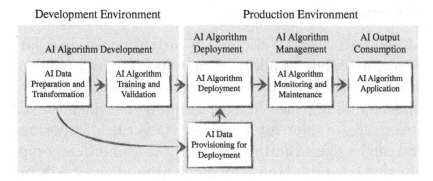

Figure 12.1 AI Pipeline Steps

The development and deployment of AI algorithms is a challenging, yet integral, task. Although the development of AI algorithms refers to the training and validation of algorithms and the preparation and transformation of data for learning, its deployment relates to consuming and managing outputs in a production environment.

AI Software Capabilities Along the AI Pipeline

As the use of AI continues to expand, a growing number of providers are stepping up to offer software solutions that support the software elements to create a full AI pipeline. Yet, for the most successful AI achievers, the customisation and flexibility of their AI software environment have been key to success. Rather than relying on a single provider or solution, they have tailored their software environment to the needs of their AI operations combining open source and commercial software solutions.

AI Output Consumption

AI's outputs can be consumed in various ways – in a dashboard, a mobile application, a vehicle, a fridge, or any other IoT device, or they can be shown in a table in Excel. Understanding which AI application type is the most suitable to create value for a use case is of critical importance and can be significantly affected by the four different types of value creation. However, the consumption of AI's output is critical to understand because it will affect the feasibility and adoption risks of AI value creation. Let us take a look at two examples.

In Chapter 3, we presented an example on how to optimise the direct mailing process through the use of AI. In that case an algorithm was applied to generate quarterly predictions of the customers who are most likely to respond to a new customer campaign from a telecommunications company. The outputs of the AI algorithm were saved in the form of a csv file, which is then conveyed to the mailing agency. From a technology perspective, the feasibility risk of the deployment was low because only minimal software requirements are needed for it to be executed on any hardware. Additionally, the adoption risk was low because the output format remained unchanged.

Drawing from the AI use case examples in Chapter 3, we also illustrated how mismatches between real-world consumption and technical implementation can create challenges for AI feasibility and adoption. Google's AI solution for diabetic retinopathy had the potential to revolutionise the way the world diagnoses and treats the condition. Despite achieving a 90% accuracy in lab tests, Google's AI product failed when exposed to the realities of the real world – including poor internet connections, low-quality photos, and the need for nurses to manually edit images in order to make them compatible with the AI solution (Douglas 2020). As a result, the product was deemed unfeasible and its adoption was hindered.

In summary, AI's value creation is significantly influenced by how the outputs of an AI algorithm get consumed by its stakeholders. Especially, any change in user consumption pattern can have a significant impact on AI's adoption risks.

AI Algorithm Management

The type of AI output consumption, the affected stakeholders of an AI use case, and the type of AI deployment have a major impact on the requirement for ongoing decision monitoring. This monitoring could involve tracking metrics such as accuracy or an algorithm's bias. If the algorithm is not performing as it should due to external changes, maintenance and retraining may be required. As illustrated by the Zillow example discussed in Chapter 8, early detection of performance issues can greatly minimise the risk of losses. In this case, the business opportunity seemed to be strongly affected by the changing environmental conditions and the resulting inaccuracy of the algorithm's predictions.

But monitoring should extend beyond the performance of an algorithm and include security of the AI system. AI security is a rapidly evolving topic, with new vulnerabilities continually arising. Common threats include system breaches – the exposure of AI algorithms to stakeholders they were not intended for – and availability attacks, in which a public-facing AI system is subject to a denial of service attack and thereby rendered unusable by a wider set of stakeholders (Hall et al. 2023). In adversarial attacks, hackers can study an algorithm's behaviour and manipulate its results. Trojans and malware are especially concerning in the open source environment of AI. Furthermore, because many AI systems are accessed via web applications and/or transmit the results of their analyses over the internet, they may be vulnerable to exploitation. In the case of public AI systems, it is possible to extract an algorithm by sending randomised input data to the system and then reconstructing the algorithm based on the output. This susceptibility could be used, for instance, to change the output of a credit algorithm in which a bank's AI system determines a customer's interest rate or credit approval. Any change in algorithm performance related to security, bias, or accuracy requires maintenance through retraining and updating the algorithm to the new conditions. Microsoft's Azure Machine Learning or Google's Cloud AI Platform include several security features to help protect AI algorithms, and IBM provides an Adversarial Robustness Toolbox, which is an open source library to defend and evaluate AI algorithms against adversarial threats.

Creating and maintaining documentation for AI algorithms is a critical but often underappreciated part of algorithm development, deployment, and maintenance. Documentation helps stakeholders understand, use, and monitor AI algorithms effectively. What should go into AI algorithm documentation? The algorithm description should include a high-level overview of its purpose and how it works. The algorithm architecture, input and output specifications, training data, and performance metrics should also be documented. Additionally, any limitations or assumptions made during the development process, use cases, deployment instructions, and maintenance guidance should be included. By documenting AI algorithms,

AI initiatives can ensure that their algorithms are well understood, properly deployed, and effectively maintained for optimal performance. There are various tools and methods that can be used for documentation. For example, Git is a version control system that is commonly used for software development. It can also be used for versioning and documenting AI algorithms and workflows (https:// git-scm.com/).

In summary, AI algorithm management is a critical but underestimated area that can help to mitigate risks of AI's application. The monitoring and documentation of AI algorithms and its use are two critical parts.

AI Algorithm Deployment

Any kind of AI decision-making we researched requires the use of AI in a production environment. In the context of AI algorithms, a production environment refers to a system where these algorithms are stored and made available for real-world applications. It's in this production environment that a trained AI algorithm is employed to process incoming data and make predictions. By contrast, a development environment is like a laboratory where AI algorithms get trained and tested.

AI algorithms are usually deployed in three different ways. Batch prediction and real-time prediction with either on-demand prediction services or embedded algorithms in IoT and mobile devices are typical viable options. Each way of algorithm deployment has its own merits and is a consequence of AI's output consumption.

Batch prediction is a method for deploying AI algorithms, in which data is collected and processed in large batches rather than in real time. Batch processing can provide several advantages over other deployment methods, including enhanced efficiency, scalability, and more consistent results. Yet, it is important to recognise that batch processing may not be suitable in applications when real-time processing is essential, such as fraud detection and monitoring of equipment. Additionally, there may be a delay between when data is collected and when predictions are made – a potential issue that must be considered when employing batch processing. Available software for AI batch prediction include Apache Spark, AWS Batch, and Apache Airflow. Apache Spark is an open source distributed computing system that can be used for batch prediction with AI algorithms, and AWS Batch is a cloud-based batch processing service that can be used to run AI batch prediction at any scale. Apache Airflow is an open source platform for programmatically authoring, scheduling, and monitoring workflows. It can be used to deploy and schedule batch processing jobs that involve AI algorithms.

Real-time prediction is supporting responsive decision-making in time-sensitive applications such as fraud detection, predictive maintenance, and chatbots. Data is processed as it arrives, rather than being collected and processed in batches. The advantages of real-time deployment go beyond its speed; it can also provide personalised decisions tailored to the specific input data. However, real-time deployment comes with its own set of challenges. It can be more resource-intensive than batch processing, requiring specialised hardware or cloud-based infrastructure to handle the increased workload. It can also introduce latency because data is processed and decisions are made, potentially affecting the speed of response. And it can be more complex to manage, because it requires careful provisioning of the input data, processing pipeline, and output results. AI initiatives that are considering real-time deployment should weigh its benefits and challenges carefully to determine if it is the right fit for their application. There are two ways of leveraging the real-time prediction capabilities of AI algorithms: on-demand prediction services or embedded algorithms in IoT and mobile devices (called EDGE computing).

Deploying AI algorithms as *on-demand prediction services* means making trained AI algorithms accessible to other software applications or end users in an efficient, effective manner. A prominent approach to deploy an AI algorithm is a lightweight, standalone executable software package, called *container*, that includes everything needed to run the algorithm. When deploying an AI model using container-based deployment, the model can be exposed to the outside world through an API (application programming interface). The API acts as an interface that allows external applications or systems to communicate with the containerised AI model. An example for that type of application could be an e-commerce website, which connects to the AI algorithm via API to provide personalised product recommendations to users based on their browsing history and previous purchasing behaviour.

Deploying AI as *embedded algorithms into IoT and mobile devices* refers to integrating pretrained algorithms into a software or hardware system so that real-time predictions and actions are enabled without access to a central server or cloud infrastructure. This is advantageous in scenarios when connectivity may be limited, such as remote areas, or when real-time processing is essential, such as in autonomous systems or real-time monitoring. Ford CEO Jim Farley underscored the importance of this when discussing their software development efforts for their new electric vehicles, emphasising that you certainly 'don't want to fire an airbag off the cloud' (Morris 2023). To optimise an AI algorithm to run on the limited resources of a device, such as memory, CPU, and power, techniques such as pruning, quantifisation, and compression are used. This reduces the complexity and size of an AI algorithm while preserving its accuracy and performance to an acceptable degree. Once the algorithm has been optimised, it can be integrated into the device's software or hardware system, either as a standalone program or part of a larger solution. From there, the device can utilise the algorithm to make predictions or take actions based on its local data, without having to access external servers or cloud infra-structure. From a software perspective, TensorFlow Lite or Core ML can be applied to deploy AI algorithms in mobile or embedded devices. TensorFlow Lite is a lightweight version of the popular TensorFlow framework, which enables efficient inference on devices with limited computer resources, and Core ML is a framework provided by Apple that enables deploying AI algorithms on iOS devices.

For the real-time deployment of AI algorithms, *data provisioning* is a crucial part of the process – and it's often challenging. To ensure that the necessary data is available and accessible to the algorithm, AI initiatives must consider how to store data in a way that makes access and use during run time easy. A feature store is managing and provisioning information for AI during an algorithm's development and especially deployment. It centralises the storage, manage-ment, and retrieval of information used by AI algorithms. Feature stores enable efficient sharing of that information across different teams and projects, help maintain consist-ency in feature engineering, and improve the overall pro-ductivity of AI development. Although there are existing open source feature store platforms such as Hopsworks, cloud providers' managed services for data storage, processing, and serving (e.g. AWS, Google Cloud, and Azure offer services) can be combined to create a feature store architecture.

The decision between batch processing and real-time deployment for AI applications is an efficiency and a responsiveness question. Batch processing may be more beneficial for applications requiring scalability for large-scale data processing and offers a lower risk of latency. However, real-time deployment may be more suitable for applications in which speed and responsiveness are paramount.

AI Algorithm Development

From an AI pipeline perspective, the development stage entails the preparation and transformation of data for and the training of an AI algorithm. The training of an AI algorithm entails the selection of the right one among a variety of algorithms (e.g. neural network, random forest), the optimisation of their training parameters (called hyperparameter tuning), and the application of techniques to reduce overfitting. All of those choices can significantly affect the output of an algorithm. The amount of data and variables have a significant impact on that training process. Although more data usually has a positive impact on an algorithm's performance, it can significantly increase its computational resource and even software requirements. However, once an algorithm has been trained, it can be saved as an object to make predictions at scale. When it comes to training AI algorithms, there is no shortage of software options. One of the most widely used tools is

TensorFlow, the open source machine learning platform developed by Google (TensorFlow 2023a). Similarly, PyTorch offers a user-friendly interface for building and training (Fridman 2022; https://pytorch.org/). Scikit-learn provides a range of tools for data preprocessing, algorithm selection, and evaluation (Scikit-Learn 2023). For deep learning, Keras is a high-level neural network API that can be used with either TensorFlow or Theano, and Caffe is a popular deep learning framework created by Berkeley AI Research (BAIR) (Caffe 2023). Finally, Microsoft's Cognitive Toolkit (CNTK) enables distributed training while supporting both CPUs and GPUs (Microsoft 2022) .

Data preparation and transformation are essential components of training an AI algorithm. The complexity of that step is usually underestimated – let us just address a couple of required steps and methods. From cleaning and transforming raw data into a format fit for the algorithm to data normalisation and scaling, feature selection, feature extraction, feature engineering, and the encoding of categorical variables, these steps require careful consideration. Raw data might contain missing values, outliers, or errors that need to be addressed before the data can be used for AI. Imputation, removal, or correction of missing values, outliers, and errors are techniques for dealing with data issues. This is an area that has benefited from new AI capabilities as well. For example, AI can be used to detect and correct data errors, identify outliers, and can even learn from user feedback and historical data to improve its efforts (LinkedIn Community 2023).

Feature selection is a method for identifying the most important features for the task and getting rid of unnecessary or redundant features (Mares et al. 2016). Feature extraction, however, involves transforming the raw data into a set of features that are more relevant for the AI algorithm. Dimensionality reduction and principal component analysis are some common feature extraction techniques. Last, feature engineering involves creating new features from existing data that may provide more valuable insights for the AI algorithm. There are several software tools and libraries that can be used to prepare and transform data. Some popular options are Pandas, Scikit-learn, and Alteryx. Pandas and Scikit-learn describe Python libraries that provide powerful data manipulation and analysis capabilities, including tools for data cleaning, preprocessing, and transformation. Alteryx is a software platform for data preparation and analysis that includes AI and predictive analytics capabilities (Witten and Tibshirani 2013).

Hardware/Compute Resources Along the AI Pipeline

Developing and deploying AI algorithms require different levels of hardware capabilities. Although the training of AI algorithms is usually significantly more hardware intensive than their deployment, the hardware needs depend on a variety of factors, such as the size and complexity of the dataset, the complexity of the algorithm, or the type of learning algorithm being used. Here are some general hardware requirements for developing an AI algorithm:

- **CPU:** The central processing unit is responsible for executing the instructions of the AI algorithm. The CPU needs to be appropriate to handle the computational load of the algorithm. For smaller datasets and less complex algorithms, a standard CPU may be sufficient. A multicore CPU with at least 8–16 cores is recommended for most commercial AI tasks.

- **GPU:** Graphics processing units can provide significant performance gains in training AI algorithms due to their ability to perform many calculations in parallel. Deep learning algorithms for natural language or image processing, in particular, often require the use of GPUs to train effectively. A high-end GPU with at least 16 GB of memory is recommended for most deep learning tasks and more for the application of generative AI.

- **RAM:** Random access memory is used to store the data and algorithm parameters during training. The amount of RAM required depends on the size of the dataset and the complexity of the algorithm. Larger datasets and algorithms require more RAM. At least 32 to 64 GB of RAM is recommended for most commercial machine learning tasks, but larger algorithms and datasets may require even more.

- **Storage:** The storage requirements depend on the size of the dataset and the number of experiments being conducted. It's important to have enough storage for the data, algorithm parameters, and results of the experiments. Solid-state drive are recommended for high-speed storage, and cloud-based storage solutions such as Amazon S3 and Google Cloud Storage are commonly used in the industry.

- **Networking:** If you're working with large datasets that are stored remotely, a fast and reliable network connection is important to ensure that data can be accessed quickly and efficiently.

Depending on the scope of the project, a CPU and a lower amount of RAM may be enough for smaller datasets and moderately complex algorithms, yet larger datasets and more intricate algorithms may require GPUs, additional RAM, and expanded storage capabilities. To ensure the successful completion of an AI training process, it's essential to accurately assess the necessary hardware requirements from the beginning. The costs associated with cloud computing providers can differ substantially, but a realistic figure for a single server based on the mentioned configurations could range from $20,000 to $40,000 annually (in 2023). This does not account for the pretraining of state-of-the-art large language algorithms, which can cost $10 million and more (Science Blog 2023). However, because that might not be the first use case for AI beginners, it might be wise to start small with a cloud provider, control cost, and scale step-by-step.

Deploying an AI algorithm typically requires fewer resources than training it, for several reasons. Inference, or using the algorithm to make predictions based on new data, is less computationally intensive than the training process, which involves iteratively updating the algorithm's parameters using larger datasets. As the algorithm is deployed, it is usually optimised to reduce its size and make it more efficient for inference, thus, reducing the hardware requirements. During deployment, the input data tends to be much smaller and so can be processed more efficiently. Additionally, during deployment, the algorithm is often deployed on a single machine or a small cluster, which further reduces the hardware requirements.

Sanjay Srivastava, Chief Digital Officer at Genpact

At Genpact, in my role as the chief digital officer, I have had the opportunity to deploy several AI solutions in diverse business processes across industries. And, as an entrepreneur and venture capitalist in the AI/generative AI ecosystem, I have built, advised, and mentored a number of AI start-ups.

Genpact transforms and manages complex business processes such as the supply chain, finance and accounting, risk and regulatory, and others. The company serves global clients across multiple industries, including manufacturing, banking, insurance, life sciences, technology, consumer goods, and more. This broad perspective has provided great insights about opportunities and challenges in deploying AI-based solutions. Additionally, my work with AI start-ups has further broadened our view of approaches and methodologies and the latest tools and techniques. This dual perspective – of enterprise opportunities, challenges, and learnings, and of emerging technologies and innovation ventures – has shaped my worldview on AI. Among the many learnings we have had, three stand out.

Build for Production at Scale, Not Pilots and POCs

AI pilots and POCs are fairly easy to build. Organisations often set up a dedicated team of bright and motivated engineers, protect them from the day-to-day distractions of the business, and have them go away and build a great answer to a critical question, such as predicting the maintenance requirement on a large engine. But the rush of getting AI off the ground doesn't always deliver the durability of using that AI solution in the enterprise – and it's because the science and the engineering of AI are two entirely different domains. In most cases, the science – the AI and the neural net modeling piece of the overall solution – represents only 10% of the total enterprise solution. The other 90%, which is the real key to success, involves the engineering of the system. This includes building the data pipeline that harmonises and continuously ingests clean data, the casing and the adaptable structuring of various AI models, the observability module and its interfaces that allows for AI governance and guardrails, and establishing the audit logs that keep track of model updates.

Be Super Intentional About the Technology Stack

At Genpact, we are right in the middle of many generative AI deployments – a technology that is still in its infancy and at a low maturity for most enterprise environments. Across the spectrum of existing approaches, we have seen various options – from a secure ChatGPT style implementation, to absorbing AI via existing software (as providers incorporate AI components increasingly into their solutions), to prompt engineering, or prompt tuning with retrieval augmented generation, to customising a foundation model, or building a proprietary LLM from the ground up.

Each of these six different approaches have completely different return on investment profiles, entirely different requirements for talent and expertise, and are positioned differently in the 'time to impact' versus 'durability of advantage' matrix. And because costs for inferencing are expensive and training requires an even higher investment, it is important to choose the right approach early.

In addition, some of these solutions require multiple technological components. Those can range from various security and tokenisation options to proprietary source or open source LLM models. Each of these components can come from a different technology provider. Thus, a very intentional and thoughtful design is critical, in which the best solution for one specific use case for a corporation (with its unique business need, talent, and capital profile) is rarely a good fit for another.

Plan for the End – Integration and Adoption Drives True Return on Investment

AI fundamentally changes business value propositions, which presents the technology's biggest opportunities as well as its single largest

(*continued*)

challenge. Unlike simple automation, where a process remains the same but becomes faster, cheaper, and better, AI transforms the entire process – reimagined at its core. These new AI-enhanced processes provide a different consumer experience, integrate in the value chain at entirely different points and in different ways, and fundamentally redefine the remaining role of its human colleagues.

And so AI projects that provide a single insight are interesting to experiment with, but AI projects that deliver actually return on investment are the ones that then seamlessly integrate the AI solution into enterprise workflows, redesign the experience based on its consumption, drive change management and pervasive adoption, and upskill the team to take advantage of it.

In summary, we have learned that there are many pieces we have to get right for achieving meaningful outcomes with AI in the enterprise. But the most significant learning we have had is that once you get it right – it can be infinitely scalable at virtually no incremental cost.

13

Data Management

Companies have tons and tons of data, but [success] isn't about data collection, it's about data management and insight.

—Prashanth Southekal (business analytics author, professor, head of the Data for Business Performance Institute)

When it comes to AI value creation requirements, data emerges as a crucial element, demanding a significant investment. However, data alone isn't enough; effective data life cycle management is crucial. The 2020 ESI ThoughtLab study of 1,200 organisations revealed that nearly all AI-mature organisations excel in data management, whereas most followers consider it their main challenge (Celi and Miles 2020). In terms of investment, the study shows that data management requires about 35% of AI spending or in absolute numbers, on average $13.3 million out of $38 million per year (Celi and Miles 2020).

However, AI beginners tend to proportionally invest more in data management compared to AI achievers (Celi and Miles 2020).

The challenge of data management goes beyond data security and quality. A 2020 McKinsey study on data management costs reveals the allocation breakdown: 38% for data sourcing, 13% for data governance, 29% for data infrastructure, and 20% for data preparation and consumption (Grande et al. 2020).

Data Management

The main objective of data management is to ensure that plans, policies, programs, and practices are effectively

279

developed, implemented, and managed to increase, control, protect, and enhance the value of data assets throughout their entire life cycle. Although there are several strategic frameworks available for data management, such as the strategic alignment model, the Amsterdam information model, and the DAMA-DMBOK framework, we will focus on breaking down the operational components and adopting a functional perspective for creating value with AI. The book *DAMA-DMBOK* is a valuable resource that focuses on this specific topic in detail (Henderson and Earley 2017).

Data management activities encompass a wide range of tasks, including data sourcing, establishing processes for data governance and data preparation, understanding the requirements for an AI-ready data infrastructure, data consumption, as well as archiving and deletion of data.

Data Sourcing

Data sourcing is the first step in data management. It involves collecting data from internal and external sources, a seemingly simple process with far-reaching implications for how it is managed. As we seek to identify the data sources needed for AI applications, let us first explore the various types of data that can be leveraged.

Raw Data Is King

Capturing and collecting data in its raw form is critical for gaining maximum value from it. Consider the example of a company that scans invoices and only extracts the total amount and the customer's name for billing purposes. By failing to retain other data points such as date, product details, and salesperson, the organisation is severely limiting the variety of insights that could be derived from the information for other purposes. The following types of data can be differentiated, with an increasing degree of structure:

- **Unstructured (raw) data:** not organised and lacks a clear format, making it challenging to analyse. Examples of unstructured data include text documents, images, and videos.
- **Semi-structured data:** has some level of organisation but is not as strict as structured data. Examples of semi-structured data include XML files and JSON data.
- **Structured data:** highly organised and easy to analyse, with a clear format and predictable patterns. Examples of structured data include databases, tables, and spreadsheets.

From a perspective of data value, the ability to apply data in various use cases with the highest degree of flexibility has the potential to yield the greatest value. This is why raw data is a highly coveted asset for organisations. However, raw data is mostly unstructured, with estimates suggesting that more than 80% of all data is available in a nonstructured format. The challenge is to transform this data into a structured form suitable for AI algorithms, which typically require a specific structured format for training purposes (Harbert 2021).

Data Creation Versus Reuse

When it comes to data sourcing, there is a decision to make: create data or leverage existing data? Primary data, which is created and collected for a specific use case with the purpose of AI value creation, offers a high quality and is an original source of information. Primary data can be collected through sensors, transactions, surveys, experiments and other sources. Secondary data describes already existing data, collected either by someone else or for another purpose. For example, secondary data can be collected through sources such as government agencies, academic institutions, commercial providers, and other organisations. However, secondary data can also come from your own organisation and be an outcome of internal processes such as billing, customer registration, employee onboarding, and manufacturing of products. Although many AI projects leverage secondary data, primary data has many advantages. Choosing between these two data sources requires an understanding of their advantages and disadvantages. Knowing the differences between them might also help to further understand the data management process. Table 13.1 shows a comparison of both forms of data.

The form of data – primary or secondary – can vary between use cases, the types of value creation, and the context. Although primary data would be ideal, it is in most cases not possible to collect, because many AI algorithms require a history of several years of data or more. Take, for example, an AI algorithm designed to predict the need for machine maintenance: in order to accurately assess the timing for the need for maintenance, many types of information (e.g. sensor data, machine use information) over a longer time period about many machines of the same type is needed. This means that data collection is not merely a time-consuming issue but also that collecting enough historic data to successfully build an AI algorithm can significantly set back a project.

Table 13.1 Comparison Primary Versus Secondary Data

Characteristic	Primary Data	Secondary Data
Purpose	Collected for the purpose of a specific use case	Collected for another purpose than the use case
Level of control	Complete control over the collection process of primary data	Limited control over the collection process of secondary data
Originality	Collected specifically for a defined purpose and is not available elsewhere	Has already been collected and is available in various sources.
Cost	Can be more expensive than collecting secondary data because it requires additional resources such as research participants, equipment, and time	Is usually less expensive because it is already available and can be accessed at a lower cost
Quality	Can be higher because the researcher can design the data collection process to ensure that the data is accurate, relevant, and reliable	May vary because it was collected for a different purpose and the researcher has no control over the data collection process
Time frame	Can be time-consuming because the researcher needs to design the data collection process and then collect and assess the data, which can take a long time	Can be accessed immediately because it is already available

Data Source Location

Given the need for historical data to train and apply AI, there are numerous sources for secondary data from which to draw. However, it is vital to comprehend the ramifications of different sources for the application of AI. For instance, many third-party data providers offer access to datasets with thousands of variables. A provider may, for instance, provide data on customer age, income, profession, and more. However, some of that information may not be originally collected, but instead be generated using AI. For example, AI can be used to predict an individual's average income based on age and profession, but that data might not be reliable or correlated with the other variables, which could pose a problem for your AI algorithm. There are three locations that can be differentiated:

- **Internal data sources** refer to information generated within an organisation – from transactional systems, customer relationship management systems, enterprise resource planning systems, and other internal data providers. For example, a retail store might have internal data sources related to inventory levels or sales data, call centers might have audio tapes from customer calls, and manufacturer data from PLC units from their machines.

- **External data sources** are those generated outside an organisation, such as public data sources, open data sources, public datasets, social media platforms, news outlets, and websites. For example, a transportation company can use external data sources to monitor traffic patterns, weather conditions, and road closures or an insurance company can leverage external data to monitor the impact of weather conditions.

- **Third-party data sources** provide access to data collected by providers, such as market research reports, surveys, and other commercial sources, which can be invaluable for companies that don't have access to the data they need or who need to augment their existing data. For example, an insurance or credit card company can use third-party data sources to uncover demographic data and other relevant information about their potential customers.

The source of data can be a key factor in understanding its quality, reliability, accuracy, and overall usefulness. A reputable source is more likely to yield trustworthy results than questionable ones and knowing its origin can also help identify and mitigate potential biases. For example, a drug store company might want to leverage (anonymised) health information about potential new customers to target their sales efforts (Thielman 2017). The acquisition of external data, however, can be a quality challenge and only be available for a group of customers, which might create a bias in an AI algorithm. Moreover, data regulations and privacy requirements vary depending on the source, so it's essential to be aware of the rules you must abide by. Furthermore, understanding the source of data can help inform decision-making; internal data can be useful for decisions regarding internal operations, while data from external sources may be more relevant for understanding and predicting industry or market trends.

Data Governance

We define AI data governance as the practices, policies, and standards organisations use to protect individuals' privacy by being compliant with the legal environment (e.g. General Data Protection Regulation [GDPR] in Europe) and ensure data security as well as high quality when collecting, storing, and using data for AI purposes. Comprehensive measures can be taken to ensure the *confidentiality, integrity, and availability* of data, such as encryption, secure data transfer, and federated learning for confidentiality; data quality and algorithm validation for algorithm integrity; and scalability, redundancy, and disaster recovery for availability (Det Norske Veritas Group 2023). Employing these safeguards protects data from unauthorised access, modification, or destruction.

Data About Data

Metadata and data lineage are two essential concepts in the world of data for AI. Although metadata helps data scientists and other stakeholders understand the characteristics and quality of the data used to develop, deploy, and manage AI algorithms, data lineage helps to ensure the accuracy and reliability of the algorithms.

Metadata can be described as data that provides information about other data. This information can include details about the source of the data, its format, and any preprocessing or cleaning that was done before it was used. Metadata helps to develop, deploy, and manage AI algorithms, providing information to ensure their accuracy, bias-free nature, and effectiveness in achieving their intended goals. Managing and organising large datasets can be a daunting task, but metadata can be used to make this task easier. By categorising data based on its type, format, or source, metadata makes it easier to locate and use data in AI projects.

The second essential concept in the context of AI data is its lineage. Data lineage refers to the process of tracing the origin, movement, and transformation of data throughout its life cycle. In the world of AI, data lineage is particularly important because it ensures the accuracy and reliability of AI algorithms. As the saying goes, 'garbage in, garbage out', meaning that the quality of the data used to train AI algorithms is directly related to the quality of the output. Therefore, by tracing the lineage of the data used in AI algorithms, data scientists and other stakeholders can identify any potential biases, errors, or inconsistencies in the data and take steps to correct them. The concept is also critical to evaluate data value. The tracking of the impact on data on business outcomes is an important element of evaluating data's ROI. In addition to ensuring the accuracy and reliability of AI algorithms, data lineage is crucial for compliance purposes. For instance, the finance industry is subject to regulations that require them to track the lineage of their data to ensure its accuracy and integrity (Gupta 2021). Data lineage, therefore, helps organisations stay compliant and avoid legal and financial penalties. Although tools for data lineage are still a new and evolving category, there are a few organisations, such as Atlan, Informatica, or Microsoft, that offer commercial solutions.

Data Confidentiality

Data privacy and security challenges can severely inhibit the ability to apply AI in various ways. As more and more personal data is amassed without consumers knowing, laws to protect the privacy of individuals are in place in many areas of the world. These rules (e.g. GDPR in Europe) and the corresponding laws create the swim lanes for AI solutions, and significant penalties exist if these are crossed.

The Cambridge Analytica scandal revealed an urgent need for data governance in the AI space in 2018 (Cadwalladr and Graham 2018). In an unprecedented violation of data privacy regulations, the British consulting firm harvested personal data of millions of Facebook users without their consent and used it for various purposes, including influencing political campaigns, such as the 2016 US presidential election (Confessore 2018). Examining the scandal from a data governance perspective, it is clear that the firm had obtained personal data from sources, such as personality quizzes and surveys, without obtaining explicit consent. Additionally, it had illegally obtained data from third-party sources, including academic researchers, and used this data to create psychographic profiles of Facebook users and target them with personalised political messages. The Cambridge Analytica scandal is a stark reminder of the importance of data governance in protecting personal data and ensuring ethical data practices (Lapowsky 2019).

The European Union's GDPR of 2018 unified consumer data protection regulations across the EU and is setting a precedent for the US (GDPR.eu 2023). Although the US has yet to introduce a comprehensive federal consumer data privacy or security law, individual states and selected industries have been driving initiatives forward. These include the US Privacy Act of 1974 and the Health Insurance Portability and Accountability Act of 1996, which define rights and restrictions on data held by government agencies and regulate health care and health insurance personal data protection, respectively (US Department of Health and Human Services 2023). The California Consumer Privacy Act (CCPA) of 2020 is the most recent example, giving consumers the right to access and delete their information, as well as opt out of processing their data. In addition, it grants California consumers a limited right to sue in the event of a data breach. Under the CCPA, personal information is defined as any piece of information that can be associated directly or indirectly with a particular consumer or household (State of California Department of Justice 2023). As such, organisations must remain vigilant when handling consumer data in the US.

The severity of fines for data breaches and consumer misinformation is a tell-tale sign that regulators are taking the issue seriously. Amazon was hit with a $887 million penalty in 2021 after being found in violation of European regulations. Despite the company's statement that 'there has been no data breach, and no customer data has been exposed to any third party', enterprises can still break GDPR rules without suffering a data breach (Shead 2021). WhatsApp was fined $270 million by Ireland's data regulators due to its failure to provide adequate descriptions of its data processing procedures in its privacy notice (Satariano 2021). Equifax's data breach in 2017 led to the exposure of 150 million people's personal and financial information. After the company failed to fix the responsible vulnerability in their web-application framework, and failed to disclose the breach to the affected customers, a settlement of $575 million was paid (Cowley 2019).

Data encryption is an essential tool for protecting sensitive data from unauthorised access or interception by hackers or malicious actors. End-to-end encryption, which involves converting data into an unreadable format and decrypting it with a specific key, is essential for ensuring secure data in transit and data at rest. Furthermore, protocols such as secure sockets layer and transport layer security enable secure communication channels between systems, further protecting data from unauthorised access or modification (IBM 2018). In addition, through the use of federated learning, organisations can train algorithms on decentralised data without compromising data confidentiality. By combining these techniques, businesses can leverage data while still protecting its integrity.

Data Integrity

Data integrity is related to its quality and one of the most important topics in preparing data for AI applications. Data quality control is essential in ensuring accurate, complete, and consistent data is used for AI applications. To ensure reliable, high-quality data, organisations can implement data profiling and cleansing mechanisms. Let us have a look at a retail company that wants to implement a recommendation system for its customers. To do this, the company used customer data such as past purchase history, search queries, and browsing history to generate personalised recommendations. To ensure the recommendations are accurate and effective, the company can implement data profiling to identify any missing or incomplete data points. This could involve identifying customer accounts with incomplete purchase histories or missing demographic information. Once identified, the company can use data cleansing mechanisms such as imputation or filling in missing values to ensure the data is complete and consistent. Additionally, the company could also use outlier detection techniques to identify any data points that fall outside of the expected range or have unusual values. By removing these outliers or adjusting them to more reasonable values, the company can ensure that the recommendation system is not affected by inaccurate or biased data. In addition to statistical characteristics of data, data quality evaluations are strongly related to domain knowledge. For instance, data can be delivered through a social media agency that is managing the social media account of an organisation. Switching the agency can have a tremendous impact on the social media data quality, which often generates problems for the algorithms built on top of it.

Another way of facilitating data integrity is by validating and testing the output of an algorithm. To do this, organisations can utilise cross-validation, a technique that splits data into multiple subsets and uses each to train and validate the algorithm. Doing this can help organisations build AI applications with reliable results.

Data Availability

Data availability is based on the accessibility and existence of data for use across diverse AI applications, analyses, and decision-making procedures. It relates the ease of access, reliability, and timeliness of data for individuals, organisations, or systems that require it. In order to have data accessible, especially for AI applications, data management efforts should evaluate data's scalability and redundancy and create disaster recovery plans.

Scalability and redundancy are two key tenets of successfully deploying AI applications. *Scalability* requires an infrastructure that can handle large volumes of data and respond rapidly to changes. An example is a social media platform that uses AI to analyse user behaviour and provide personalised recommendations. As the platform grows and more users join, the amount of data that needs to be processed and analysed increases rapidly. If the infrastructure is not scalable, it may not be able to handle the large volumes of data, leading to slow response times and poor user experience. To ensure scalability, the social media platform could use a cloud-based infrastructure that can scale up or down based on demand.

Redundancy involves implementing backup systems and fail-over mechanisms to keep AI applications available in the event of a disruption (e.g. a mobile network failure). An example where redundancy is important in AI applications is in autonomous vehicles. Autonomous vehicles rely heavily on AI algorithms to process data from various sensors and make decisions in real time. A disruption in the AI system, such as a hardware or a software failure, can lead to a catastrophic event. For instance, an autonomous vehicle can have multiple sensors for detecting objects and obstacles, and if one sensor fails, the backup sensors take over or the vehicle is stopped. The vehicle can also have redundant systems for processing the sensor data and making decisions, so that if one system fails, the backup system can take over.

Disaster recovery plans are standard to ensure the availability of data (and AI algorithms) in the event of a disaster. For example, a health care organisation that uses data and AI to analyse patient information to provide personalised treatment recommendations should have a disaster recovery plan. If the AI algorithm fails or the data is lost, patient care cannot be compromised. To ensure disaster recovery, the organisation can implement data backup and replication systems, and use cloud-based disaster recovery solutions that can quickly restore data and algorithms in the event of a disaster.

Data Ownership and Responsibility

Data ownership refers to the identification of roles or individuals within an organisation who have the authority and accountability for specific datasets. Data owners are responsible for overseeing the integrity, availability, and confidentiality of data under their stewardship. Centralising this ownership in IT has often failed to produce the desired results (Torrekens 2023). It often creates a bottleneck due to the amount of data to oversee and the lack of domain knowledge for quality evaluation from a functional perspective. As a result, organisations are increasingly sharing data ownership across departments, looking to maximise data integrity, availability, and confidentiality. With a more decentralised ownership, there is an opportunity to tackle further domain-specific challenges: data representativeness and its ethical application for AI purposes. Data representativeness is critical to ensure that AI algorithms are trained on unbiased data to avoid algorithm bias and discrimination. Knowledge exchange and transparency about how AI algorithms are trained, what data is used, and how decisions are made are requirements for that. This includes providing clear explanations of how AI algorithms work and how decisions are reached, as well as providing access to data subjects who wish to review or correct their data. Data's ethical contribution requires the establishment of clear policies and procedures for the collection, use, and sharing of data in AI applications. Its purpose is to ensure that AI systems are designed and used in a way that is consistent with ethical principles, such as avoiding harm to individuals and communities, respecting privacy, and promoting fairness and justice as well, as being compliant with the applicable legal environment.

The responsibility for data within organisations can be divided into different categories, depending on the context in which data is being used:

- **Data user:** the organisation or individual who determines the purposes and means of data processing. This could be a company, a department, or any other entity that applies data for decision-making.
- **Data processor:** an organisation or individual that processes data. This could include service providers, such as cloud providers or payment processors.
- **Data regulator:** a government agency or regulatory body that is responsible for enforcing data protection laws and regulations.
- **Data subject:** the organisation or individual to whom the data belongs. They have a right to know how their data is being collected, processed, and used. They also have the right to access, correct, and delete their data, as well as the right to control how their data is shared with third parties.

With the distinct roles come distinct responsibilities – yet too often, these are not adequately outlined, leading to value creation issues down the line. The roles have to be clarified throughout an organisation to gain control over data during collection and use, which makes it easier to stay on top of data-related responsibilities.

Data Infrastructure for AI

Data infrastructure is the technical foundation of data management. It comprises technical components, such as data storage (e.g. data warehouse, data lakes, data lake house), data processing (e.g. data pipelines, data integration platforms) significantly affecting data security and privacy (e.g. through data encryption, access controls), and data analytics capabilities (e.g. business intelligence, AI development and deployment, data visualisation).

Data Storage

Organisations rely on various data storage systems to store and manage large amounts of data, ranging from data warehouses to data lakes and distributed file systems to cloud storage. While data warehouses take structured data from various databases and create a layer optimised for and dedicated to reporting and business analytics, data lakes are utilised to store big volumes of raw, unprocessed data mostly leveraged for data science and AI. Distributed file systems enable data to be stored across multiple nodes in a cluster, while Cloud services like Amazon Web Services, Google Cloud Platform, and Microsoft Azure offer cloud storage solutions. By leveraging the right mix of data storage systems, organisations can reap the benefits for the training or deployment of AI applications.

Data lakes and data warehouses offer different advantages for AI applications. The highly scalable and flexible data storage of data lakes makes them ideal for storing vast amounts of structured and unstructured data, enabling organisations to combine multiple data sources for training AI algorithms. At the same time, data warehouses are built on top of databases such as MySQL, PostgreSQL, offered by for example Snowflake or Oracle for robust data consistency, fast access, and transactional processing capabilities, which can be beneficial for the deployment of certain types of AI applications. Both types of data storage technologies provide advantages for the application of AI. That is the reason why the usage of multiple data storage technologies for the application of AI has become a common approach – including data lakes, data warehouses and other specialised systems such as streaming, graph and image databases.

The increasing complexity and delays associated with utilising multiple systems for data management have driven organisations to seek a new data management architecture. The data lake house, offered by Amazon, databricks and Oracle, is a combination of data warehouses and data lakes, offering improved oversight and governance. Experian and Generali are two organisations that have successfully adopted this new architecture and seen measurable results (Oracle 2023).

A data lake house Is a comprehensive architecture for building and managing data lakes that provides a unified, integrated view of all the data within an organisation (Databricks 2021). Within a data lake house architecture, data lake zones are used to organise and manage different types of data. A data lake zone is a logical area within a data lake that is dedicated to a specific type of data or data processing activity. A lake zone organises data based on factors like source, quality, security, and access requirements, creating efficiencies in data management, processing, and analysis. For example, one zone might be used for real-time transactional data, while another holds historical data used for reporting and analysis. From a data processing perspective for AI, there could be three zones:

1. **Raw zone:** where all the data is initially ingested into the data lake, without any processing or transformation. It contains all the data in its original format, such as log files, sensor data, social media data, and more.
2. **Processed zone:** where the data is processed and transformed into a format that is easier to work with. It may include data that has been cleaned, enriched, or aggregated. It may also include data that has been transformed into a specific data model or schema.
3. **Analytics and AI zone:** where the data is analysed, visualised, and used to generate insights. It is typically where data scientists and analysts work with the data to identify patterns, trends, and insights that can help the organisation make better decisions.

Cloud storage services such as Amazon S3, Google Cloud Storage, and Microsoft Azure provide highly secure and scalable data storage solutions for AI datasets and algorithms. Features such as data encryption, access controls, and data redundancy ensure data integrity and availability. In addition, distributed file systems such as Hadoop distributed file system provide fault-tolerant storage for large-scale datasets, making it easier for AI initiatives to scale AI algorithms as needed. By leveraging these features of cloud storage and distributed file systems, AI initiatives can ensure the security and scalability of their AI algorithms and datasets (Databricks 2021).

Data Processing

Data processing is essential for organisations to transform data into usable formats for the application of AI (Kahn 2022). From an AI perspective, data processing systems enable the *ingestion, cleaning, transformation,* and *labeling* of data necessary for effective training or prediction of an AI algorithm. Here a brief overview that those functions entail:

- **Data ingestion** involves the process of acquiring and bringing data from various sources into the data processing system. The data can come from sources such as databases, data warehouses, data lakes, file systems, and APIs. For the application of AI, the data is typically labeled data or raw data and needs to be labeled before it can be used for training algorithms (Esppenchutz 2023).

- **Data cleaning** is the process of removing noise, errors, inconsistencies, and outliers from the data. Data cleaning is important for the application of AI because algorithms are sensitive to noise, and having bad data in the training set can lead to inaccurate or biased algorithms. Common techniques used for data cleaning include outlier detection, imputation, and data profiling (Stedman, 2022).

- **Data transformation** involves converting data from its original format into a format that is suitable for AI algorithms. Data transformation techniques may include feature extraction, feature engineering, normalisation, and more (Zheng and Casari 2018).

- **Data labeling** is the process of annotating the data with relevant metadata, such as class labels or tags.

Data labeling can be done manually or using automated tools, such as image recognition software or natural language processing algorithms. Labeling is essential for supervised learning algorithms, where the algorithm learns from examples that are labeled with the correct output (Amazon AWS 2023).

To eventually leverage AI in a production environment, data processing workflows have to be automated. Data processing after the application of AI relates to the consumption of its outcomes, which we address in the previous chapter.

Data Archiving and Deletion

The significance of data archiving and deletion in the data life cycle is critical in the age of AI, when privacy, security, and legal compliance are of utmost importance. Today, organisations are grappling with massive amounts of data, and their archiving, retention, and deletion strategies can significantly affect their business operations.

Data archiving is the process of storing data for future retrieval, and it is vital in the AI context. AI initiatives must ensure that the data used to train and refine AI algorithms is properly archived and easily accessible for future use. This is crucial because AI algorithms may need to be retrained or updated over time, and historical data can help improve the accuracy and effectiveness of these algorithms. It is therefore important for AI initiatives to establish robust archiving protocols that cater to the needs of the AI use cases. Data deletion involves the permanent removal of data from an organisation's systems. This is especially important in the AI context, because organisations must ensure that they do not retain data that is no longer necessary or that may pose a privacy or security risk. For example, organisations that collect personal data for a specific purpose but no longer require it must delete it to comply with privacy regulations such as those imposed by the GDPR or the CCPA.

Data retention – the length of time an organisation keeps data before deletion or archiving – is also a critical consideration in the AI context. Organisations should ensure that they retain data for an appropriate length of time to comply with legal and regulatory requirements. For example, financial organisations might be obligated to retain customer transaction data for a certain number of years to comply with regulations. Failing to establish an appropriate retention policy might result in costly legal and regulatory penalties. To effectively manage the data life cycle, organisations must establish comprehensive data governance policies that include robust archiving, deletion, and retention protocols. These policies should be tailored to meet the specific needs of their AI use cases and comply with the relevant legal and regulatory requirements.

The Trend to a Decentralised Data Management

Centralised data management has been a common practice for large organisations. However, it often fails to deliver the expected results due to problems such as siloed datasets, duplication of effort, and inconsistent data quality.

Although data silos aren't necessarily the problem and some organisations can operate just fine, it becomes problematic for the enterprise-wide application of AI, which requires a more holistic and functional data view across data silos for many of its use cases and applications.

To address these issues, a new concept has emerged in the world of data management called *data mesh*. Developed by Zhamak Dehghani from Thoughtworks, this approach promotes a decentralised model of data management, while still providing centralised governance and standardisation (Thoughtworks 2023). Through the use of a shared and harmonised self-serve data infrastructure, data mesh is designed to provide organisations with a secure and efficient data management platform that overcomes the common challenges associated with traditional centralised models. Although in a traditional data management system, a centralised data team is responsible for managing all data flows, in a decentralised data mesh, the responsibility for data quality, governance, and delivery is put into the hands of the teams that create and use the data to facilitate the sharing of data across departments. One real-world example of a data mesh is at Zalando, a European online fashion retailer (Litchlien 2022). They faced challenges in managing their data as the company grew, and they decided to adopt the data mesh approach. Zalando's data mesh is designed to enable autonomous teams to own their data and to make it easily accessible and understandable to other teams. The company has created a data platform that supports data discovery, access, and governance, and it has empowered teams to build and own data products (Databricks 2023).

The data mesh approach integrates domain-driven design principles, and together with a functional data infrastructure approach through data lake houses, enables AI initiatives to manage AI opportunities and risks on the data level.

Vikas Kumar, Head of AI and Data at CNA Insurance

As a leader in the data and AI ecosystem, I've had the privilege to build numerous data and AI products, as well as self-serve data and AI platform solutions. Although AI technology continues its rapid advancement and an increasing number of AI products and applications are shaping our daily work environment, it's essential to recognise that data remains the cornerstone of these solutions.

Although many organisations invest considerable efforts and resources into areas of data storage and endeavours aimed at simplifying data consumption, mostly for business intelligence purposes, data management remains a significant hurdle. Missing data management efforts often leads to data residing in isolated silos, plagued by inconsistencies and diminished quality. However, it's crucial to understand that, in the absence of high-quality data available at the moment of decision-making, AI cannot deliver the expected value. Reducing the feasibility risk of AI solutions significantly hinges on a dedicated focus on data management. When data is easily discoverable, accessible, and consumable, data management becomes a potent force for improving both the quality and the time-to-value proposition of any AI solution.

In addressing the data management challenges for AI implementation, I've encountered several successful best practices. First and foremost, it's crucial to have a comprehensive understanding of the entire data life cycle, from its origin to its eventual consumption and deletion based on compliance and regulatory requirements. This means tracing the data's journey through the organisation's AI environment.

To accomplish this, it's imperative to connect data to meaningful business and technical contexts, clearly defining how data is utilised within the organisation's AI ecosystem. This contextual information is essential for stakeholders to understand how data contributes to AI solutions. Furthermore, providing metadata about the data is crucial for building trust in AI solutions. This metadata includes details about data value, data lineage (its origin and transformations), and data transformations. Making this information accessible in a repository that can be easily accessed by data consumers has proven highly effective. Although these best practices may sound straightforward, their implementation has yielded remarkable results, with efficiency improvements ranging from 20% to 30%. This increased efficiency has significantly accelerated the speed at which AI solutions can be brought to market.

Furthermore, even as many organisations shift their data operations to cloud environments, it's important to recognise that the challenges of data management cannot be resolved by this move. Migrating data from various on-prem storage environments to the cloud can inadvertently create a data swamp that organisations struggle to navigate. Additionally, with the ever-growing volumes of data, the associated costs from cloud providers can undermine the overall value generated by this strategic asset. Deliberate data asset management is one of the key factors in cultivating a data-driven culture.

14

Talent

No institution can possibly survive if it needs geniuses or supermen to manage it.

—Peter Drucker (management consultant, educator, and author, laying the foundations of modern management theory)

AI talent is one of the key capabilities to create value with AI. However, many organisations new to AI are missing out on the value it can create due to a failure to invest in it. From a budget allocation perspective, it is the investment in talent that differentiates AI achievers and AI beginners. Although the more mature AI organisations invest 27% of their AI budget on talent, those just beginning to explore it allocate about 15% (Celi and Miles 2020). However, it is not just investment in talent, it is the investment in the right talent pool that differentiates AI achievers from beginners. Although AI is traditionally associated with STEM fields and experts (physicists, mathematicians, computer scientists, and data scientists), the experience of AI achievers has shown that successful value creation requires more than just that. AI value creation will need to acquire a diverse set of competencies, including technical and nontechnical abilities.

Evidence for that requirement comes from the shifted expectations at the leadership level of AI initiatives. In the early 2010s, many enterprises began their data-driven journey by appointing chief data officers (CDOs). Initially, CDOs were expected to have a background in data management and data governance, but now they require expertise in data science, advanced analytics, and cultural change management with the goal to create business value across the organisation. This is why the role of CDO is highly sought after and has a high turnover rate, because the requirements for the role are increasingly complex and the competencies needed are expanding (Weldon 2016).

But it's not just leadership positions that have experienced such changes. The roles of data scientists and data engineers have shifted and continue to evolve as organisations grow more proficient in AI. Data professionals are facing increasing levels of pressure and stress due to poorly defined roles, responsibilities without the corresponding authority, and a lack of training to meet role expectations (SAS 2014). This kind of environment has led to a high job dissatisfaction among data professionals, with many of them feeling burned out in their current roles, contemplating leaving their current employer or the industry entirely (Kahuha 2022; Wilson 2022).

From Tasks to Competencies and Skills to Roles

The challenge of identifying and defining roles and job expectations for AI value creation amidst constantly changing needs and priorities of AI initiatives can be daunting. We present an approach that can help organisations along their AI journey to find success in this endeavor.

That approach is starting from the task perspective – delineating the various tasks that need to be completed to create value with AI. Then, create descriptions for needed skills and competencies, and combine them to form well-defined roles and responsibilities for AI value creation (see Figure 14.1).

That approach cannot only be used for bringing on the right talent to launch an AI initiative but also for equipping current employees with the right competencies and skills. By adding the necessary AI value-related competencies and

Figure 14.1 From Tasks to Roles

skills to those of existing employees across the organisation, AI initiatives cannot just educate an organisation's workforce to fulfill specific AI value creation tasks; it can also leverage their organisational and domain-specific competencies. Research shows more mature AI organisations value internal talent development the most, whereas AI beginners mostly outsource their AI work and team up with technology or consulting firms before they start hiring and build capabilities internally (Celi and Miles 2020).

Identifying Competencies and Skills

No matter how hard data leaders and data professionals strive to fulfill the intensifying demands of AI and data initiatives, they cannot possess all the competencies and skills necessary for AI value creation. To steer clear of the burnout of AI leadership, it is essential to assess the competencies and skills needed and delegate roles that can effectively deliver them. To do that, let's explore the necessity for competencies and skills to overcome the challenges of and to create value with AI.

Critical Competencies and Skills Across AI Value Creation Tasks

Although many of the competencies required for AI value creation are present in many AI initiative's talent pools, the challenge lies in weighting and connecting them to the appropriate job roles. To do that, it is essential to understand the competencies and skills required for various tasks across the AI value creation areas. For example, the business alignment and use case prioritisation as part of the AI strategy requires a variety of technical and nontechnical competencies and soft skills whereas AI hardware enablement mostly requires technical competencies. The relevant groups of technical and nontechnical competencies and soft skills can be further broken down in areas such as competencies in mathematics and statistics, programming skills, and AI technology knowledge as part of the technical competency group. However, business and domain knowledge and product development describe rather nontechnical competencies.

To gain an understanding of the necessary individual skills across AI value creation areas, let's take a look at Table 14.1. It outlines the competencies and skills needed for various tasks in AI strategy, AI technology enablement, AI data management, AI project management, AI culture cultivation, and AI initiative leadership. Each of those AI value creation areas is broken down further in specific tasks.

What insights and patterns can be found by laying out the technical and nontechnical competencies and soft skills needed to create value with AI across relevant areas? We found that soft skills are the most essential of all and a prerequisite for most tasks related to AI value creation. Fulfilling any task across the AI value creation areas seems to combine technical as well as nontechnical competencies. Following close behind are technical and nontechnical competencies, indicating that both categories are equally important and should be given their due. That aligns with the findings from McKinsey, which revealed that 87% of

Table 14.1 Tasks × Competencies/Skills

AI Value Creation Areas and Tasks		Technical Competencies						Nontechnical Competencies					Soft Skills		
		Mathematics, Statistics, Computer Science	Programming	AI Technology Knowledge	Data Infrastructure, Processing, and Storage	Data Manipulation, Transformation, and Visualisation	Software Engineering and Application Development	Business and Domain Knowledge	Project Management	Experience and Skills in Organisational Psychology	Data and AI Governance	Strategy and Leadership	Problem-Solving and Critical Thinking	Communication and Collaboration	Creativity and Curiosity
AI Strategy	AI strategy and definition of an operating model	**	*	**	*	**	*	**	*	*	*	**	**	**	**
	Business alignment and use case prioritisation	**				**		**		**	**	**	**	**	**
Technology enablement	Hardware AI enablement	*	**	**	*	*	*	*					**	*	*
	Software AI enablement	*	**	**	*	*	*	*			*		**	*	*
	AI algorithm deployment		**	**	**	**	**	*			**		*	*	
	AI algorithm monitoring	**	**	*	*	*	*	*			**		**	**	**

(continued)

AI Value Creation Areas and Tasks		Technical Competencies						Nontechnical Competencies					Soft Skills		
		Mathematics, Statistics, Computer Science	Programming	AI Technology Knowledge	Data Infrastructure, Processing, and Storage	Data Manipulation, Transformation, and Visualisation	Software Engineering and Application Development	Business and Domain Knowledge	Project Management	Experience and Skills in Organisational Psychology	Data and AI Governance	Strategy and Leadership	Problem-Solving and Critical Thinking	Communication and Collaboration	Creativity and Curiosity
Data Management	Data storage and processing	*	**	*	**	**	*				*		*		*
	Data quality and governance				*	*		**			**	*	**	**	*
Project Management	Change management/ stakeholder trust and value creation	*				**	*	**	*	**		*	**	**	**
	Value scoping, solution design, and delivery planning	**	*	*		**	*	**	*	*	**	*	**	**	**
	AI algorithm and solution development	**	**	*	*	**	**	**	*	*	*	*	**	*	**
	AI solution deployment	*	**		**	**	*	**	*	**	*	*	**	**	**
	Project management	*	*			*	*	*	**	**	*	*	**	**	**

Culture Cultivation	AI culture management/ evangelism	*			*		**	*	**	**	**
	Communication and knowledge exchange	*		**	*		*	**	**	**	**
Leadership	Talent management	*	*	*	*		*	**	**	**	**
	Department resource planning and allocation	*	*	*	*	**	*	**	**	**	**

Notes: ** strong requirement, * weak requirement, no * means no requirement. Evaluation is based on our experience.

AI achievers spend about half of their analytics budget on nontechnical tasks connecting with employees, a clear indicator that technical and nontechnical competencies are equally essential (McKinsey 2021).

Description of Required Competencies

From the outlined tasks essential for AI value creation, we can deduce the various competencies and skills relevant for their effective execution. In detail, *technical competencies* are required to evaluate and set up AI technological capabilities for algorithm development and deployment; to be able to load, process, and transform data for AI applications; and to be able to build those applications. We can differentiate the following technical competence areas (see Table 14.2).

Table 14.2 Technical Competencies Overview

Competencies	Description
Mathematics and statistics	• Strong foundation in mathematics and statistics, including probability theory and statistical inference • Expertise in machine learning algorithms, including supervised and unsupervised learning • Possible expertise in specialised areas such as natural language processing, computer vision, or deep learning
Programming	• Strong programming skills in Python, R, and SQL • Ability to write efficient, production-ready code • Proficiency with frameworks like TensorFlow, PyTorch, and Scikit-learn

Competencies	Description
AI technology knowledge	• Understanding AI hardware and software requirements • Familiarity with AI pipeline development and deployment • Knowledge of distributed computing technologies in AWS, Azure, or Google Cloud
Data storage, infrastructure, and processing	• Proficiency in SQL databases, NoSQL databases, and data lakes • Knowledge of distributed computing technologies: Hadoop, Spark, Kafka • Experience with data management for AI purposes
Data manipulation, transformation, and visualisation	• Proficiency in handling large and complex datasets • Algorithmic understanding of AI-centric data processing • Data visualisation skills for deriving insights
Software engineering and application development	• Proficiency in software engineering principles • Experience in application development

Although technical competencies are usually the first ones that come to mind for AI value creation, *nontechnical competencies* are equally important. The challenges of AI value creation and AI's enterprise integration to scale AI value creation throughout the organisation direct us to determine what skills and knowledge is required to drive AI value creation. The required nontechnical competence areas are shown in Table 14.3.

The *soft skills* are focussed on the capabilities to understand stakeholders and to connect AI to its stakeholders, which are shown in Table 14.4.

Table 14.3 Nontechnical Competencies Overview

Competencies	Description
Business and domain knowledge	• Business domain expertise • Industry-specific knowledge • Process understanding
Project management	• Project management skills • Planning and budgeting • Stakeholder collaboration and negotiation • Talent pool management, team building
Creation of trust and psychological competencies	• Building trust • Understanding stakeholder motivation • Facilitating discussions • Designing value-driven AI solutions
Data and AI governance	• Data and AI risk understanding • Data and AI compliance and regulations • Data quality evaluations
Strategy & leadership	• AI–business strategy alignment • Capability deployment across projects • Cross-project leadership • Organisational connectivity

Table 14.4 Soft Skills Overview

Soft Skill	Description
Problem-solving and critical thinking	• Problem analysis • Pattern identification • Solution proposal
Communication and collaboration	• Effective communication • Cross-functional teamwork
Creativity and curiosity	• Curiosity and innovation • Willingness to explore new ideas

Interconnection Between Competencies and Skills

Another insight that can be gained from the task versus competencies/skills overview is that some of them seem to be connected and that their combination is required for various value creation tasks. It seems obvious that technical competencies are mostly required for AI technology enablement and that those are connected. However, the combination of seemingly disparate competencies and skills between groups can be essential for succeeding in various tasks. Mathematical and statistical competencies alongside business and domain knowledge, data knowledge, and various soft skills are paving the way for actionable insights and the creation of business opportunities, for overcoming feasibility risks, and for integrating AI in the enterprise. Combining business and domain knowledge with the creation of trust and psychological competencies can yield value for facilitating AI adoption throughout the enterprise. It also seems of importance to have mathematical and statistical competencies as well as a solid understanding of data manipulation across the board as technical competencies seem to be a requirement for almost all tasks across the AI value creation areas. As such, having the ability to knit together these different skill sets is becoming increasingly important for the success of AI initiatives and is of crucial importance in defining various roles of the AI initiative to fulfill tasks across the AI value creation chain.

Defining the Roles for AI Value Creation

The question of how to define roles within an organisation is key. It is important to consider the tasks required and the specific competencies and skills needed to fulfill each role. It's important to consider each employee's capacity to effectively perform a role, taking into account the maximum number of tasks that can be managed, as well as the maximum number of competencies and skills that an individual is able to hold. The best way to allocate AI responsibilities across value creation areas and tasks is to reduce overlap. This ensures that there are no competing roles or authority issues, and it can reduce capacity limitations caused by centralised decision-making dominated by a single leader or small group of individuals. With a clear delineation of duties and responsibilities, organisations can maximise their performance and limit the risk of friction or confusion. Table 14.5 provides an overview of potential roles and their tasks alignment for AI value creation.

There are only minor intersections among tasks in the proposed roles. It's critical to understand which roles are most essential and which can be replaced by others or supplied by external partners (e.g. technical enablement) to a successful AI initiative. Table 14.6 provides an overview of those roles, encompassing their tasks and requisite skills and knowledge.

The core roles of AI initiatives are vital, but there might be more roles necessary to augment the talent pool. Consider product tester roles for AI solution quality testing and support roles in HR, marketing, or specialised software design roles for AI applications on mobile and web devices.

In enterprises new to building AI solutions, a small but well-rounded team of AI specialists with multiple complementary skills and knowledge is essential to successfully tackle the multifaceted challenge of creating and

Table 14.5 Tasks × Roles

AI Value Creation Areas and Tasks		Very Technical Roles				Less Technical Roles					
		Data Scientist	Data Engineer	MLOps Engineer	Application Designer/Front-End Developer	AI Product Manager/AI Consultant	AI Project Manager	Cultural Change Agent/AI Evangelist	Legal Counsel and Risk Auditor	AI Strategic Leadership	AI Operational Leadership
AI Strategy	AI strategy and definition of an operating model						*			**	*
	Business alignment and use case prioritisation						*			**	
Technology Enablement	Hardware AI enablement		**	**							
	Software AI enablement	*	*	**	**						
	AI algorithm deployment	*		**	*						
	AI algorithm monitoring			**					**		
Data Management	Data storage and processing		**								
	Data quality and governance		**	**		*			**	*	

(continued)

AI Value Creation Areas and Tasks		Very Technical Roles				Less Technical Roles					
		Data Scientist	Data Engineer	MLOps Engineer	Application Designer/Front-End Developer	AI Product Manager/AI Consultant	AI Project Manager	Cultural Change Agent/AI Evangelist	Legal Counsel and Risk Auditor	AI Strategic Leadership	AI Operational Leadership
Project Management	Change management/stakeholder trust and value creation	*				**	**	**			*
	Value scoping, solution design, and delivery planning	**			**	**	**	**			
	AI algorithm and solution development	**				*	**	*	**		
	AI solution deployment	**			**	**	**		*		
	Project management	*				**	**	*			
Culture Cultivation	AI culture management/evangelism							**			
	Communication and knowledge exchange							**		**	*
Leadership	Talent management						*			*	**
	Department resource planning and allocation						*			**	**

Notes: ** strong involvement, * weak involvement, no * means no requirement. Evaluation is based on our experience.

Table 14.6 AI Value Creation Role Overview

Role	Tasks	Skills and Knowledge Requirements
Data scientist	▪ Advanced analytics and machine learning ▪ Collaboration with data engineers and business stakeholders ▪ Data analysis and predictive algorithm development ▪ Problem understanding and solution development using data	▪ Strong mathematical and statistical knowledge ▪ Proficiency in Python, R, and SQL ▪ Expertise in machine learning algorithms ▪ Understanding of hardware and software requirements ▪ Proficiency in data storage and distributed computing technologies ▪ Ability to write optimised code ▪ Familiarity with frameworks like TensorFlow, PyTorch, and Scikit-learn ▪ Domain expertise and problem-solving skills ▪ Effective communication abilities ▪ Innovation and willingness to explore new ideas

(continued)

Role	Tasks	Skills and Knowledge Requirements
Data engineer	• Infrastructure design, construction, and maintenance • Support for data collection, storage, processing, and analysis • Vital role in AI algorithm effectiveness and efficiency	• Proficient in SQL and Python programming languages • Knowledgeable in data storage and distributed computing technologies • Competence in handling large and complex datasets • Familiarity with data storage technologies such as SQL databases, NoSQL databases, and data lakes • Understanding of distributed computing technologies • Risk assessment for data storage, processing, and AI solutions • Data quality evaluation to mitigate AI feasibility risks • Complex problem analysis, pattern identification, and solution proposal

Role	Responsibilities	Skills
MLOps engineer	<ul><li>Infrastructure and tools design, construction, and maintenance</li><li>Support for AI algorithm and application development, testing, and deployment</li><li>Ensuring smooth and efficient AI system operation throughout its life cycle</li></ul>	<ul><li>Strong programming skills in Python, R, and SQL</li><li>Knowledge of distributed computing and data storage technologies</li><li>Experience with containerisation (e.g. Docker) and orchestration tools (e.g. Kubernetes)</li><li>Familiarity with infrastructure automation tools</li><li>Understanding of software engineering principles</li><li>Analytical problem-solving abilities</li><li>Awareness of AI application data risks</li><li>Knowledge of security best practices</li></ul>
Application designer/ front-end developer	<ul><li>User interface and experience design</li><li>Creation of the front end for AI applications for an intuitive user experience</li><li>Ensuring usability and accessibility of AI applications</li></ul>	<ul><li>Proficiency in HTML, CSS, JavaScript, and UI frameworks</li><li>Experience with data visualisation and design principles</li><li>Proficiency in design tools such as Sketch or Adobe Creative Suite</li><li>Effective communication skills for technical and nontechnical stakeholders</li><li>Curiosity and innovation in problem-solving</li><li>Willingness to explore new ideas and techniques</li></ul>

(continued)

Role	Tasks	Skills and Knowledge Requirements
AI product manager/AI consultant	- Leading development and delivery of AI products or services - Collaboration with data scientists, engineers, and application designers - Defining AI solution requirements - Prioritising features for successful project delivery - Customer-centric approach to meet business outcomes	- Technical and nontechnical competencies and soft skills required - Domain knowledge and understanding of stakeholder motivation - Leadership skills for aligning business and AI strategy - Analytical abilities for problem-solving - Proficiency in mathematics and statistics - Effective communication skills for technical and nontechnical stakeholders - Curiosity and innovation in approach to problem-solving
AI project manager	- Project planning and resource allocation - Assemble and lead a cross-functional team - Maintain effective communication with stakeholders - Ensure AI solutions meet quality standards	- Technical understanding of AI concepts and tools and proficiency in data handling and preprocessing - Domain expertise related to the industry and awareness of industry-specific AI regulations - Strong project management skills and efficient time management - Knowledge of ethical considerations in AI - Excellent communication and interpersonal skills and strong leadership abilities

	- Manage project budgets and monitor project time lines - Implement change management processes - Assess the impact of AI solutions and identify areas for improvement	- Effective problem-solving skills capacity to adapt to changing project requirements - Ability to think critically and solve business problems - Skills to manage conflicts within the project team - Preferably project management certification: PMP or PRINCE2
Cultural change agent/AI evangelist	- Facilitate AI integration into organisational culture - Align AI initiatives with organisational goals and values - Collaborate with stakeholders across the organisation - Identify areas for AI-driven operational improvement, efficiency, and innovation	- Facilitate stakeholder discussions and derive value-oriented AI solutions - Profound knowledge of psychology and organisational behaviour - Analyse complex problems and communicate findings effectively - Collaborate effectively within diverse teams - Exhibit curiosity, innovation, and openness to new ideas and techniques - Possess the vision to align business and AI strategies - Foster connections with leaders across the organisation

(continued)

Role	Tasks	Skills and Knowledge Requirements
Legal counsel and risk auditor	<ul><li>Offer legal guidance and advice to organisations</li><li>Specialise in AI product and service development, use, and marketing</li></ul>	<ul><li>Understand legal and regulatory frameworks for AI</li><li>Review and advise on legal and regulatory requirements</li><li>Conduct risk assessments for legal and ethical AI risks</li><li>Draft and review legal documents for AI development and deployment</li><li>Provide compliance guidance for AI industry standards</li><li>Collaborate with cross-functional teams to ensure legal and ethical AI compliance</li></ul>
AI strategic leadership	<ul><li>Oversee AI strategy development and implementation</li><li>Align AI initiatives with business goals</li><li>Ensure legal and regulatory compliance for AI</li><li>Build and manage AI talent pool</li></ul>	<ul><li>Broad knowledge of AI, tech, business operations, and data management</li><li>Connect business to AI strategy for value creation</li><li>Strong communication and leadership skills for strategy dissemination</li></ul>

| AI operational leadership | <ul><li>Oversee AI algorithm development, deployment, and maintenance</li><li>Manage a team of individual contributors</li></ul> | <ul><li>Deep understanding of machine learning, data science, and AI technologies</li><li>Understanding of the organisation's goals and objectives</li><li>Leadership skills for team management and stakeholder engagement</li><li>Effective communication of technical concepts to nontechnical stakeholders</li><li>Resource management and project planning for complex projects with multiple stakeholders</li></ul> |

enabling value with AI. The highly skilled talent team typically requires a higher seniority and expensive financial investment per employee. However, as AI matures and standardised processes become more common and the organisation learns more about AI, the need for very senior personnel may diminish. The salaries required to attract and retain this level of skill and knowledge are essential. In the competitive landscape of today's job market, roles in data science and engineering are in high demand, with salaries ranging from an average of $100,000 to $125,000 per year for a base salary to more than $400,000 per year for experienced subject matter experts in data science and engineering in larger cities such as New York and San Francisco.

Organising an AI initiative

Having the right organisational structure for an AI initiative is a critical strategic decision that can have far-reaching implications and influences the planning of AI capabilities in various ways (Fountaine et al. 2019). Drawing from the AI journey from various organisations, there are three major types of organisational structures:

- **Centralised:** consolidating the majority of the capabilities in a central department
- **Decentralised:** decentralising the capabilities and embedding them in the business units of the stakeholders
- **Hybrid:** creating a hybrid model where core capabilities are centralised and others reside with individual business units

Although there might be no best organisational structure to AI initiatives and their success within an organisation, it is critical to evaluate potential impacts of the chosen structure and its ability to drive the desired outcomes of an AI initiative. It is difficult to answer which model is best for driving AI adoption and value creation, because it appears to be context specific and contingent on, for example, an enterprise's AI and data maturity, business strategy and the desired type of AI value creation, as well as the economic conditions and industry affiliation of an organisation. Organisations such as Deutsche Bank, Pfizer, J.P. Morgan Chase, Procter & Gamble, Anthem, or Farmers Insurance have centralised their efforts in the field of AI whereas Google, Microsoft, or Meta pursue the path of a decentralised organisational integration of AI (Davenport 2019).

A *centralised AI initiative*, led by a chief data/analytics/product officer, is taking the charge on all facets of AI. This department consolidates core capabilities such as AI data management, project management, cultural transformation, and technical capabilities such as AI infrastructure. Even domain capabilities related to the subject matter expertise of a business unit are centralised, and the AI initiative mostly works in partnership with business units on an individual project basis. Those centralised initiatives are branded as competence centers or centers of excellence.

This organisational model offers tremendous advantages for scaling AI across an enterprise, from consolidating functions to reducing risks, sharing knowledge, and generating cost savings. Further, it provides companies the opportunity for a centralised learning strategy and to define standards related to AI, while developing a transparent process for value calculation and creation. Despite the obvious advantages of a centralised structure for the AI initiative, it brings its own challenges. At the outset of a journey into AI, trust can be difficult to cultivate and value creation for individual stakeholders is complex, given that the relevant key stakeholders may be in other business units. Also, there is the problem of how to share credit for enterprise value creation between the AI initiative and the business unit. Additionally, there is a conflict of resource allocation, because resources from the business unit are expected to be shared with the AI initiative, and vice versa.

In contrast to the centralised organisation model for AI initiatives, a *decentralised approach* places the majority of its capabilities (domain specific, functional, and core capabilities) in the hands of each business unit. This enables the business unit-specific AI initiative to report directly to each unit's leadership, creating trust and allocating credit as value is created in each unit separately. But there are further benefits to decentralised AI initiatives. Teams learn deep business domain and process knowledge, whereas project management has less friction and requires less planning because business and AI teams are able to work more closely together.

Despite potential benefits for individual business units, decentralisation of AI initiatives can create drawbacks on an enterprise level. Knowledge sharing is limited, costly overhead is generated by a decentralised AI infrastructure to cater to the needs of each business unit, key competencies and skills that are crucial for value creation might be absent (e.g. AI engineers, product development managers, etc.), business leaders may overestimate their AI value creation expertise, transparency of value calculation and communication can be affected, data knowledge can be siloed, and duplicated efforts in supporting functions such as IT and HR can occur. To ensure a successful AI deployment, enterprises must carefully consider the potential impacts of decentralised models.

The *hybrid AI initiative* has become a popular model for leveraging centralised AI technical and core capabilities while maintaining domain expertise and business-level responsibilities in individual business units. A central 'hub' is led by a C-level executive, and is responsible for governance, infrastructure, hiring, training, and overall initiative management. At the same time, the business units maintain their specialists and responsibilities for adoption and implementation, AI solution definition, project/stakeholder management, and tracking of value creation. This model provides a way to combine AI and function-specific business strategies to drive success.

The hybrid model seems to combine the advantages of centralised and decentralised models while reducing the impact of their drawbacks. Although the hybrid model appears to be superior at the beginning, it still poses certain challenges when it comes to reporting structure, prioritising the long-term objectives of AI projects over short-term business goals, and assigning clear responsibilities between hub and business units. The biggest benefit of a hybrid approach compared to a decentralised one is the lower investment required from business stakeholders, resulting in a lower commitment of resources and time. Many practitioners have stated that cross-functional project teams are well suited for implementing AI in an enterprise. It is an effective approach for leveraging the benefits of hybrid models, as demonstrated by companies such as Harley-Davidson or John Deere (Kiron 2017; Rigby et al. 2015). Despite having a more centralised organisational structure, these companies adopt a hybrid organisational approach by assembling project teams with diverse functional expertise. John Deere, the leader in agriculture technology, initiated a transformative program called xTreme Innovation in which cross-functional teams were empowered to solve problems from end to end. As a result, they were able to significantly compress the idea-to-prototype time line by over 75% compared to traditional processes, allowing for the development of a working prototype for a new machine form in just eight months. George Tome, the company's chief technology officer, reported that these results were supported by data indicating improvements in team happiness, work quality, and velocity, resulting in better innovative product development projects (Rigby et al. 2015).

Sripathi Sripada, Vice President Wealth Management Platforms and Digital at Tech Mahindra

Over the past decade, my responsibility has been designing digital solutions for numerous global Fortune 500 companies, mainly leading financial services organisations, health care, as well as banks in the US and Australia. In this capacity, I have overseen the implementation of AI solutions, providing guidance and support to executive teams eager to realise substantial returns on their significant investments in AI initiatives.

One of the most critical factors for success in these endeavors is having the right talent with a clear understanding of the essential roles and skills required for value creation with AI. Although many leaders recognise the importance of technical AI talent, they often underestimate the significance of skills beyond the technical aspects. Given that AI is still a relatively new field, new roles are continuously emerging.

However, one particular role that I have found to be crucial and frequently lacking in many AI initiatives is that of an AI consultant, serving as a bridge between the business and AI. This subject matter expert possesses a deep understanding of the business domain along with a profound knowledge of AI analytics and technology.

A few years ago, I collaborated with a global health care financial service company in Asia to transform their customer call center experience. The company had been receiving numerous unfavorable reviews due to customers having to make multiple calls to obtain relevant and accurate information. An AI solution was developed to support their knowledge management and automate information retrieval. However, the solution faced significant challenges when applied in a real-world business context. For instance, it was less accurate than human counterparts in approximately 30% of cases. Progress was achieved through numerous interactions, a slow learning process, and the collaborative efforts of various business leaders across departments.

These challenges and delays could have been avoided, and the project time line significantly reduced if we had someone with expertise in both the business process and AI analytics and technology. As a result, we have now made it standard practice to include such a role in every AI project. This AI business consultant plays a pivotal role in bridging the gap between business requirements and AI capabilities, facilitating smoother and more successful AI integration.

Conclusion

We hope this book equips you with a comprehensive framework for leveraging AI to create value. Technology, including AI, is advancing rapidly, presenting new daily opportunities. However, despite the ever-evolving AI landscape, we've observed that the framework for value creation has been relatively stable. Although some of the AI value creation challenges appear to be unique to the technology, approaches employed by AI achievers to harness business potential and mitigate technological risks are not new but have evolved and matured over time.

In essence, we highlight two crucial elements for your consideration:

- **Understanding AI's value contribution:** It's essential to grasp the current and evolving AI technology landscape to fully understand its capabilities to create value.
- **Applying the value creation framework:** Implement the framework provided in this book to successfully execute your AI projects and build your AI initiative.

By combining these two aspects, you can both avoid common mistakes and maximise your potential for creating value with AI. We genuinely appreciate your time and effort in reading this book. As lifelong learners, we wholeheartedly embrace your perspective and look forward to learning from your experiences. We apologize for all mistakes we made in this book. But there is no perfect project and we live the adaptive project development approach. Please let us know what we need to change for the next edition and don't hesitate to reach out to us through www. aivaluesecrets.com. We eagerly anticipate continuing the dialogue. Until our next conversation . . .

About the Authors

Michael Proksch

Michael Proksch is a highly accomplished expert and industry leader, celebrated for his remarkable ability to generate substantial business value with AI across a broad spectrum of organisations. His expertise spans from agile start-ups to multinational Fortune 2000 corporations. Michael is widely respected for his deliberate, holistic, systematic, and forward-looking approach to driving successful AI implementations, drawing from his profound knowledge of AI strategy and operations. His academic background features both an MBA and a PhD in economics. Furthermore, he is actively engaged in mentoring students at universities globally, sharing his wealth of knowledge and expertise.

Nisha Paliwal

Nisha Paliwal is a visionary technologist, a mother of two beautiful girls, and a passionate advocate for human-centered thinking. With more than 20 years of experience in leveraging technology and data insights to create true business value, Nisha has established herself as a trailblazer in the tech industry. Throughout her career, Nisha has held various leadership roles in top financial institutions.

Nisha's philosophy of learning, unlearning, and relearning has forced some of the top technologists in the industry to truly examine the real business value they are creating with data. She is extremely passionate in democratising mentoring and dedicates her time to several nonprofit companies in a mission to drive female representation in the tech industry.

Wilhelm 'Wil' Bielert

Wilhelm 'Wil' Bielert is a distinguished figure in the world of digital transformation, with more than two decades of significant contributions. Currently serving as the senior vice president and chief information officer of the Canadian multinational company Premier Tech, Rivière-du-Loup, Quebec, Canada, since 2022. Since 2017, Wil has been instrumental in guiding Premier Tech's digital direction. His prior roles include vice president operations and chief digital officer at Premier Tech from 2017 to 2021, where he amplified the company's digital growth. He played a key role in founding Premier Tech Digital. He was a pivotal figure at Capgemini from 2013 to 2017, leading digital transformation initiatives for various industries including telecommunication, media, and manufacturing. In academia, Wil has been a lecturer in digital transformation at the University of Hamburg since 2014. Named a top 25 global Industrial Internet of Things (IIoT) thought leader by CBT in 2021, Wil seamlessly merges academic wisdom with innovative business strategies. He is dedicated to advancing corporate digital transformation, ensuring businesses are prepared for the present and future. His expertise, coupled with his multilingual leadership capabilities in English, French, and German, and global work experience across four continents, positions him as a standout voice in the digital transformation domain.

About the Contributors

We express our sincere appreciation to our industry experts and leaders who have enriched this book with their unique insights, best practices, and personal stories. Their contributions not only enrich our understanding but also serve as a source of inspiration, demonstrating the practical application and transformative impact of AI in the real world. Their experiences, ranging from overcoming challenges to achieving breakthroughs, provide invaluable lessons and guidance for anyone looking to leverage AI for business value creation.

Our esteemed industry experts and leaders provided contributions to the following chapters:

Chapter 1: Radha Subramanyam
Chapter 2: Bibhuti Anand
Chapter 3: Dr. Adam Bujak
Chapter 4: Dr. Das Dasgupta
Chapter 5: Karan Dhawal
Chapter 6: Paul Hurlocker
Chapter 7: Scott Brooker
Chapter 8: Dr. Ambar Sengupta
Chapter 9: Dr. Marcell Vollmer
Chapter 10: Phanii Pydimarri
Chapter 11: Scott Hallworth
Chapter 12: Sanjay Srivastava
Chapter 13: Vikas Kumar
Chapter 14: Sripathi Sripada

References

Abdulkader, Ahmad, Aparna Lakshmiratan, and Joy Zhang. 2016. "Introducing DeepText: Facebook's Text Understanding Engine – Engineering at Meta." Engineering at Meta. https://engineering .fb.com/2016/06/01/core-data/introducing-deeptext-facebook-s-text-understanding-engine/.

Abril, Danielle. 2022. "Future of Work: Computer Vision and Machine Learning May Soon Bolster Restaurant Jobs." *Washington Post* (January 4). https://www.washingtonpost.com/technology/2022/01/04/chipotle-brian-niccol-future-of-work/.

Accenture. 2014. "Satisfaction with Insurance Claims Settlements Not Enough to Keep Customers Loyal, According to Accenture's Global Insurance Customer Survey." https://newsroom.accenture .com/news/satisfaction-with-insurance-claims-settlements-not-enough-to-keep-customers-loyal-according-to-accentures-global-insurance-customer-survey.htm.

Accenture. 2022. "Emerging Group of "Organized Consumers" Looking to Spread Holiday Spending Over Several Months, Accenture Survey Finds | Accenture." https://newsroom.accenture.com/news/emerging-group-of-organized-consumers-looking-to-spread-holiday-spending-over-several-months-accenture-survey-finds.htm.

Acemoglu, Daron. 2021. "Opinion | The AI We Should Fear Is Already Here." *Washington Post*. https://www.washingtonpost.com/opinions/2021/07/21/ai-we-should-fear-is-already-here/.

Ackoff, Russel L. 1989. "From Data to Wisdom." *Journal of Applied Systems Analysis* 16: 3–9.

Ajao, Esther. 2022. "Chipotle Pilots AI Systems to Assist Workers and Diners." *TechTarget* (September 27). https://www.techtarget.com/searchenterpriseai/news/252525452/Chipotle-pilots-AI-systems-to-assist-workers-and-diners.

Alfonseca, Manuel, M. Cebrian, A. F. Anta, L. Caviello, A. Abeliuk, and I. Rahwan. 2016. "Superintelligence Cannot Be Contained: Lessons from Computability Theory." Arxiv.org. https://arxiv.org/pdf/1607.00913.pdf.

Al-Heeti, Abrar. 2019. "Google and Verily Use AI to Screen Patients for Diabetic Eye Conditions." CNET. https://www.cnet.com/science/google-and-verily-using-ai-to-screen-patients-for-diabetic-eye-conditions/.

Amazon. 2017. "Jeff Bezos' 2016 Letter to Amazon Shareholders." About Amazon. https://www.aboutamazon.com/news/company-news/2016-letter-to-shareholders.

Amazon. 2023. "Amazon Ranks No.1 for Value and Selection in the Latest American Customer Satisfaction Index (ACSI)." About Amazon. https://www.aboutamazon.com/news/company-news/amazon-ranks-no-1-for-value-and-selection-in-the-latest-american-customer-satisfaction-index-acsi.

Amazon AWS. 2023. "What Is Data Labeling?" https://aws.amazon.com/sagemaker/data-labeling/what-is-data-labeling/.

American Litho. 2022. "Direct Mail Marketing for Telecommunications – Alitho." https://www.alitho.com/industries/direct-mail-marketing-for-telecommunications/.

Andersen Consulting. 1996. "Where to Look for Incremental Sales Gains: The Retail Problem of Out-of-Stock Merchandise." https://www.ccrrc.org/wp-content/uploads/sites/24/2014/02/Where_to_Look_for_Incremental_Sales_Gains_The_Retail_Problem_of_Out-of-Stock_Merchandise_1996.pdf.

Anyoha, Rockwell. 2017. "The History of Artificial Intelligence." *Science in the News* (Harvard University). https://sitn.hms.harvard.edu/flash/2017/history-artificial-intelligence/.

Appugliese, Carlo. 2020. "Accelerate Your AI Project with an Agile Approach." IBM. https://www.ibm.com/blog/accelerate-your-ai-project-with-an-agile-approach/.

Aten, Jason. 2021. "This Was Steve Jobs's Most Controversial Legacy. It Was Also His Most Brilliant." *Inc. Magazine.* https://www.inc.com/jason-aten/this-was-steve-jobs-most-controversial-legacy-it-was-also-his-most-brilliant.html.

B&R Industrial Automation. 2023. "Integrated Machine Vision." https://www.br-automation.com/en-in/products/vision-systems/.

Bates, Tom. 2011. "Everybody Needs a Coach – Eric Schmidt – Google CEO." YouTube. https://www.youtube.com/watch?v=kngyyeMel5c.

Bean, Randy. 2022. "Why Becoming a Data-Driven Organization Is So Hard." *Harvard Business Review*. https://hbr.org/2022/02/why-becoming-a-data-driven-organization-is-so-hard.

Bechtel, Mike. 2023. "Podcast Mike, Deloitte." Deloitte Consulting. https://open.spotify.com/episode/5QIiYGDrTb1z5rCyMFlHnU.

Beckett, Emma L. 2022. "Chipotle Tests Chippy, a Tortilla Chip-Making Robot" (March 16, 2022). https://www.restaurantdive.com/news/chipotle-tests-chippy-a-tortilla-chip-making-robot/620477/.

Belinski, Ippolit. 2016. "Slavoj Zizek on Niels Bohr and Ideology." https://youtu.be/lTAp3KZwYl0?si=Cbb7qvr8i5qm8r-h.

Berthiaume, Dan. 2021. "Chipotle Spices Up Personalization with Centralized Data Platform." *Chain Store Age* (January 12). https://chainstoreage.com/chipotle-spices-personalization-centralized-data-platform.

Blagec, K., G. Dorfner, M. Moradi, and M. Samwald. 2019. "A Critical Analysis of Metrics Used for Measuring Progress in Artificial Intelligence." arxive.org. https://arxiv.org/ftp/arxiv/papers/2008/2008.02577.pdf.

Bloch, Michael, Sven Blumberg, and Jurgen Laartz. 2012. "Delivering Large-Scale IT Projects on Time, on Budget, and on Value." McKinsey. https://www.mckinsey.com/capabilities/mckinsey-digital/our-insights/delivering-large-scale-it-projects-on-time-on-budget-and-on-value.

Boyd, Stowe. 2017. "Decision Making Not Decision Faking." Cloverpop. https://www.cloverpop.com/hubfs/Whitepapers/%20Cloverpop_Decision_Making_White_Paper.pdf.

Brandon, John. 2017. "Coca-Cola Reveals AI-Powered Vending Machine App." *VentureBeat* (July 11). https://venturebeat.com/ai/coca-cola-reveals-ai-powered-vending-machine-app/.

Brown, Sara. 2022. "Why It's Time for 'Data-Centric Artificial Intelligence'" (June). https://mitsloan.mit.edu/ideas-made-to-matter/why-its-time-data-centric-artificial-intelligence.

Buckingham, Marcus, and Curt Coffman. 2005. *First, Break All the Rules: What the World's Greatest Managers Do Differently*. Pocket Books.

Burns, Ed. 2013. "Coca-Cola Overcomes Challenges to Seize BI Opportunities." TechTarget. https://www.techtarget.com/search businessanalytics/tip/Coca-Cola-overcomes-challenges-to-seize-BI-opportunities.

Burns, Ed. 2018. "Davenport: AI-Based Projects Should Be Focused in Scope." TechTarget. https://www.techtarget.com/searchenter priseai/feature/Davenport-AI-based-projects-should-be-focused-in-scope.

Business Wire. 2019. "IDC Survey Finds Artificial Intelligence to Be a Priority for Organizations but Few Have Implemented an Enterprise-Wide Strategy" (July 8). https://www.businesswire.com/ news/home/20190708005039/en/IDC-Survey-Finds-Artificial-Intelligence-to-be-a-Priority-for-Organizations-But-Few-Have-Implemented-an-Enterprise-Wide-Strategy.

Cadwalladr, Carole, and Emma Graham. 2018. "Revealed: 50 Million Facebook Profiles Harvested for Cambridge Analytica in Major Data Breach." The Guardian (March 17). https://www .theguardian.com/news/2018/mar/17/cambridge-analytica-facebook-influence-us-election.

Caffe. 2023. "Caffe | Deep Learning Framework." https://caffe .berkeleyvision.org/.

Candelon, François. 2022. "Critics Warned Employees Would Hate Using A.I. Data Proves Them Wrong." Fortune. https://fortune.com/ 2022/11/04/artificial-intelligence-ai-employee-empowerment/.

Capoot, Ashley. 2023. "Microsoft Announces New Investment in ChatGPT-Maker OpenAI." CNBC. https://www.cnbc.com/2023/01 /23/microsoft-announces-multibillion-dollar-investment-in-chatgpt-maker-openai.html.

Carstens, Glenn, Kevin Carmichael, Victoria Wells, Jake Edmiston, and Gabriel Friedman. 2021. "Over 1 Billion People Worldwide Use a MS Office Product or Service." Financial Post. https:// financialpost.com/personal-finance/business-essentials/over-1-billion-people-worldwide-use-a-ms-office-product-or-service.

Celi, Loui, and Daniel Miles. 2020. "Driving ROI Through AI." ESi Though Lab (September). https://s41256.pcdn.co/wp-content/uploads/ 2020/09/ESITL_Driving-ROI-through-AI_FINAL_September-2020.pdf.

Chatterjee, Sheshadri, and Kalyan Bhattacharjee. 2020. "Adoption of Artificial Intelligence in Higher Education: A Quantitative Analysis Using Structural Equation Modelling." *Education and Information Technologies* 25: 3443–63. https://link.springer.com/article/10.1007/s10639-020-10159-7.

Chaturvedi, Mita. 2021. "How Coca-Cola and PepsiCo Use AI to Bubble Up Innovation." *Analytics India Magazine.* https://analyticsindiamag.com/how-coca-cola-and-pepsico-use-ai-to-bubble-up-innovation/.

Chen, Brian X. 2011. "Review: With Siri, iPhone Finds Its Voice." *CNN,* October 12, 2011. https://edition.cnn.com/2011/10/12/tech/mobile/review-siri-iphone-voice-wired/index.html.

Chipotle. 2018. "Chipotle Announces Growth Strategies Focused on Winning Today and Cultivating a Better Future" (June 27). https://ir.chipotle.com/2018-06-27-Chipotle-Announces-Growth-Strategies-Focused-On-Winning-Today-And-Cultivating-A-Better-Future.

Chipotle. 2021. "A Better World." https://www.chipotle.com/content/dam/chipotle/global-site-design/en/documents/sustainability/Chipotle_SustainabilityReport_Final.pdf.

Chipotle. 2022. "Cultivate a Better World." https://www.google.com/url?q=https://www.chipotle.com/content/dam/chipotle/global-site-design/en/documents/sustainability/2022/Chipotle_2022_Executive Summary.pdf&sa=D&source=docs&ust=1696498055634692&usg=AOvVaw2qQ5ECLkB20IHjViSbN_YT.

Chipotle. 2023. "Chipotle Announces First Quarter 2023 Results" (April 25). https://ir.chipotle.com/2023-04-25-CHIPOTLE-ANNOUNCES-FIRST-QUARTER-2023-RESULTS.

Choi, Youngkeun. 2020. "A Study of Employee Acceptance of Artificial Intelligence Technology." *European Journal of Management and Business Economics.* https://www.emerald.com/insight/content/doi/10.1108/EJMBE-06-2020-0158/full/html.

Christensen, Clayton M. 2013. *The Innovator's Dilemma: When New Technologies Cause Great Firms to Fail.* Harvard Business Review Press.

Chui, Michael, Bryce Hall, Helen Mayhew, Alex Singla, and Alex Sukharevsky. 2022. "The State of AI in 2022—And a Half Decade

in Review." *McKinsey Survey* (December). https://www.mckinsey
.com/capabilities/quantumblack/our-insights/the-state-of-ai-in-
2022-and-a-half-decade-in-review#/.

Citizen Tribune. 2023. "Financial Literacy Increases with Age and
Educational Level." https://www.citizentribune.com/news/business/
financial-literacy-increases-with-age-and-educational-level/
image_54429e67-2290-5c65-9f37-5da8c321cc5a.html.

Clark, Dori. 2021. "Google's '20% Rule' Shows Exactly How
Much Time You Should Spend Learning New Skills—And Why
It Works." CNBC. https://www.cnbc.com/2021/12/16/google-20-
percent-rule-shows-exactly-how-much-time-you-should-spend-
learning-new-skills.html.

Clifford, Catherine. 2017. "Elon Musk: 'Robots Will Be Able to
Do Everything Better Than Us.'" CNBC. https://www.cnbc.com/
2017/07/17/elon-musk-robots-will-be-able-to-do-everything-
better-than-us.html.

The Coca-Cola Company. 2023a. "About Us." https://www.coca-
colacompany.com/about-us.

The Coca-Cola Company. 2023b. "Life at Coca-Cola." https://www
.coca-colacompany.com/careers/life-at-coca-cola.

Colodony, Lora. 2017. "Deere Is Acquiring Blue River Technology for
$305 Million." CNBC. https://www.cnbc.com/2017/09/06/deere-
is-acquiring-blue-river-technology-for-305-million.html.

Commonwealth Bank of Australia. 2023. "Foresight Webinar Series."
https://www.commbank.com.au/business/foresight/webinars
.html?ei=tl_webinar-series.

Confessore, Nicholas. 2018. "Cambridge Analytica and Facebook: The
Scandal and the Fallout So Far." *New York Times* (April 4). https://
www.nytimes.com/2018/04/04/us/politics/cambridge-analytica-
scandal-fallout.html.

Costa, Cameron. 2020. "The Newest Fintech Unicorn Is a Credit
Card, and It's Betting Against Big Banks." CNBC. https://www
.cnbc.com/2020/08/13/newest-fintech-unicorn-is-a-credit-card-
betting-against-big-banks.html.

Cowley, Stacy. 2019. "Equifax to Pay at Least $650 Million in
Largest-Ever Data Breach Settlement." *New York Times* (July 22).
https://www.nytimes.com/2019/07/22/business/equifax-settlement
.html.

Cremer, David, and Garry Kasparov. 2021. "AI Should Augment Human Intelligence, Not Replace It." *Harvard Business Review.* https://hbr.org/2021/03/ai-should-augment-human-intelligence-not-replace-it.

Chui, Michael, Bryce Hall, Alex Singla, and Alex Sukharevsky. 2021. "Global Survey: The State of AI in 2021." McKinsey. https://www.mckinsey.com/capabilities/quantumblack/our-insights/global-survey-the-state-of-ai-in-2021.

Dastin, Jeffrey. 2018. "Amazon Scraps Secret AI Recruiting Tool That Showed Bias Against Women." Reuters (October 10). https://www.reuters.com/article/us-amazon-com-jobs-automation-insight-idUSKCN1MK08G.

Dastin, Jeffrey. 2023. "Google Unveils 'Magic Wand' to Draft Documents as AI Race Tightens." Reuters. https://www.reuters.com/technology/google-unveils-magic-wand-draft-documents-ai-race-tightens-2023-03-14/.

Databricks. 2021. "eBook - Data Management 101 on Databricks." Squarespace. https://static1.squarespace.com/static/634818d8d6e57e290ceee8f9/t/63886692e873f17c552e20bd/1669883547947/data-management-101-on-databricks-ebook-v6-0891421.pdf.

Databricks. 2023. "Databricks." YouTube. https://www.youtube.com/c/Databricks.

Davenport, Thomas H. 2019. "How to Set Up an AI Center of Excellence." *Harvard Business Review* (January 16). https://hbr.org/2019/01/how-to-set-up-an-ai-center-of-excellence.

Davenport, Thomas, Mathias Holweg, and Dan Jeavons. 2023. "How AI Is Helping Companies Redesign Processes." *Harvard Business Review.* https://hbr.org/2023/03/how-ai-is-helping-companies-redesign-processes.

Davenport, Thomas H., and Nitin Mittal. 2023. *All-In on AI: How Smart Companies Win Big with Artificial Intelligence.* Harvard Business Review Press.

Davis, Kathleen. 2023. "ChatGPT Won't Take This Job: The Most In-Demand Skill Is Something Only Humans Can Do." Fast Company. https://www.fastcompany.com/90851293/most-in-demand-skills-2023-linkedin-management-chatgpt-cant-do.

Deci, E. L., R. Koestner, and R. M. Ryan. 1999. "A Meta-Analytic Review of Experiments Examining the Effects of Extrinsic

Rewards on Intrinsic Motivation." *Psychology Bulletin* (November): 627–28. https://pubmed.ncbi.nlm.nih.gov/10589297/.

Deci, Edward L., Anja Olafsen, and Richard Ryan. 2017. "Self-Determination Theory in Work Organizations: The State of a Science." *Annual Reviews*. https://www.annualreviews.org/doi/pdf/10.1146/annurev-orgpsych-032516-113108.

Deloitte. 2019. "AI Transformation and Culture Shifts." https://www2.deloitte.com/us/en/pages/technology/articles/build-ai-ready-culture.html.

Deloitte. 2020. "Data Valuation: Understanding the Value of Your Data Assets." https://www2.deloitte.com/content/dam/Deloitte/global/Documents/Finance/Valuation-Data-Digital.pdf.

Deloitte and Google Cloud. 2017. "Business Impacts of Machine Learning." https://www2.deloitte.com/content/dam/Deloitte/tr/Documents/process-and-operations/TG_Google%20Machine%20Learning%20report_Digital%20Final.pdf.

Denning, Steve. 2016. "What Is Agile." *Forbes* 8. https://www.forbes.com/sites/stevedenning/2016/08/13/what-is-agile/?sh=75a087726e3d.

Det Norske Veritas Group. 2023. "The Three-Pillar Approach to Cyber Security: Data and Information Protection." https://www.dnv.com/article/the-three-pillar-approach-to-cyber-security-data-and-information-protection-165683.

Díaz, Alejandro, and Tamim Saleh. 2018. "Why Data Culture Matters." McKinsey. https://www.mckinsey.com/~/media/McKinsey/Business%20Functions/McKinsey%20Analytics/Our%20Insights/Why%20data%20culture%20matters/Why-data-culture-matters.ashx.

Dol, Quinten. 2021. "22 Companies Spearheading Digital Innovation in Their Industries in 2021." Built In. https://builtin.com/corporate-innovation/corporate-digital-innovation-transformation-2021.

Douglas, Will. 2020. "Google's Medical AI Was Super Accurate in a Lab. Real Life Was a Different Story." *MIT Technology Review*. https://www.technologyreview.com/2020/04/27/1000658/google-medical-ai-accurate-lab-real-life-clinic-covid-diabetes-retina-disease/.

Drucker, Peter F. 1974. *Management: Tasks, Responsibilities, Practices*. Harper & Row.

Duhigg, Charles. 2016. "What Google Learned from Its Quest to Build the Perfect Team." *New York Times*. https://www.nytimes.com/2016/02/28/magazine/what-google-learned-from-its-quest-to-build-the-perfect-team.html.

Eckert, Adam. 2023. "Coca-Cola CEO Compares Age of AI to the Smartphone Revolution: 'This Is Just the Beginning.'" Benzinga. https://www.benzinga.com/news/earnings/23/04/31965334/coca-cola-ceo-compares-age-of-ai-to-the-smartphone-revolution-this-is-just-the-beginning.

Edelman, David, and Mark Abraham. 2023. "Generative AI Will Change Your Business. Here's How to Adapt." *Harvard Business Review*. https://hbr.org/2023/04/generative-ai-will-change-your-business-heres-how-to-adapt.

Eggers, William D., Tina Mendelson, Bruce Chew, Pankaj K. Kishnani, and Traci Daberko. 2019. "Crafting an AI Strategy for Government Leaders." Deloitte. https://www2.deloitte.com/content/dam/insights/us/articles/6436_crafting-an-ai-strategy-for-govt-leaders/DI_Crafting-an-AI-strategy-for-govt-leaders.pdf.

Elias, Jennifer. 2022. "Google Employees Are Becoming Unhappy with Pay, Promotions and Execution, Survey Results Show." CNBC. https://www.cnbc.com/2022/03/14/google-employees-growing-unhappy-with-pay-and-promotions-survey-shows.html.

Erman, Michael. 2015. "Automated Lenders Threaten to Eat Banks' Lunch." Reuters. https://www.reuters.com/article/us-usa-banks-automation-insight-idUSKBN0OR0BC20150611.

Esppenchutz, Gláucia. 2023. *Data Ingestion with Python Cookbook: A Practical Guide Helping You Ingest, Monitor, and Identify Errors in the Data Ingestion Process*. Packt Publishing.

Experian. 2023. "My Credit Score." https://www.experian.com/blogs/ask-experian/credit-education/score-basics/my-credit-score/.

FANUC America. 2023. "Picking & Packing Industry's Most Trusted Robots." https://www.fanucamerica.com/solutions/applications/picking-and-packing-robots.

Fernandez, Elizabeth. 2022. "AI Is Not Similar to Human Intelligence. Thinking So Could Be Dangerous." *Forbes*. https://www.forbes.com/sites/fernandezelizabeth/2019/11/30/ai-is-not-similar-to-human-intelligence-thinking-so-could-be-dangerous/?sh=72e36d36c22f.

Fernando, Jason, and Khadija Khartit. 2022. "What Is Financial Literacy, and Why Is It So Important?" *Investopedia*. https://www.investopedia.com/terms/f/financial-literacy.asp.

Field, Emily, Bryan Hancock, Ruth Imose, and Lareina Yee. 2023. "Middle Managers Hold the Key to Unlock Generative AI." McKinsey. https://www.mckinsey.com/capabilities/people-and-organizational-performance/our-insights/the-organization-blog/middle-managers-hold-the-key-to-unlock-generative-ai#.

Forbes Technology Council. 2022. "14 Common Missteps to Avoid When Pursuing Digital Transformation." *Forbes*. https://www.forbes.com/sites/forbestechcouncil/2022/01/07/14-common-missteps-to-avoid-when-pursuing-digital-transformation/?sh=26c7ddb97d2e.

Fountaine, Tim, Brian McCarthy, and Tamim Saleh. 2019. "Building the AI-Powered Organization." *Harvard Business Review*. https://hbr.org/2019/07/building-the-ai-powered-organization.

Fridman, Adam. 2016. "The Massive Downside of Agile Software Development." *Inc. Magazine*. https://www.inc.com/adam-fridman/the-massive-downside-of-agile-software-development.html.

Fridman, Lex, dir. 2022. *Jeremy Howard: Deep Learning Frameworks–TensorFlow, PyTorch, fast.ai | AI Podcast Clips*. https://www.youtube.com/watch?v=XHyASP49ses.

Fuller, Joseff, and William Kerr. 2022. "The Great Resignation Didn't Start with the Pandemic." *Harvard Business Review*. https://hbr.org/2022/03/the-great-resignation-didn't-start-with-the-pandemic.

Future of Life Institute. 2023. "Pause Giant AI Experiments: An Open Letter." Future of Life Institute. https://futureoflife.org/open-letter/pause-giant-ai-experiments/.

Gade, Krishna, S. Geyik, Krishnaram Santapadi, Varun Mithal, and Ankur Taly. 2019. "Explainable AI in Industry." ACM Digital Library. https://dl.acm.org/doi/abs/10.1145/3292500.3332281.

Gallo, Amy. 2014. "The Value of Keeping the Right Customers." *Harvard Business Review* (October 29). https://hbr.org/2014/10/the-value-of-keeping-the-right-customers.

Gallo, Amy. 2017. "A Refresher on A/B Testing." *Harvard Business Review*. https://hbr.org/2017/06/a-refresher-on-ab-testing.

Gartenberg, Chaim. 2017. "How Does Google Assistant Stack up Against Siri on an iPhone?" The Verge. https://www.theverge.com/2017/5/19/15655558/google-assistant-vs-siri-iphone-ios-apple-locked-down-sandbox.

Gartner. 2017. "Gartner Says by 2020, Artificial Intelligence Will Create More Jobs Than It Eliminates." https://www.gartner.com/en/newsroom/press-releases/2017-12-13-gartner-says-by-2020-artificial-intelligence-will-create-more-jobs-than-it-eliminates.

Gartner. 2018. "Gartner Says Nearly Half of CIOs Are Planning to Deploy Artificial Intelligence." https://www.gartner.com/en/newsroom/press-releases/2018-02-13-gartner-says-nearly-half-of-cios-are-planning-to-deploy-artificial-intelligence.

Gartner. 2019a. "Avoid These 9 Corporate Digital Business Transformation Mistakes." https://www.gartner.com/en/articles/avoid-these-9-corporate-digital-business-transformation-mistakes.

Gartner. 2019b. "Gartner Survey Reveals Leading Organizations Expect to Double the Number of AI Projects in Place Within the Next Year." https://www.gartner.com/en/newsroom/press-releases/2019-07-15-gartner-survey-reveals-leading-organizations-expect-t.

Gartner. 2021. "How to Improve Your Data Quality." https://www.google.com/url?q=https://www.gartner.com/smarterwithgartner/how-to-improve-your-data-quality?_its%3DJTdCJTIydmlkJTIyJ-TNBJTIyOGM5MTZiMmUtZmJlNy00OTQ5LWJmZDMtZDUyZTg2NjIyOGMxJTIyJTJDJTIyc3RhdGUlMjIlM0ElMjJybHR%252BMTY5NTY3MTgzMX5sYW5kfjJfMTY0NjVf.

GDPR.eu. 2023. "FAQ." https://gdpr.eu/faq/.

Gerbis, Nicholas. 2022. "What Is the Actual Cost of Auto Insurance?" Auto | HowStuffWorks. https://auto.howstuffworks.com/under-the-hood/cost-of-car-ownership/cost-of-auto-insurance.htm.

Gillis, Alexander S. 2021. "What Is Customer Retention? Importance and Metrics." TechTarget. https://www.techtarget.com/searchcustomerexperience/definition/customer-retention.

Global Data. 2022. "Deere & Co Company Profile – Deere & Co Overview." https://www.globaldata.com/company-profile/deere-co/.

Gomez, Javier, Pablo Hernandez, and Rafael Ocejo. 2019. "Four Success Factors for Workforce Automation." McKinsey. https://www.mckinsey.com/capabilities/operations/our-insights/four-success-factors-for-workforce-automation.

Google AI. 2023. "Making AI Helpful for Everyone." https://ai.google/.

Google Blogs. 2019. "A Letter from Larry and Sergey." The Keyword. https://blog.google/alphabet/letter-from-larry-and-sergey/.

Google Finance. 2023. "Deere & Company." https://www.google .com/finance/quote/DE:NYSE?sa=X&ved=2ahUKEwiyobXMu52 AAxU1cmwGHZGGDgsQ3ecFegQIKhAh.

Gosiewska, Alicja, Anna Kozask, and Przemyslaw Biecek. 2021. "Simpler Is Better: Lifting interpretability-Performance Trade-Off via Automated Feature Engineering." ScienceDirect. https://www .sciencedirect.com/science/article/pii/S016792362100066X# bb0045.

Grande, Davide, George Machado, Bryan Petzold, and Marcus Roth. 2020. "Reducing Data Costs Without Sacrificing Growth" (July). https://www.mckinsey.com/capabilities/mckinsey-digital/our-insights/reducing-data-costs-without-jeopardizing-growth.

Greenhouse, Steven. 2023. "US Experts Warn AI Likely to Kill Off Jobs – And Widen Wealth Inequality." *The Guardian*. https:// www.theguardian.com/technology/2023/feb/08/ai-chatgpt-jobs-economy-inequality.

Grennan, Liz, Andreas Kremer, Alex Singla, and Peter Zipparo. 2022. "Why Businesses Need Explainable AI—And How to Deliver It." McKinsey (September 29). https://www.mckinsey.com/capabilities/ quantumblack/our-insights/why-businesses-need-explainable-ai-and-how-to-deliver-it.

Griggio, Carla F., Midas Neuwens, and Clemens N. Klokmose. 2022. "Caught in the Network: The Impact of WhatsApp's 2021 Privacy Policy Update on Users' Messaging App Ecosystems." ACM Digital Library. https://dl.acm.org/doi/10.1145/3491102.3502032.

Gupta, Ankur. 2021. "Data in Financial Services." Collibra. https:// www.collibra.com/us/en/blog/the-importance-of-data-quality-in-financial-services.

Gupta, Atin, and Geoffrey Parker. 2023. "How Will Generative AI Disrupt Video Platforms?" *Harvard Business Review*. https://hbr .org/2023/03/how-will-generative-ai-disrupt-video-platforms.

Haan, Kathy. 2023. "Over 75% of Consumers Are Concerned About Misinformation from Artificial Intelligence." *Forbes*. https://www .forbes.com/advisor/business/artificial-intelligence-consumer-sentiment/.

Hall, Patrick, James Curtis, and Parul Pandey. 2023. *Machine Learning for High-Risk Applications*. O'Reilly Media.

Harbert, Tam. 2021. "Tapping the Power of Unstructured Data." *MIT Sloan* (February 1). https://mitsloan.mit.edu/ideas-made-to-matter/tapping-power-unstructured-data.

Heaven, Will D. 2020. "Google's Medical AI Was Super Accurate in a Lab. Real Life Was a Different Story." *MIT Technology Review* (April 27). https://www.technologyreview.com/2020/04/27/1000658/google-medical-ai-accurate-lab-real-life-clinic-covid-diabetes-retina-disease/.

Helmore, Edward. 2022. "Tesla's Self-Driving Technology Fails to Detect Children in the Road, Group Claims." *The Guardian*. https://www.theguardian.com/technology/2022/aug/09/tesla-self-driving-technology-safety-children.

Henderson, Deborah, and Susan Earley. 2017. *DAMA-DMBOK: Data Management Body of Knowledge*. Data Management Association.

Hiatt, Jeff. 2006. *ADKAR: A Model for Change in Business, Government, and Our Community*. Prosci Learning Center Publications.

Horwitz, Lauren. 2020. "Making IoT Data Meaningful at John Deere." *IoT World Today*. https://www.iotworldtoday.com/iiot/making-iot-data-meaningful-in-agriculture-at-john-deere.

Huang, Sonya, and Pat Grady. 2023. "Generative AI's Act Two." Sequoia Capital. https://www.sequoiacap.com/article/generative-ai-act-two/.

IBM. 2010. "How Organizations Can Predict Future Events to Drive Better Business Outcomes with IBM SPSS Solutions." *IBM Redbooks*. https://www.redbooks.ibm.com/redpapers/pdfs/redp4710.pdf.

IBM. 2018. "Secure Sockets Layer (SSL) and Transport Layer Security (TLS) Concepts." https://www.ibm.com/docs/en/ibm-mq/7.5?topic=cspts-secure-sockets-layer-ssl-transport-layer-security-tls-concepts.

IBM. 2022a. "A History of Progress." https://www.ibm.com/ibm/history/interactive/ibm_history.pdf.

IBM 2022b. " IBM Global AI Adoption Index 2022." https://www.ibm.com/downloads/cas/GVAGA3JP.

IBM. 2022c. "IBM + Palantir Lunch and Learn: Transforming Business with AI." IBM Community. https://community.ibm.com/community/user/datamanagement/events/event-description?CalendarEventKey=5188ca3f-2a61-4585-af0e-fc875a5abea0&CommunityKey=5f34857e-d55b-404b-9806-a571c485c1ff&Home=%2Fcommunity%2Fuser%2Fibmcommunity%2Fhome.

IBM. 2023a. "Build a Garage Culture and Squads." https://www.ibm.com/garage/method/practices/culture/practice_building_culture/.

IBM. 2023b. "IBM AI Fairness 360." IBM AI. https://aif360.mybluemix.net/.

IBM 202Intel® AI Academy. 2022. "AI Courses and Certifications." https://www.intel.com/content/www/us/en/developer/topic-technology/artificial-intelligence/training/overview.html.

Intelligent Insurer. 2023. "80% of Underwriters Worry AI Will Reshape Roles." https://www.intelligentinsurer.com/news/80-of-underwriters-worry-ai-with-reshape-roles-32785.

Isaacson, Walter. 2023. "How Elon Musk Set Tesla on a New Course for Self-Driving." CNBC. https://www.cnbc.com/2023/09/09/ai-for-cars-walter-isaacson-biography-of-elon-musk-excerpt.html.

Ismail, Mariam, A. Walters, Mohamed Khater, and Mohamed Zaki. 2017. "Digital Business Transformation and Strategy | Cambridge Service Alliance." Cambridge Service Alliance. https://cambridgeservicealliance.eng.cam.ac.uk/news/2017NovPaper.

Jaser, Zahira. 2021. "The Real Value of Middle Managers." *Harvard Business Review*. https://hbr.org/2021/06/the-real-value-of-middle-managers.

Javerbaum, Mollie, and Meghan Houghton. 2020. "Google Supports COVID-19 AI and Data Analytics Projects." Google Blogs. https://blog.google/outreach-initiatives/google-org/google-supports-covid-19-ai-and-data-analytics-projects/.

Jennings, John. 2020. "Want to Become a Better Investor? Look to the Wisdom Hierarchy." *Forbes*. https://www.forbes.com/sites/johnjennings/2020/05/06/want-to-become-a-better-investor-look-to-the-wisdom-hierarchy/?sh=24ca3fb16bc1.

John Deere. 2022a. "John Deere Reveals Fully Autonomous Tractor at CES 2022." https://www.deere.com/en/news/all-news/autonomous-tractor-reveal/.

John Deere. 2022b. "Tech@Work." https://www.deere.com/en/publications/the-furrow/2022/summer-2022/tech-at-work/.

Johnson, Carolyn Y., and Carolyn Johnson. 2019. "Scientists Detected Racial Bias in a Product Sold by Optum, but the Problem Likely Extends to Algorithms Used by Major Health Systems and Insurers" *Washington Post* (October 24). https://www.washingtonpost.com/health/2019/10/24/racial-bias-medical-algorithm-favors-white-patients-over-sicker-black-patients/.

Kahn, Jeremy. 2022. "Deep Learning Pioneer Andrew Ng Says Companies Should Be 'Data-Centric' to Find A.I. Success." *Fortune*. https://fortune.com/2022/06/21/andrew-ng-data-centric-ai/.

Kahneman, Daniel, Andrew Rosenfield, Linnea Gandhi, and Tom Blaser. 2016. "Noise: How to Overcome the High, Hidden Cost of Inconsistent Decision Making." *Harvard Business Review*, 10: 16. https://hbr.org/2016/10/noise.

Kahuha, Eric. 2022. "How to Avoid Burning Out If You Are a Data Scientist" (September 16). https://blog.dataiku.com/how-to-avoid-burning-out-if-you-are-a-data-scientist.

Kanter, Rosabeth M. 2012. "Ten Reasons People Resist Change." *Harvard Business Review*. https://hbr.org/2012/09/ten-reasons-people-resist-chang.

Kar, Arpan K., and Amit K. Kushwaha. 2021. "Facilitators and Barriers of Artificial Intelligence Adoption in Business – Insights from Opinions Using Big Data Analytics." *Information Systems Frontiers* 25: 1351–74. https://link.springer.com/article/10.1007/s10796-021-10219-4.

Kelley, Sage, S. Kaye, and Oscar Oviedo-Trespalacios. 2023. "What Factors Contribute to the Acceptance of Artificial Intelligence? A Systematic Review." ScienceDirect. https://www.sciencedirect.com/science/article/pii/S0736585322001587.

Keswin, Erica. 2021. *Rituals Roadmap: The Human Way to Transform Everyday Routines into Workplace Magic*. McGraw-Hill Education.

Kiron, David. 2017. "Why Your Company Needs More Collaboration." *MIT Sloan Management Review*. https://sloanreview.mit.edu/article/why-your-company-needs-more-collaboration/.

Kloumann, Isabel. 2021. "How We're Using Fairness Flow to Help Build AI That Works Better for Everyone." *Meta AI* 3. https://ai.facebook.com/blog/how-were-using-fairness-flow-to-help-build-ai-that-works-better-for-everyone/.

Kolmar, Chris. 2023. "25+ Amazing Cold Calling Success Statistics [2023]: Data, Trends, Opinions and More." Zippia. https://www.zippia.com/advice/cold-calling-statistics/.

Kotter, John P. 1995. "Leading Change: Why Transformation Efforts Fail." *Harvard Business Review* (June). https://hbr.org/1995/05/leading-change-why-transformation-efforts-fail-2.

Kotter, John P. 2012. *Leading Change*. Harvard Business Review Press.

Kotter, John, and Leonard Schlesinger. 2013. "Choosing Strategies for Change." Projects at Harvard. https://projects.iq.harvard.edu/files/sdpfellowship/files/day3_2_choosing_strategies_for_change.pdf.

Krauth, Olivia. 2018. "9 Ways to Overcome Employee Resistance to Digital Transformation." TechRepublic. https://www.techrepublic.com/article/9-ways-to-overcome-employee-resistance-to-digital-transformation/.

Kuhberger, Anton, Michael Shulte-Muklemberk, and Joseph Perner. 1999. "The Effects of Framing, Reflection, Probability, and Payoff on Risk Preference in Choice Tasks." *Organizational Behavior and Human Decision Process*, 6. https://www.sciencedirect.com/science/article/abs/pii/S0749597899928303.

Lafley, Alan G., and Roger L. Martin. 2013. *Playing to Win: How Strategy Really Works*. Harvard Business Review Press.

Lambert, Lance. 2023. "CEO of Fortune 1000 Builder: U.S. Housing Market Bottom Should Hold, but If It Doesn't This Key Metric Will Warn Us." *Fortune*. https://fortune.com/2023/09/02/housing-market-home-price-bottom-should-hold-kb-home-ceo-says-but-if-not-inventory-will-warn-us/.

Lapowsky, Issie. 2019. "How Cambridge Analytica Sparked the Great Privacy Awakening." *WIRED* (March 17). https://www.wired.com/story/cambridge-analytica-facebook-privacy-awakening/.

Larson, Eric. 2018. "Don't Fail at Decision Making Like 98% of Managers Do." *Forbes*. https://www.forbes.com/sites/eriklarson/2017/05/18/research-reveals-7-steps-to-better-faster-decision-making-for-your-business-team/?sh=6a378cae40ad.

Lee, Julie. 2023. "Unlocking the Future of Credit Underwriting." Experian. https://www.experian.com/blogs/insights/2023/01/unlocking-the-future-of-credit-underwriting/.

Lee, Peter. 2016. "Learning from Tay's Introduction." *The Official Microsoft Blog* (March 25). https://blogs.microsoft.com/blog/2016/03/25/learning-tays-introduction/.

Leswing, Kif. 2023. "Only 9% of Americans Think A.I. Development Will Do More Good Than Harm." CNBC. https://www.cnbc.com/2023/02/15/only-9percent-of-americans-think-ai-development-will-do-more-good-than-harm-.html.

Levy, Ari. 2021. "Zillow Plunges 25% to Lowest Since July 2020, After Company Exits Home-Buying Business." CNBC (November 3). https://www.cnbc.com/2021/11/03/zillow-stock-plunges-24percent-after-company-exits-home-buying-business.html.

Levy, Nat. 2017. "Microsoft's New Corporate Vision: Artificial Intelligence Is In and Mobile Is Out." GeekWire. https://www.geekwire.com/2017/microsofts-new-corporate-vision-artificial-intelligence-mobile/.

Lin, Judy T., Christopher Bumcart, Gary Mottola, Olivia Valdes, Robert Ganem, Chriestine Kiefer, Gerri Walsh, and Annamaria Lusardi. 2022. "Financial Capability in the United States." *Finra Investor Education Foundation* (7). https://www.finrafoundation.org/sites/finrafoundation/files/NFCS-Report-Fifth-Edition-July-2022.pdf.

LinkedIn Community. 2023. "How AI Improves Data Quality and Consistency." https://www.linkedin.com/advice/0/how-can-ai-improve-data-quality-consistency.

Litchlien, Judith. 2022. "The Data Mesh Concept at Zalando." DATA Festival. https://data-festival.com/the-data-mesh-concept-at-zalando/.

Loizos, Connie. 2019. "Sam Altman's Leap of Faith." TechCrunch. https://techcrunch.com/2019/05/18/sam-altmans-leap-of-faith/.

Lowry, Stella, and Gordon Macpherson. 1988. "A Blot on the Profession." *British Medical Journal* 296 (623): 657–58.

Lowsen, Ben, and Shannon Tiezzi. 2022. "How Reliable Are China's Statistics?" The Diplomat. https://thediplomat.com/2022/03/how-reliable-are-chinas-statistics/.

Lundberg, Scott, Sun I. Lee, and Gabriel Erion. 2019. "Consistent Individualized Feature Attribution for Tree Ensembles." arXiv (March 7). https://arxiv.org/pdf/1802.03888.pdf.

Luscher, Lotte, and Marianne Lewis. 2008. "Organizational Change and Managerial Sensemaking: Working Through Paradox." *Academy of Management.* https://journals.aom.org/doi/10.5465/amj.2008.31767217.

MacKinzie, Ian, Chris Meyer, and Steve Noble. 2013. "How Retailers Can Keep Up with Consumers." McKinsey (October 1). https://www.mckinsey.com/industries/retail/our-insights/how-retailers-can-keep-up-with-consumers.

Malik, Aisha. 2023. "Amazon Achieved Its 'Fastest Prime Speeds Ever' Last Quarter, Plans to Double Same-Day Delivery Sites." Tech Crunch. https://techcrunch.com/2023/07/31/amazon-achieved-fastest-prime-speeds-last-quarter-plans-double-same-day-delivery-sites/?guccounter=1&guce_referrer=aHR0cHM6Ly93d3cuZ29vZ2xlLmNvbS8&guce_referrer_sig=AQAAAHATJbKeecCXXpkjQCldrqsXgugziiKSmtDViz3mIGR-jj6wSosKV.

Mares, Michaela, Shicai Wang, and Yike Guo. 2016. "Combining Multiple Feature Selection Methods and Deep Learning for High-Dimensional Data." Imperial College London. https://spiral.imperial.ac.uk/handle/10044/1/34535.

Markets and Markets. 2018. "Artificial Intelligence" White Paper.

Marr, Bernard. 2017a. "The Amazing Ways Coca-Cola Uses Artificial Intelligence and Big Data to Drive Success." *Forbes.* https://www.forbes.com/sites/bernardmarr/2017/09/18/the-amazing-ways-coca-cola-uses-artificial-intelligence-ai-and-big-data-to-drive-success/?sh=4438f33b78d2.

Marr, Bernard. 2017b. "28 Best Quotes About Artificial Intelligence." *Forbes* 7: 17. https://www.forbes.com/sites/bernardmarr/2017/07/25/28-best-quotes-about-artificial-intelligence/?sh=596c3b6f4a6f.

Marr, Bernard. 2020. "The Amazing Ways John Deere Uses AI And Machine Vision to Help Feed 10 Billion People." https://bernardmarr.com/the-amazing-ways-john-deere-uses-ai-and-machine-vision-to-help-feed-10-billion-people/.

Marr, Bernard. 2023. "The Amazing Ways Coca-Cola Uses Generative AI in Art and Advertising." *Forbes.* https://www.forbes.com/sites/bernardmarr/2023/09/08/the-amazing-ways-coca-cola-uses-generative-ai-in-art-and-advertising/?sh=794c1eee2874.

Maverick, J. B. 2022. "Average Profit Margin for Telecommunications Agency: Overview." *Investopedia*. https://www.google.com/url?q=https://www.investopedia.com/ask/answers/060215/what-average-profit-margin-company-telecommunications-sector.asp%23:~:text%3DKey%2520Takeaways,approximately%252012.5%2525%2520as%2520of%25202022&sa=D&source=docs&ust=168741166038.

McAfee, Andrew, and Erik Brynjolfsson. 2012. "Big Data: The Management Revolution." *Harvard Business Review* 10: 12. https://hbr.org/2012/10/big-data-the-management-revolution.

McKinsey. 2018a. "The Keys to a Successful Digital Transformation." https://www.mckinsey.com/capabilities/people-and-organizational-performance/our-insights/unlocking-success-in-digital-transformations.

McKinsey. 2018b. "Notes from the AI Frontier: Modeling the Impact of AI on the World Economy." https://www.mckinsey.com/~/media/McKinsey/Featured%20Insights/Artificial%20Intelligence/Notes%20from%20the%20frontier%20Modeling%20the%20impact%20of%20AI%20on%20the%20world%20economy/MGI-Notes-from-the-AI-frontier-Modeling-the-impact-of-AI-on-the-world-economy-September-2018.pdf.

McKinsey. 2018c. "Sizing the Potential Value of AI and Advanced Analytics" (April 17). https://www.mckinsey.com/featured-insights/artificial-intelligence/notes-from-the-ai-frontier-applications-and-value-of-deep-learning.

McKinsey. 2021. "Scaling AI: How Leaders Capture Exponential Returns." https://www.mckinsey.com/industries/technology-media-and-telecommunications/our-insights/tipping-the-scales-in-ai.

McKinsey. 2023. "The Economic Potential of Generative AI." https://www.mckinsey.de/~/media/mckinsey/locations/europe%20and%20middle%20east/deutschland/news/presse/2023/2023-06-14%20mgi%20genai%20report%202023/the-economic-potential-of-generative-ai-the-next-productivity-frontier-vf.pdf.

McKinzie, Ian, Chris Meyer, and Steve Noble. 2013. "How Retailers Can Keep Up with Consumers." McKinsey. https://www.mckinsey.com/industries/retail/our-insights/how-retailers-can-keep-up-with-consumers.

Meffert, Jurgen, and Anand Swaminathan. 2017. "Digital @ Scale: The Playbook You Need to Transform Your Company." McKinsey. https://www.mckinsey.com/capabilities/mckinsey-digital/our-insights/digital-at-scale-the-playbook-you-need-to-transform-your-company.

Mergr. 1999. "NavCom Technology, Acquired by Deere & Co. on November 22nd, 1999." https://mergr.com/navcom-technology-acquired-by-deere.

Miao, Jianyu, and L. Niu. 2016. "A Survey on Feature Selection." ScienceDirect. https://www.sciencedirect.com/science/article/pii/S1877050916313047.

Microsoft. 2022. "The Microsoft Cognitive Toolkit." Microsoft Learn. https://learn.microsoft.com/en-us/cognitive-toolkit/.

Mikko, Riikkinen, Hannu Saarijärvi, Peter Sarlin, and Ilkka Lähteen-mäk. 2018. "Using Artificial Intelligence to Create Value in Insurance." *International Journal of Bank Marketing.* https://www.emerald.com/insight/content/doi/10.1108/IJBM-01-2017-0015/full/html.

MIT Sloan Podcast. 2021. "No Need for AI Unicorns: PepsiCo's Colin Lenaghan." *MIT Sloan Management Review* (June 8). https://sloanreview.mit.edu/audio/no-need-for-ai-unicorns-pepsicos-colin-lenaghan/.

Morris, Charles. 2023. "CEO Jim Farley Explains How Ford Is Learning from Tesla, Marketing EVs as "Digital Products." Charged EVs. https://chargedevs.com/newswire/ceo-jim-farley-explains-how-ford-is-learning-from-tesla-marketing-evs-as-digital-products/.

Murthy, Rathi. 2023. "Making 600 Billion Decisions with AI: Expedia Group's Rathi Murthy." *MIT Sloan Management Review.* https:// loanreview.mit.edu/audio/making-600-billion-decisions-with-ai-expedia-groups-rathi-murthy/.

Nakai, Junta. 2022. "Return on Data Assets: A New Way for CFOs to Think About Data Value." *CFO Magazine.* https://www.cfo .com/technology/2022/11/return-on-data-assets-metrics-capital-technology/.

National Defense University. 2020. "Concept of Organization Culture: Why Bother?" https://www.ndu.edu/Portals/59/Documents/Incoming/AY21%20Briefings/CIC%206014/Sample%20Reading%20-%20The%20Concept%20of%20Organizational%20Culture%20-%20Why%20Bother.pdf?ver=2020-08-10-134253-903.

Naughton, John. 2022. "Alexa, How Did Amazon's Wrong Call on Voice Assistants Tee Up a $10bn Loss?" *The Guardian* (November 27). https://www.theguardian.com/commentisfree/2022/nov/26/alexa-how-did-amazons-voice-assistant-rack-up-a-10bn-loss.

Netflix Research. 2023. "Netflix Research." https://research.netflix.com/research-area/experimentation-and-causal-inference.

Netflix Techblog. 2022. "Experimentation Is a Major Focus of Data Science Across Netflix." Netflix TechBlog. https://netflixtechblog.com/experimentation-is-a-major-focus-of-data-science-across-netflix-f67923f8e985.

Nunez, Steve. 2021. "Why AI investments Fail to Deliver." *InfoWorld*. https://www.infoworld.com/article/3639028/why-ai-investments-fail-to-deliver.html.

O'Brien, Matt. 2023. "Microsoft CEO Satya Nadella on AI: 'Human Preferences.'" *Fortune* (February 7). https://fortune.com/2023/02/07/microsoft-ceo-satya-nadella-ai-chatgpt-bing-human-preferences-societal-norms/.

OECD Statistics. 2023. "Insurance Indicators: Retention Ratio." https://stats.oecd.org/index.aspx?queryid=25441.

OpenAI. 2023. "Research Index." https://openai.com/research.

Oracle. 2023. "What Is a Data Lakehouse?" https://www.oracle.com/in/big-data/what-is-data-lakehouse/.

Ore, Oystein. 1960 "Pascal and the Invention of Probability Theory." *The American Mathematical Monthly* 67, no. 5: 409–19.

Parry, Glenn, Linda Newens, and Xiaoxi Huang. 2011. "Goods, Products and Services." ResearchGate. https://www.researchgate.net/publication/225830366_Goods_Products_and_Services.

Peng, Lily. 2016. "Detecting Diabetic Eye Disease with Machine Learning." Google Blogs (November 29). https://blog.google/technology/ai/detecting-diabetic-eye-disease-machine-learning/.

Perez, Johanna. 2021. "IBM and Microsoft Have Integrated AI Ethical Standards into Their Operations, So Can You." *IEEE Spectrum* 4, no. 28: 21. https://spectrum.ieee.org/ibm-and-microsoft-have-integrated-ai-ethical-standards-into-their-operations-so-can-you.

Placek, Martin. 2022. "USPS – Mail Volume 2022." *Statista*, November 21, 2022. https://www.statista.com/statistics/320234/mail-volume-of-the-usps/.

Poletti, Therese. 2023. "Tesla Beat Earnings Thanks to $300 Million from 'Full Self Driving,' a Product That Still Doesn't Live Up to

Its Name." MarketWatch. https://www.marketwatch.com/story/tesla-beat-earnings-thanks-to-300-million-from-full-self-driving-a-product-that-still-doesnt-live-up-to-its-name-11674767405.

Pope, Carol. 2022. "Average Cost of Car Insurance in May 2023." Bankrate. https://www.bankrate.com/insurance/car/average-cost-of-car-insurance/.

Porter, Michael E. 1985. "Competitive Advantage." Amazon.in. https://www.amazon.in/Competitive-Advantage-Creating-Sustaining-Performance/dp/0684841460.

Porter, Michael E. 1998. *Competitive Strategy: Techniques for Analyzing Industries and Competitors*. Free Press.

Porter, Michael E. 2008. *Competitive Advantage: Creating and Sustaining Superior Performance*. Free Press.

Power, Brad. 2018. "How to Get Employees to Stop Worrying and Love AI." *Harvard Business Review*. https://hbr.org/2018/01/how-to-get-employees-to-stop-worrying-and-love-ai.

Press, Gill. 2022. "A Very Short History of Artificial Intelligence (AI)." *Forbes*. https://www.forbes.com/sites/gilpress/2016/12/30/a-very-short-history-of-artificial-intelligence-ai/?sh=3df4eab16fba.

Prime, G. W. 2021. "The Story of Coca-Cola and Its AI-Powered Vending Machines." Geospatial World. https://www.geospatialworld.net/prime/case-study/the-story-of-coca-cola-and-its-ai-powered-vending-machines/.

Project Management Institute (PMI). 2021. "A Guide to the Project Management Body of Knowledge (PMBOK® Guide) – Seventh Edition and The Standard for Project Management (ENGLISH)."

Project Management Institute (PMI). 2022. "PMBOK® Guide." https://www.pmi.org/pmbok-guide-standards/foundational/pmbok.

Project Management Works. 2021. "Project Failure Statistics: The Shocking Truth." Project Management (October 14). https://www.projectmanagementworks.co.uk/project-failure-statistics/.

PwC. 2017. "PwC's Global Artificial Intelligence Study." https://www.pwc.com/gx/en/issues/data-and-analytics/publications/artificial-intelligence-study.html.

Ram, Aliya. 2019. "Alphabet's Life Sciences Arm Verily Raises $1Bn from Investors." *Financial Times* (January 4). https://www.ft.com/content/1402ee00-100f-11e9-acdc-4d9976f1533b.

Ransbotham, Sam. 2021. "The Cultural Benefits of Artificial Intelligence in the Enterprise." *MIT Sloan Management Review*. https://sloanreview.mit.edu/projects/the-cultural-benefits-of-artificial-intelligence-in-the-enterprise/.

Rash, Wayne. 2023. "Tech Leaders Ask for Pause in AI Development." *Forbes*. https://www.forbes.com/sites/waynerash/2023/03/29/tech-leaders-ask-for-pause-in-ai-development/?sh=3ceb4bdc6eee.

Rayome, Alison D. 2018. "How IBM Wants to Use Watson AI to Reduce Bias in Hiring." TechRepublic (September 24). https://www.techrepublic.com/article/how-ibm-wants-to-use-watson-ai-to-reduce-bias-in-hiring/.

Rayome, Alison D. 2019. "Why 85% of AI Projects Fail." TechRepublic. https://www.techrepublic.com/article/why-85-of-ai-projects-fail/.

Redman, Thomas C. 2016. "Bad Data Costs the U.S. $3 Trillion per Year." *Harvard Business Review*. https://hbr.org/2016/09/bad-data-costs-the-u-s-3-trillion-per-year.

Reichert, Tom, Patric Forth, Romain Laubier, and S. Chakrabarthy. 2020. "Flipping the Odds of Digital Transformation Success." Boston Consulting Group. https://www.bcg.com/publications/2020/increasing-odds-of-success-in-digital-transformation.

Reichheld, Fred. 2001. "Prescription for Cutting Costs." Bain & Company. https://media.bain.com/Images/BB_Prescription_cutting_costs.pdf.

Rescue One. 2023. "Can Artificial Intelligence Predict Heart Disease?" Rescue One Training for Life. https://rescue-one.com/can-artificial-intelligence-predict-heart-disease/.

Richardson, Douglas. 2016. "Viewpoint: What We Can Learn from Google About Collaboration." SHRM. https://www.shrm.org/resourcesandtools/hr-topics/organizational-and-employee-development/pages/viewpoint-what-we-can-learn-from-google-about-collaboration.aspx.

Rigby, Darrell K., Steve Berez, Greg Caimi, and Andrew Noble. 2015. "Agile Innovation." Bain & Company. https://media.bain.com/Images/BAIN_BRIEF_Agile_innovation.pdf.

Rigby, Darrell, Jeff Sutherland, and Hirekuta Takeuchi. 2016. "The Secret History of Agile Innovation." *Harvard Business Review*. https://hbr.org/2016/04/the-secret-history-of-agile-innovation.

Rose, Charlie. 2015. "Every Company Has to Be a Software Company." https://youtu.be/OgO4I3_B0Js.

Roth, Emma, and Alex Castro. 2022. "Elon Musk's Raising the Cost of Tesla's Full Self-Driving Software to $15k." The Verge. https://www.theverge.com/2022/8/21/23315270/tesla-full-self-driving-fsd-feature-price-increase-electric-vehicle-elon-musk.

Rothfeder, Jeffrey. 2017. "Detroit's Urgent Embrace of Self-Driving Cars." *The New Yorker*. https://www.newyorker.com/business/currency/detroits-urgent-embrace-of-self-driving-cars.

Rudin, Cynthia. 2019. "Stop Explaining Black Box Machine Learning Models for High Stakes Decisions and Use Interpretable Models Instead." *Nature*. https://www.nature.com/articles/s42256-019-0048-x.

Rudin, Emily. 2020. "The Value of Loyalty for Telecoms Brands." Oracle Blogs. https://blogs.oracle.com/marketingcloud/post/the-value-of-loyalty-for-telecoms-brands.

Samson, Ashley, Duncan Simpson, Cindra Kampoff, and Adrienne Langlier. 2015. "Think Aloud: An Examination of Distance Runners' Thought Processes." *International Journal of Sports and Exercise Psychology* 15, no. 2 (July): 176–89. https://www.tandfonline.com/doi/full/10.1080/1612197X.2015.1069877?scroll=top&needAccess=true&role=tab.

SAS. 2014. "What Makes a Great Data Scientist?" *SAS Survey Reports*: 5–7. https://www.sas.com/content/dam/SAS/en_gb/image/other1/events/WMAGDS/DataScientist-survey-report-web%20FINAL.pdf.

Satariano, Adam. 2021. "Facebook's WhatsApp Fined for Breaking E.U. Data Privacy Law." *New York Times* (September 3). https://www.nytimes.com/2021/09/02/business/facebook-whatsapp-privacy-fine.html.

Schein, Edgar H. 2010. *Organizational Culture and Leadership*. Wiley.

Schmelzer, Ron. 2022. "You Need to Stop Doing This on Your AI Projects." *Forbes*. https://www.forbes.com/sites/cognitiveworld/2022/08/07/you-need-to-stop-doing-this-on-your-ai-projects/?sh=6f20d4e54c99.

Scholkmann, Antonia. 2021. "1 Dimensions of Learning, Nonlearning, and Resistances to Change . . . . | Download Scientific Diagram."

ResearchGate. https://www.researchgate.net/figure/Dimensions-of-learning-nonlearning-and-resistances-to-change-Based-on-Illeris-2009a_fig1_342130277.

Schulz, Matt, and Dan Shepard. 2023. "2023 Credit Card Debt Statistics." LendingTree. https://www.lendingtree.com/credit-cards/credit-card-debt-statistics/.

Schwartz, Mark. 2018. "Shiny Objects and Professionalism." Amazon AWS (November 8). https://aws.amazon.com/blogs/enterprise-strategy/shiny-objects-and-professionalism/.

Science Blog. 2023. "There's a Faster, Cheaper Way to Train Large Language Models." https://scienceblog.com/538599/theres-a-faster-cheaper-way-to-train-large-language-models/.

Scikit-Learn. 2023. "About Us—Scikit-Learn 1.3.0 Documentation." https://scikit-learn.org/stable/about.html.

Scrum Inc. 2023. "Agile Unleashed at Scale: John Deere Case Study." https://www.scruminc.com/agile-unleashed-scale-john-deere-case-study/.

Shazi, Rhamat, Nocle Gillespie, and John Steen. 2015. "Trust as a Predictor of Innovation Network Ties in Project Teams." *Science Direct* 33, no. 1. https://www.sciencedirect.com/science/article/abs/pii/S0263786314000970.

Shead, Sam. 2021. "Amazon Hit with $887 Million Fine by European Privacy Watchdog." CNBC (July 30). https://www.cnbc.com/2021/07/30/amazon-hit-with-fine-by-eu-privacy-watchdog-.html.

Sheehy, Kelsey, Rick VanderKnyff, Courtney Neidel, and Hal M. Bundrick. 2020. "Verizon Family Cell Phone Plans." NerdWallet. https://www.nerdwallet.com/article/finance/verizon-family-cell-phone-plans.

Silver, David, J. Schrittwieser, K. Simonyan, and Joannis Antonoglou. 2017. "Mastering the Game of Go Without Human Knowledge." *Nature* 550: 354–59. https://doi.org/10.1038/nature24270.

Smith, Tim, Ben Stiller, Jim Guszcza, and Tom Davenport. 2019. "Analytics and AI-Driven Enterprises Thrive in the Age of With." Deloitte Insights. https://www2.deloitte.com/content/dam/Deloitte/ec/Documents/technology-media-telecommunications/DI_Becoming-an-Insight-Driven-organization%20(2).pdf.

Soper, Spencer. 2017. "Bezos Says Artificial Intelligence to Fuel Amazon's Success." *Economic Times*. https://economictimes.indiatimes.com/small-biz/security-tech/technology/bezos-says-artificial-intelligence-to-fuel-amazons-success/articleshow/58163468.cms?from=mdr.

Spiteri, Maria, and George Azzopardi. 2018. "Customer Churn Prediction for a Motor Insurance Company." Pure. https://pure.rug.nl/ws/files/238924399/Customer_Churn_Prediction_for_a_Motor_Insurance_Company.pdf.

State of California Department of Justice. 2023. "California Consumer Privacy Act (CCPA)." https://oag.ca.gov/privacy/ccpa.

Stedman, Craig. 2022. "What Is Data Cleansing (Data Cleaning, Data Scrubbing)?" TechTarget. https://www.techtarget.com/searchdatamanagement/definition/data-scrubbing.

Stevenson, Megan, and Christopher Slobogin. 2018. "Algorithmic Risk Assessments and the Double-Edged Sword of Youth." *Washington University Open Scholarship*. https://openscholarship.wustl.edu/law_lawreview/vol96/iss3/6/.

Super, Tom. 2019. "Auto Insurance Customer Loyalty Is Declining. Here's Why." *Insurance Journal*. https://www.insurancejournal.com/news/national/2019/10/15/545458.htm.

Sutherland, Jeff. 2014. *Scrum: A Revolutionary Approach to Building Teams, Beating Deadlines, and Boosting Productivity*. Random House.

Svare, Helge, Anne Haugen, and Guido Mollering. 2019. "The Function of Ability, Benevolence, and Integrity-Based Trust in Innovation Networks." *Industry and Innovation* 27, no 6: 585–604.

Swartz, Jon. 2021. "Zillow to Stop Flipping Homes for Good as It Stands to Lose More Than $550 million, Will Lay Off a Quarter of staff." *Market Watch* 11, no. 3. https://www-marketwatch-com.cdn.ampproject.org/c/s/www.marketwatch.com/amp/story/zillow-to-stop-flipping-homes-for-good-as-it-stands-to-lose-more-than-550-million-will-lay-off-a-quarter-of-staff-11635885027.

Taylor, Bill. 2017. "How Coca-Cola, Netflix, and Amazon Learn from Failure." *Harvard Business Review*. https://hbr.org/2017/11/how-coca-cola-netflix-and-amazon-learn-from-failure.

TensorFlow. 2022. "Implement Differential Privacy with TensorFlow Privacy | Responsible AI Toolkit." https://www.tensorflow.org/responsible_ai/privacy/tutorials/classification_privacy.

TensorFlow. 2023a. "An End-to-End Machine Learning Platform." https://www.tensorflow.org/.

TensorFlow. 2023b. "Federated Learning." https://www.tensorflow.org/federated/federated_learning.

Tesla. 2023. "AI & Robotics." https://www.tesla.com/AI.

Tett, Gillian. 2019. "What Anthropologists Can Teach Tech Titans." *Financial Times* (January 2). https://www.ft.com/content/7f5f53e2-08b1-11e9-9fe8-acdb36967cfc.

Thanawala, Hiral. 2023. "What Triggers Your Bank to Shrink Your Credit Card Limit?" Moneycontrol. https://www.moneycontrol.com/news/business/personal-finance/what-triggers-your-bank-to-shrink-your-credit-card-limit-11148151.html.

Thesing, Theo, and C. Feldman. 2021. "Agile Versus Waterfall Project Management: Decision Model for Selecting the Appropriate Approach to a Project." *Procedia Computer Science* 181: 746–56. https://www.sciencedirect.com/science/article/pii/S1877050921002702?ref=pdf_download&fr=RR-2&rr=80874cc29ec39377.

Thielman, Sam. 2017. "Your Private Medical Data Is for Sale – And It's Driving a Business Worth Billions." *The Guardian*. https://www.theguardian.com/technology/2017/jan/10/medical-data-multibillion-dollar-business-report-warns.

Thomas, Rob. 2019. "AI Is Not Magic – It's Time to Demystify and Apply." *InformationWeek*. https://www.informationweek.com/machine-learning-ai/ai-is-not-magic-it-s-time-to-demystify-and-apply.

ThoughtSpot. 2021. "Dashboards Are Dead." *Intelligent Tech Channels*. https://www.intelligenttechchannels.com/wp-content/uploads/sites/20/2021/07/ThoughtSpot-Dashboards-are-Dead-WP.pdf.

Thoughtworks. 2023. "Data Mesh." https://www.thoughtworks.com/en-de/what-we-do/data-and-ai/data-mesh.

Threewitt, Cherise, and J. DePietro. 2023. "What Does Tesla's Full-Self Driving Mode Do? *US News*. https://cars.usnews.com/cars-trucks/advice/tesla-full-self-driving.

Todtling, Franz, Ron Ashiem, and Bjorn Boschma. 2013. "Knowledge Sourcing, Innovation and Constructing Advantage in Regions of Europe." *European Urban and Regional Studies*, 161–69.

Torrekens, Rani. 2023. "The Impact of Data Mesh on Organizational Data." KPMG. https://kpmg.com/be/en/home/insights/2023/03/lh-the-impact-of-data-mesh-on-organizational-data.html.

Trax. 2016. "Real-Time Cooler Data and Analytics Without an Actual Visit to the Store." https://traxretail.com/wp-content/uploads/2016/01/Trax-Smart-Cooler.pdf.

21 Century Equipment. 2013. "Farm Forward by John Deere." YouTube. https://www.youtube.com/watch?v=t08nOEkrX-I.

Twitter. 2023. "Coca-Cola (@CocaCola)." https://twitter.com/CocaCola?ref_src=twsrc%5Egoogle%7Ctwcamp%5Eserp%7Ctwgr%5Eauthor.

UNC Lineberger Cancer Center. 2015. "Partnering with IBM and Watson to Accelerate DNA Analysis and Inform Personalized Treatment." https://unclineberger.org/news-archives/partnering-with-ibm-and-watson-to-accelerate-dna-analysis-and-inform-personalized-treatment/.

Urban, Steve, Jennifer Shin, and Tejas Shikhare. 2016. "It's All A/Bout Testing: The Netflix Experimentation Platform." Netflix TechBlog. https://netflixtechblog.com/its-all-a-bout-testing-the-netflix-experimentation-platform-4e1ca458c15.

US Department of Health and Human Services. 2023. "HIPAA Home." https://www.hhs.gov/hipaa/index.html.

Vahaba, Dan. 2023. "AI Companion Robots: A Potential Remedy for Loneliness Epidemic." *Neuroscience News*. https://neurosciencenews.com/ai-robot-loneliness-23616/.

Vasunandan, Aditi, and Sumathi Annamalai. 2023. "Parallel Mediation Analysis of Self-Image and Perceived Usefulness Between Job Security, Habit, Organizational Culture and Intention to use AI Technologies." *Scandinavian Journal of Information Systems*. http://sjisscandinavian-iris.com/index.php/sjis/article/view/613.

Vincent, James. 2017. "John Deere Is Buying an AI Startup to Help Teach Its Tractors How to Farm." The Verge. https://www.theverge.com/2017/9/7/16267962/automated-farming-john-deere-buys-blue-river-technology.

Vincent, James. 2021. "Alexa Is Nagging You More Because Amazon Knows You Don't Care About Its New Features." The Verge (December 23). https://www.theverge.com/2021/12/23/22851451/amazon-alexa-by-the-way-use-case-functionality-plateaued.

Vincent, James, and Amelia H. Krales. 2021. "Siri's 10-Year Anniversary Is a Reminder of Apple's Wasted Head Start." The Verge. https://www.theverge.com/22704233/siri-apple-digital-assistant-10-years-development-problems-why.

Vohra, Sanjeev, Ajay Vasal, Philippe Rosiere, Praveen Tangutiri, and Lan Guan. 2019. "The Art of AI Maturity." *Accenture Articles*. https://www.accenture.com/us-en/insights/artificial-intelligence/ai-maturity-and-transformation?c=acn_glb_aimaturityfrompmediarelations_13124019&n=mrl_0622.

Vreede, Triparna, Mukunth Raghavan, and Gert-Jan Vreede. 2021. "Design Foundations for AI Assisted Decision-Making: A Self Determination Theory Approach." *Scholar Space*. https://scholarspace.manoa.hawaii.edu/server/api/core/bitstreams/a5ca7fd6-39c6-47ae-8f17-ef6ceed41117/content.

Walch, Kathleen. 2022. "What a Research Firm Learned from Hundreds of AI Project Failures." *Forbes*. https://www.forbes.com/sites/cognitiveworld/2022/08/29/what-a-research-firm-learned-from-hundreds-of-ai-project-failures/?sh=73235d256af1.

Wang, Xuanhui, Nadav Golbandi, Michael Bendersky, and Donald Metzler. 2018. "Position Bias Estimation for Unbiased Learning to Rank in Personal Search." Google Research. https://static.googleusercontent.com/media/research.google.com/en//pubs/archive/46485.pdf.

Weldon, David. 2016. "Study Defines the CDO Reason, Role, and Responsibilities for 2017 | Insights." Bloomberg.com (December 14). https://www.bloomberg.com/professional/blog/study-defines-cdo-reason-role-responsibilities-2017/.

Wikipedia. 2023. "Principal-Agent Problem." https://en.wikipedia.org/wiki/Principal%E2%80%93agent_problem.

Wilson, Adam. 2022. "Why Are So Many People Burning Out of the 'Sexiest Job of the 21st Century'?" *IDG Connect* (August). https://www.idgconnect.com/article/3669890/why-are-so-many-people-burning-out-of-the-sexiest-job-of-the-21st-century.html.

Witten, Daniela, and Robert Tibshirani. 2013. *An Introduction to Statistical Learning with Applications in R*, 2nd ed. Springer.

Yampolskiy, Roman V. 2019. "Unexplainability and Incomprehensibility of Artificial Intelligence." Philarchive.org (June). https://philarchive.org/archive/YAMUAI.

Zest AI. 2022. "Improve Risk Assessment Across the Entire Credit Spectrum." https://www.zest.ai/solutions/increase-approvals.

Zheng, Alice, and Amanda Casari. 2022. "Feature Engineering for Machine Learning: Principles and Techniques for Data Scientists." Amazon.in. https://www.amazon.in/Feature-Engineering-Machine-Learning-Principles-ebook/dp/B07BNX4MWC.

Zhou, Li, Jianfeng Gao, Di Li, and Heung-Yeung Shum. 2020. "The Design and Implementation of XiaoIce, an Empathetic Social Chatbot." *Computational Linguistics* 46: 53–93. https://doi.org/10.1162/coli_a_00368.

Zillow. 2023. "What Is a Zestimate? Zillow's Zestimate Accuracy." https://www.zillow.com/z/zestimate/.

Zillow Group. 2021. "Q3 2021 Shareholder Letter." https://s24.q4cdn.com/723050407/files/doc_financials/2021/q3/Zillow-Group-Q3%2721-Shareholder-Letter.pdf.

Zillow Group. 2022. "Zillow Group, Inc. - Investors - Financials - Quarterly Results." https://investors.zillowgroup.com/investors/financials/quarterly-results/default.aspx.

Index